THE EUROPEAN HIGH-SPEED TRAIN AND URBAN DEVELOPMENT

This book is one of a series to be published by Ashgate under the auspices of EURICUR, the European Institute for Comparative Urban Research, Erasmus University Rotterdam. Titles in the series are:

Leo H Klaassen, Leo van den Berg and Jan van der Meer (eds), *The City: Engine behind Economic Recovery*

Leo van den Berg, H. Arjen Klink and Jan van der Meer, *Governing Metropolitan Regions*

Leo van den Berg, Jan van der Borg and Jan van der Meer, *Urban Tourism*

The European High-Speed Train and Urban Development

Experiences in fourteen European urban regions

LEO VAN DEN BERG
PETER POL

European Institute for Comparative Urban Research
Erasmus University Rotterdam
The Netherlands

Ashgate

Aldershot • Brookfield USA • Singapore • Sydney

Published by
Ashgate Publishing Ltd
Gower House
Croft Road
Aldershot
Hants GU11 3HR
England

Ashgate Publishing Company
Old Post Road
Brookfield
Vermont 05036
USA

British Library Cataloguing in Publication Data
Berg, Leo van den
    The European high-speed train and urban development
    : experiences in fourteen European urban regions
    1. High speed trains - Europe 2. Urban transportation -
    Europe 3. Cities and towns - Europe - Growth 4. Community
    development, Urban - Europe
    I. Title II. Pol, Peter
    303.4'832'094

Library of Congress Catalog Card Number: 98-73749

ISBN 1 84014 532 3

Printed and Bound by Biddles Short Run Books, King's Lynn

Contents

List of Figures and Tables

Preface

In May 1997, the Eurocities Working Group for High-Speed Train (HST) matters completed an investigation into the urban implications of HST integration. This investigation was initiated and led by the Communauté Urbaine de Lyon. The aim was to study and exchange information about interactions between high-speed train stations and the spatial-economic development of urban regions. Main elements of the study are the strategic dimension of the HST integration, the configuration of the station-areas and secondary transport, and urban planning and development.

In the first stage of the study, the participants from the 14 cities involved all carried out a study of their situation. That resulted in 14 monographs presenting a wealth of facts on the integration of the HST in these cities. In regular meetings the progress of the study was discussed and experiences exchanged. These meetings were held in the participating cities, so that attendants could also take note of actual practice. By visiting HST stations and related urban locations, the participants from the cities involved were able to get acquainted with important HST developments. At the second stage of the investigation EURICUR (the European Institute for Comparative Urban Research) carried out a comparative study, taking the monographs written by the participating cities as basis. Besides, EURICUR visited all the participating cities to discuss the local HST integration with key personalities.

An inspiring exchange of knowledge and experiences has been achieved and the investigation has produced important results, which have been communicated in various ways to relevant actors. A colourful booklet was issued in the French and English language. It recapitulates the results and illustrates them with colour plates and maps. The brochure has proved to be a useful vehicle for communicating information among the relevant actors, such as local, regional and national governments, European institutions, railway companies, and private investors. To complete the investigation, a major congress was staged in Lyon. That congress was attended by representatives from many European countries. Among the speakers were Bram Peper, Mayor of Rotterdam and president of Eurocities, and Raymond Barre, President of the urban region of Lyon.

The results of the investigation have been laid down in this book. It contains a theoretical introduction to the research, 14 case-studies of metropolitan regions, the final conclusions, and background information on the 14 participating cities. The information for the research has been gathered by desk research and from interviews. The most important information source for the desk research was the monographs written by the representatives of the participating cities. Summaries of the monographs are integrated in the annex of the book. The cities were represented by the following persons: Mr Ton Buffing (on behalf of the city of Amsterdam), Mr Frank de Bruyne (Antwerp), Ms Marie Zezulkova and Mr Jaroslav Josífek (Brno), Mr Claude van den Hove (Brussels), Mr Lars Möller (Cologne), Mr Michel Jaques and Mr S. Manzoni (Geneva), Mr Jean-François Sleijpen (Liège), Mr Damien Caudron (Lille), Mr Jean-Loup Molin (Lyon), Mr Vincent Touze (Marseilles), Mr Jean-Paul Jacquet (Nantes), Mr Jan van Teeffelen (Rotterdam), Mr Jean-Yves Meunier and Mr Michel Reverdy (Strasbourg), Mr Biagio Burdizzo, Mr Allessandro Faraggiana and Mr Ilario Signoretti (Turin). They also organised the meetings with discussion partners of, amongst others, representatives of cities, regions, public transport companies, railway stations, airports and Chambers of Commerce. We wish to thank the representatives of the cities for their valuable and pleasant cooperation. We want to express our gratitude to all the discussion partners. Their information and opinions have added much value to the material that was available on the subject.

Three other EURICUR researchers contributed to this study. Thanks are due to Drs Erik Braun, who participated to the case-studies of Amsterdam and Antwerp, Drs Peter de Langen, co-author of the case-study of Amsterdam, and Drs Willem van Winden, co-author of the case-studies of Brussels and Marseille, for their much-appreciated contribution to this research project. Naturally only the two authors are responsible for the contents of the full report.

We want to express our gratitude to Jean-Loup Molin who enthusiastically and with great efforts initiated and coordinated the research-project. We also thank Ms Attie Elderson-de Boer for translating the Dutch parts of the report and checking the English parts, Ms Mel Lewis for translating the French parts, and Ms Arianne van Bijnen, the EURICUR secretary, for her indispensable help during all the phases of the investigation.

Leo van den Berg
Peter Pol
Rotterdam, April 1998

Theoretical Introduction on the Integration of the HST in European Cities

Transport and Urban Development

The increasing importance which economic activities attach to the exchange of information and the fast development of new information techniques are affecting the location patterns of business companies. Labour-intensive activities tend to disperse across space, while knowledge-intensive ones, on the contrary, seem to concentrate in a limited number of zones. There is a process of locational disarticulation, whereby the physical production disperses to a wider and wider range of locations worldwide, while control and command functions concentrate in a few global cities (Sassen, 1991). Economic activities that are dependent on the use of modern information technology need workers with a high level of education, and will therefore be attracted to urban regions with an ample supply of highly-qualified labour. Besides, such innovative activities often want to locate near such important sources of information as universities, consulting engineers, government agencies and others (Van den Berg, 1987), which tend to be established in major urban regions. A distinction can be made between standardised and non-standardised activities. People working with information and knowledge that cannot easily be standardised are very sensitive to the facilities and the environment that permits them to talk with their peers and keep an eye on what others are doing (Lambooy, 1996). Such an environment is apt to be found in economically, socially and administratively prominent regions. In that respect, Hall (1995 and 1996) expects key economic sectors in leading urban areas to be in command and control of functions, financial and business services, urban tourism and creative and cultural industries.

New information technology partly replaces physical transport. Fax, e-mail and the Internet are to some degree alternatives for physical transport, and teleconference meetings could in part be a substitute for face-to-face

1

meetings. However, as Hall (1996) reminds us, ever since the invention of the telephone in 1876, but above all in the last half-century, the growth of telecommunication has marched in unison with the growth of personal business travel, including both in-business trips and business tourism in the form of conferences, fairs and conventions. Likewise, the growth of electronic data interchange (EDI) can be expected to generate new flows of physical transport. The expectation is that there will always be an urgent great demand for face-to-face contacts, in spite of – or even thanks to – the development of new transport technology.

As prosperity increases and incomes rise, people want to travel further and faster. They want to live far from their workplace in a pleasant living environment; companies want economic interaction with other actors further afield; and individuals want to travel on holiday to ever more remote areas. Zahavi argued that people devote on average a constant fraction of their day to travel – what he called the travel-time budget (see Schafer and Victor, 1997). From that starting point, Schafer and Victor have developed the hypothesis that the typical travel-time budget stretches between one and one and a half hours a person per day in a wide variety of economic, social and geographic settings. If people keep their travelling time constant but also demand more mobility as their income rises, they must select faster modes of transport to cover more distance in the same stretch of time (Schafer and Victor, 1997). Accordingly, with rising prosperity, a more or less continuous development of faster transport modes can be observed. Schafer and Victor expect high-speed transport (HSTs and aircraft) to account for about two-fifths of all passenger-kilometres travelled in 2050 (in 1990 the share was nine per cent).

New communication and information technology is not introduced everywhere at the same moment. There are time lags among areas in the availability of new infrastructure and know-how. As a rule, the existing prominent economic centres are the first to avail themselves of new techniques. Naturally, that serves to strengthen the hierarchical distribution of economic activities among urban areas. In that connection, Janelle (1969) spoke about a time-space convergence process. His argument was that new forms of infrastructure tend to be constructed where there is already much interaction. The most intensive interaction occurs among economic key areas. Economic key areas are linked up by ever faster communication systems, bringing them closer together in terms of time. Key areas in this respect are the Boston-Washington corridor, the Tokyo-Osaka-corridor and the so-called European 'blue banana'.

For regions, a pleasant living environment is becoming more and more an important precondition for economic growth. As they grow more prosperous, people increasingly value living, working and spending their leisure in an attractive and clean environment. Business companies, in particular those needing highly-qualified staff, will prefer to establish in regions where the living environment is good in terms of built-up areas as well as natural beauty. To create an enjoyable living environment the presence of sufficient relatively environmentally-friendly transport, such as high-grade railways, is desirable. Then a more frequent use of these kind of transport modes can be stimulated, through which negative external effects of transport can decrease. Also, airports should be laid out in such a way as to avoid as much as possible nuisance to residential areas. For this kind of transport infrastructure, which is often an important location factor for economic activities, is mostly generating a considerable nuisance to inhabitants. For some densely populated urban regions, underground construction of rail and road infrastructure is desirable to minimise negative effects of transport. Examples are the underground motorways along the Rhine in the centres of the German cities Düsseldorf and Cologne, and the underground railway network now under construction in Turin.

To repress as much as possible nuisance from traffic – and also crime – is essential, but on the other hand a city must be alive if it is to count as an attractive urban environment. The presence of an appealing urban centre where people can feel happy is important. The city centre should be a place where people can meet casually and informally, and which induces a creative and stimulating exchange of ideas. Such an environment can be the breeding ground for economic activities to which creativeness and innovativeness are vital.

We can expect that the high-speed train (HST) will obtain an important position in this growing market for high-speed transport. For, on the one hand air transport will face more and more environmental restrictions and, on the other hand, new rail technologies promise adequate alternative high-speed services. Especially at medium distances, the HST can become an adequate substitute for the aeroplane.

The HST is not faster than air transport, but it has the advantage of connecting the centres of cities, less time being lost in transfers to destinations in city centres. The effects of the developing HST network will therefore be most noticeable in urban areas. In comparison with air travel, the HST has also the advantages of avoiding time-consuming check-in procedures as well as better possibilities for in-board working for travellers.

In comparison with conventional rail transport, the innovative elements are first, the high quality of the trains (the rolling stock), offering a combination of high speed with high comfort, and second, the new *dedicated* infrastructure. This infrastructure is constructed with as few curves and hills as possible, thus enabling the rolling stock effectively to reach the high speeds envisaged.

Another important factor for the European system is the improved organisation of frontier-crossing transport. For a long time international rail services were quite poor, due to differing technical features of the national rail networks and a lack of cooperation between the national railway companies. Now, because of better international cooperation and construction of rolling stock which can be used in different countries, better international rail services are provided.

The possibility of integration with the conventional rail system promises synergetic effects and reduces, at some locations, the need for new infrastructure. Unlike the magnetic levitation train, the 'normal' HST can also run on conventional rail infrastructure. Therefore, the HST system can easily penetrate the heart of city centres using the already-existing rail infrastructure. New, dedicated HST infrastructure is often constructed between, but seldom within, cities. A major advantage is that, at an early stage of the HST network development, a relatively large amount of HST services to different destinations can be offered, partly by using conventional infrastructure. Furthermore, more peripheral urban regions, to which the construction of dedicated infrastructure is not economic feasible, can also be served by HSTs on existing rail.

The Influence of the HST on Regional-Economic Development

There is no unequivocal causal relationship between transport infrastructure and regional-economic development. *Transport infrastructures do not generate economic development any more than rain produces vegetation or fertiliser produces crops* (Plassard, 1992). Transport infrastructure can work as a catalyst, however, helping to set in motion an economic evolution which otherwise would not have started. Indeed, infrastructure can in some cases be a necessary, although it is never a sufficient, condition for economic growth.

Many cities in Western Europe have reached a phase of reurbanisation in which major cities regain status as places for people to live in and for businesses to locate in. An increasing polarisation of economic activities can be observed in major cities and metropolitan areas. At this stage, inter-regional (intercity) as well as intraregional connections are important. Good access to the principal European cities is a weighty location condition for many organisations.

By joining the European network of high-speed railways an urban region enhances its relative attraction as a settling place for persons and organisations, which will influence its regional-economic development. Joining the HST network improves a region's international and multi-modal accessibility. The high-speed railway is particularly interesting for 'one-day return trips'; in intra-European business traffic, these distances are crucial. To be able to travel there and back between two locations in one day (and have time to do what one has come to do) is regarded as an important threshold value for generating new transport. To enhance international and multi-modal accessibility is important in a period of increasing international spatial interaction, notably between metropolitan regions.

The Influence of the HST on the Competition among Metropolitan Areas

Every city has its specific configuration of functions. An urban system is a structure of cities or agglomerations mutually connected by functional-spatial relations (commuting relations, cultural relations, commercial relations, and so on). There are two trains of thought with respect to the functioning of towns in an urban system: the hierarchical or central-places model and the network model.

In the central-places model, cities are elements of a vertically-oriented urban system with (rigid) regional delimitation. In such a hierarchical urban system, the position of an individual town (that is, its degree of centrality within the urban system) is determined by the number of its functions. The urban structure is dominated by one single central city.

The network model, on the contrary, assumes a horizontally-oriented urban system, where the network is a decentralised structure of towns. The position of a town in an urban network is determined by the exclusiveness of its functions with respect to other cities in the network. Function specialisation rather than function cumulation is what counts.

In practice, the European urban system displays features of the hierarchical as well as the network model. Nor is the European urban system a rigid one. It is an interdependent system: the development of one city affects the position and development of other cities in the system. Certain fundamental developments in the surroundings of the cities and the cities' reaction to those developments affect the position of the cities and urban regions. Cities tend to pursue a strategic policy aimed at satisfying the requirements of companies and individuals, thus strengthening their competitive position as business or residence location.

The construction of the HST network affects the development of the European urban system, and thus the competition among cities and metropolitan areas. The influence manifests itself along the two trains of thought distinguished above: on the one hand the HST reinforces the urban hierarchy, on the other it promotes the formation of a network of cities. The two lines of influence will be commented upon below.

An HST station increases the attractiveness of the city for certain activities for which (international) interaction is essential. High-quality services such as the supply and processing of information, publicity, research and advice come to mind particularly. Activities from a relatively extensive area will (want to) establish themselves in the neighbourhood of the HST station. The connection of a town to the high-speed railway makes it more central to its surroundings. It strengthens the city's competitive position.

The hierarchical distance to cities lacking such a connection is lengthened: the regional economy tends to polarise. The HST reinforces the discontinuous distribution of economic and social activities. In a ring around the HST stopping-places new spatial border lines are formed, delimiting areas of deteriorating accessibility. Cities failing to connect to the network of high-speed railways are put at a disadvantage. Their competitive position is marred.

The disadvantage can be relieved by improving the connection with the nearest HST station. Shuttle services between cities with and without HST stations allow the latter to benefit to some extent from the enhanced accessibility of the HST locations. On the other hand, urban areas with a relatively poor economic potential may find the non-connection protective of their local industry, because the remaining transport barriers prevent draining effects.

Cities linked by the network of high-speed railway lines will become a network of their own. Each having its own speciality, they are to some extent each other's complement. With improved mutual access, the cities can capitalise the complementarity and develop some degree of function specialisation. To give an example, with easier access an internationally-operating financial service firm no longer needs an office in every European capital, and is able to concentrate its activities at the location offering the most advantageous conditions. With respect to financial services, London, Frankfurt and Amsterdam come to mind. By specialising their functions, the cities can become more attractive locations for their specialisms, thus bettering their competitive position.

The Case Studies

This study is based on an international comparative investigation in 14 European cities: Amsterdam, Antwerp, Brno, Brussels, Cologne, Geneva, Liège, Lille, Lyon, Marseilles, Nantes, Rotterdam, Strasbourg and Turin. Some of these cities are already connected to the European HST network; others expect to be within one or two decades.

All participating cities in this research are members of Eurocities, an association of more than 70 medium-sized European cities (larger than 250,000 inhabitants). Tpe 14 cities of this research chose to participate in the HST working group to exchange information about and to study the HST integration in their regions.

The cities involved give a good picture of the HST cities in northwest continental Europe. Seven out of the 14 cities are part of the so-called PBKAL-network (Paris, Brussels, Cologne, Amsterdam and London). This is the most important cross-border HST network in Europe. Many of the until-now-realised *dedicated* HST lines are situated within European member states. Instances are Lyon-Paris, Paris-Le Mans, Hanover-Würzburg, Mannheim-Stuttgart and Madrid-Sevilla. The PBKAL-network, therefore, constitutes a positive exception to the still-dominating national developments. This network can have a major influence on the European integration process, for which interweaving of national markets is vital. The cities participating in this study who consitute the PBKAL-network are Amsterdam, Antwerp, Brussels, Cologne, Liège, Lille anl Rotterdam. At present, all these cities are served by HSTs. However, as yet only two cities are connected via *dedicated* lines: Brussels and Lille.

From the case study sample, Lyon is the city with the longest experience with connection to a *dedicated* HST line. This urban region has been served by the HST since 1981. This goes for the City of Geneva also, although it is not connected by *dedicated* lines. The cities of Marseilles, Nantes, Lille and Brussels have already been connected to the HST network for more than five years. Therefore, empirical effects of the HST integration can be noticed in these urban regions also.

Two participating cities have a major airport in their direct vicinity: Schiphol in the Amsterdam region and Zaventem in the Brussels region. Both airports generate more than 10 million passengers a year and accommodate relatively many intercontinental passengers (see Table 1). Amsterdam, Brussels, Cologne, Geneva and Lyon see the high-speed train as a tool to contribute to the development of their airports. On the other hand, Antwerp,

Liège, Lille and Rotterdam will benefit from their good access to the continent's major hubs (Amsterdam, Brussels, Paris) once the HST network is completed.

Lyon, Amsterdam and Turin will have three HST stations in their region. Therefore, they have to make choices with respect to the way the region is served by the HST, how secondary transport services are connected to the different transport nodes, and how the different stations influence the spatial development of the urban region. Lille and Cologne will have two HST stations that are located close to each other. They must foster good coordination between those two nodes. For both cities, it may even be preferable to speak about one HST station with two terminals. Interconnection of those terminals is a major point of attention.

Brno, Liège, Lille, Lyon, Strasbourg and Turin view the construction of new lines as an opportunity to continue their development within a true network of cities, enabling them to counterbalance the influence exerted upon them by the major metropolises of Prague, Brussels, Paris and Milan. Brussels, Cologne, Lille, Lyon and Strasbourg can hope to take advantage in the long term of their strategic position as crossroads cities within the developing network.

Table 1   Population and airports of the participating cities

| | | Inhabitants | | Airport | |
	City	Region	Year[1]	Passengers	Year[1]
Amsterdam	722,400	1,376,900	1995	24,800,000	1995
Antwerp	466,000	1,139,000	1993	250,000	1994
Brno	390,000	770,965	1996	120,000	1996
Brussels	950,000	1,700,000	1997	13,600,000	1996
Cologne	1,000,000	1,978,000	1993	4,842,000	1985
Geneva	171,042	379,190[3]	1991	6,270,000	1995
Liege	195,000	447,123	1986	100,000	1996
Lille	172,149	1,157,113	1990	800,000	1990
Lyon	415,487	2,476,004[2]	1990	4,445,576	1995
Marseilles		1,087,276	1995	5,400,000	1996
Nantes		520,000	1996	1,149,428	1995
Rotterdam	596,000	1,100,000	1993	317,000	1994
Strasbourg	251,000	423,000	1990	1,700,000	1996
Turin	942,076	1,719,647	1994	1,836,407	1995

1   Year of data collection.
2   1990, region urbaine de Lyons.
3   90–91, espace franco-valdo-genevois.

Methodology

EURICUR has written 14 case studies on the HST integration in Eurocities based on the monographs written by the representatives of the participating cities and the discussions held in these cities. EURICUR discussed the local HST integration with key personalities, such as, among others, representatives of the urban and regional authorities, chambers of commerce, railway companies and airports. The list of the discussion partners can be found in the annexes.

This book deals with the question: how can the high-speed train make an optimum contribution to the long term development of well-being in urban regions? To be more specific, how can the HST system be fitted into an urban region to contribute efficiently and effectively to a socially and spatially balanced and sustainable urban economic growth? From this question the following proposition can be deduced: an optimal contribution by the high-speed train to the well-being of an urban region can only be striven for by an integral approach. This research tries to elaborate this integral approach of HST integration in urban regions.

To describe and analyse the HST integration in the 14 Eurocities, EURICUR used six criteria that were deduced from the statement of the problem: accessibility, economic potential, quality of the living environment, balanced spatial distribution of the activities, balanced social distribution of the effects and organising capacity. These criteria, shown in Figure 1, constitute the basic framework of the research. All the case studies and the conclusions are structured by these criteria. The criteria are further elaborated below.

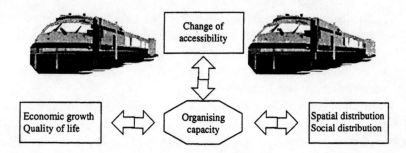

Figure 1   Integral analysis of the HST integration in urban regions

Criterion 1: Accessibility

The HST is only one element of the total transport system in an urban area that determines its accessibility. The fast train mostly constitutes only a link in the transport chain of the traveller, who needs more transport modes to get from origin to destination. To benefit of the HST connection, other – competing as well as complementary – transport services have to be adapted. An urban area can only benefit in an optimum way from the HST if there is a coherent transport system. For this, decisions have to be made with respect to the location of the HST station and how to connect the fast train with the available external and internal transport services of an urban region.

The Choice of the Location of a HST Station

The HST station area can develop as a spatial-economic gravity centre and main junction of passenger transport flows of an urban region. Its location choice is, therefore, an important determining factor of urban spatial development. A wrong choice might create a *locked-in* situation, which can only be corrected with relative high costs and radical spatial changes.

In many cities, the choice is between a peripheral and a central location. The first kind of station often stimulates a (further) suburbanisation of economic activities. At a peripheral station, secondary public transport services are often underdeveloped but there is usually good accessibility for cars. A central station stimulates a concentration of activities in the inner city. A central stopping place mostly offers admission to a high-grade package of secondary public transport, but lacks easy access by car.

Clearly, there are intermediary solutions, like a HST stopping place at the fringe of the centre. More space is often available there, or it is easily cleared to accommodate new economic activities. Such a location can also improve the socioeconomic functioning of the inner city, provided there are adequate interconnecting transport links.

The ultimate choice depends particularly on the configuration of the rail infrastructure, the internal accessibility, the available space in the urban area, the level of the developing costs of the different alternatives and the desired spatial-economic development.

External Accessibility

To increase the benefits of connection to the HST network, it is desirable for an urban region to be linked to a multitude of HST lines. The more lines converge in an urban region, the more attractive this transport system is. In comparison with air travel, the HST is a quite rigid system, since the degree of accessibility improvement depends on the availability of an adequate rail infrastructure. But when an urban region possesses an airport, any city can be reached, in principle.

By linking different external transport systems, such as aeroplane, train and car, travel time gains can be realised, as travellers can change more easily between transport modes and have a greater flexibility to choose the most adequate solution for each journey. Moreover, by mutual connection the attractiveness of the junctions of the different sub-transport systems will increase. For instance, travelling by HST instead of by car to an intercontinental airport may save travel time and – as a consequence – the attractiveness of the airport might increase through this HST connection.

The vulnerability of the total transport system might decrease when different transport modalities are adequately interconnected. If one subsystem drops out (for instance, the air system because of strikes), another subsystem (such as the HST) can form an adequate substitute.

Internal Accessibility

Often, internal transport systems has to be improved when an urban region is connected to the HST system. The HST is generally an additional transport system and, therefore, will generate larger transport flows to more remote areas in the urban region. On the one hand, these larger streams are a consequence of the supply of a new transport service; on the other, these increased transport flows are necessary to make the HST services economically viable. Usually the car and the public transport system have to be improved. The degree to which adaptation of these transport-systems is necessary and feasible depends on the location of the HST station. For, as we stated earlier, a central location – as opposed to a peripheral one – generally offers better public transport and worse car accessibility.

Good accessibility by car of the HST stopping place seems to be important for stimulating the use of the HST, as the car is an adequate complementary mode with respect to quality features, like speed, comfort and reliability. Therefore, it can be expected that some of the potential HST travellers will only use the fast train if the stations are adequately accessible by car. This will especially apply for the business traveller, who attaches a high value to comfort and short travel time. Especially for those transport relations which compete with air travel, good car accessibility to the HST junctions might be a decisive factor in chosing between these two high-speed transport modes. Therefore, a kind of environmental paradox seems to arise: it might be necessary to create excellent car accessibility to the HST stations to influence the modal split in favour of the HST.

With respect to car accessibility to the HST station, two elements can be distinguished: connecting infrastructure and parking facilities. The HST stopping-place has to be adequately connected by car infrastructure to the whole urban region and with – if available – the airport. Furthermore, in the direct vicinity of the station there must be car parking space available. To accommodate the larger passenger flows new infrastructure and parking facilities are often needed. The degree to which both elements are used can be influenced by the government. If they consider an unlimited car accessibility desirable and feasible they can supply the infrastructure and free parking space. But if the government wants the station accessible by car for those who attach high value to this, they can influence the use of the infrastructure and parking facilities by price instruments (road-pricing and parking fees).

Improvement of the secondary public transport system of an urban region that obtains a HST connection often implies adapting the capacity, quality and range. The capacity of the public transport system has to be adapted to the expected increase of passengers travelling via the HST station. This may imply an increase of the frequency of services, the use of larger equipment and the addition of new services. The offered public transport services have to form an adequate complement to the HST services. This means that in principle they have to have similar quality features with respect to speed and comfort. To stimulate the business traveller (let's use the same example) to use the HST instead of the aeroplane, the concessions to be made with respect to these quality elements may not be too great. Therefore, the availability of high-quality public transport at metropolitan HST stations, such as underground and light rail, is often desirable. It can be expected that the HST will attract passengers from a larger region than the conventional train since it is a rail service that is only provided in a limited amount of cities. Therefore, a logical consequence is that the range of the additional public transport services has to be extended.

Criterion 2: Economic Potential

The area around HST stations, as around airports, is bound to attract economic activities that are sensitive to status. The HST bestows an aura of modernity and dynamism on its places of call. Investigations into location factors have shown that status is an important motive for companies to locate near an airport or an HST station. From French experience, economic effects – in the shape of new activity attracted by the arrival of the HST – appear to be strongest in the direct vicinity of the HST stations. Also, the possibility of cutting transaction costs makes the zone around an HST station an attractive location for organisations to which international interactions are essential. A station in the HST network can therefore exert a powerful appeal on activities thriving on communication. A necessary condition is that other location factors in the area are adequate as well. The size of the urban area benefiting of the improved accessibility depends on the quality and capacity of the secondary public as well as private transport networks. In Figure 2, the influence of the high-speed railway on the regional economy is first schematically presented and then elaborated.

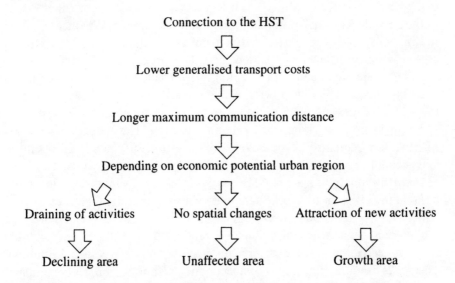

Figure 2   Influence of the high-speed railway on the regional economy

The direct effect of connecting an urban region to the European network of high-speed railways is to reduce the generalised transport costs, expressed in monetary costs, time costs and sacrifice. That effect is due mostly to the phenomena indicated in the theory as time-space convergence and cost-space convergence. The high-speed railway brings cities closer together in terms of travel time and (direct) transport costs. In particular the direct access to the centres of major towns will be improved, because many HST stations are in town centres. The generalised transport costs will also be reduced by competition between transport modes serving the same intercity connections in Europe, notably air and rail. Such competition spells greater choice and flexibility as well as lower prices for the travellers.

Reduction of the generalised transport costs extends the maximum communication distance from the location newly connected to the HST network. Given the maximum acceptable travel time (per day, for instance) and the travel costs, individuals can either travel further or reach their destinations earlier. The relevant region for individuals and organisation – the area that can be reached in a given length of time – is extended. Against the same generalised transport cost level more remote locations can be reached. Therefore, the welfare potential of the city will increase; within its relevant region, more welfare elements are available. On the other hand, a city linked to the HST network can attract new activities and visitors. The 'market value' of the city and its location climate can, therefore, improve. Whether an urban region will draw economic profits from the realised longer maximum communication distance in practice depends on its economic potential.

The economic potential of a region is determined by many other factors besides its accessibility, such as the average educational level of the population, the level of wages and salaries, the mentality of the population and the quality of the residential, working and living environment. The economic activities in the urban region involved have to operate in a sufficiently competitive way, at inter-regional as well as international level. In other words, they have to supply products with a relatively good price-quality relation and they must be able to sell them to appropriate markets. Furthermore, there has to be a sufficient diversification of economic functions to limit the vulnerability of the regional economy to the decline of certain activities.

Their economic potential determines whether a region will face: 1) draining effects; 2) the attraction of new socioeconomic activities; or 3) no appreciable spatial-economic effects (see Figure 2).

The first case deals with a declining area. The location of an HST station does not always work out positively on the location attractiveness of an urban region. The degree to which an HST connected city profits from its enhanced accessibility depends, among other things, on its own potentialities and those of competing nodal points in the vicinity. When the city's own potential is relatively poor, its connection to the HST system may well result in economic activities being drained away to other urban regions. Therefore, for a proper estimate of a town's development chances, a strength-weakness analysis of the city's own and any neighbouring junctions is necessary.

The second-mentioned case is a growth area, where the urban area in question has sufficient economic potential to attract new activities. In spatial-economic terms, this will lead to scale-enlargement and concentration of economic activities. Business companies can extend the scale of their activities to the greater relevant market. The range of economic and social relations of cities linked to the HST network will increase.

The third case deals with an area of indifference. There is a neutral spatial-economic effect as a result of the HST integration. On balance socioeconomic activities are neither attracted nor drained away. Therefore, the investments in the new transport infrastructure are not or hardly profitable for the urban area in question.

Criterion 3: Quality of the Living Environment

To achieve sustainable economic growth, the HST has to improve the quality of the urban living environment. A balanced division of welfare between present and future generations should be aimed for. The HST, the necessary secondary traffic modes and the new social and economic activities attracted by the HST must not damage the urban living environment, and should preferably enhance it.

The HST is looked upon as a fairly environmentally-friendly transport mode. By partly substituting car and air transport, the HST makes a positive contribution to the quality of the living environment. On the other hand, the same living environment may be harmed by dedicated HST lines cutting through landscapes and producing a lot of noise. That the construction of new HST lines should call forth so much resistance may be due in part to the fact that the very people who suffer the nuisance are not the ones who will directly profit from the system.

If the HST system is to make a long-term positive contribution to the quality of the living environment, it must be of the highest quality and constructed so as to produce maximum intermodal substitution effects, and minimum negative environmental effects.

By supplying high-grade HST services people can be stimulated to use the relative environmentally-friendly HST instead of the car or aeroplane. This would contribute to improving the quality of life in the urban region involved.

To minimise negative environmental effects will often imply higher short-time construction costs due to, for instance, subterranean construction and construction of soundproof barriers. However, the extra investment will serve to make the area around the HST station more attractive as a location to settle, for the living environment is becoming more and more an important location factor, next to easy access.

The successful fitting of the HST into the urban space hinges upon the attention given to the living environment. As it is necessary to create sufficient social support for the HST integration, it is a necessary precondition to attract and retain companies and citizens and it is important for the city's image-building. An HST station is a major aspect of the city. A high-quality location with a pleasant living environment can add much to the city's image.

The effect of the HST on the quality of the living environment around the station may be either positive or negative. The construction of new secondary transport services and the attraction of new economic activities and more traffic may negatively influence the quality of life of the HST station-area. That applies in particular to vehicles such as private cars and buses that are relatively polluting but still necessary to optimise the junction's logistic function. To limit negative effects possible measures are the construction of subterranean infrastructure and use of flexible price instruments for car traffic. The latter can be useful to sort out economically necessary and unnecessary car traffic: for those who are willing to pay for it, good accessibility by car to the HST station can be created. This has to be an important point of attention when connecting an urban region to the HST network and especially when choosing the HST stopping-place. Unacceptably high negative effects on the quality of life in an urban centre might be a fair reason not to chose a central location for the stopping place of the fast train, but instead to chose a more peripheral one.

But the arrival of the HST can also produce an impulse to rehabilitate the, mostly outdated, surroundings of the station in the city centre. By making the public space more attractive and arranging secondary transport modes in an environmentally-friendly way, the transition of a station to an HST junction may have a positive effect on the living environment. Therefore, for each specific city to be connected to the HST network the net effect on the quality of life in the city areas in question has to be considered.

Criterion 4: Balanced Spatial Distribution of Activities

The HST stimulates a polarisation of the spatial distribution of activities. Because of the improved accessibility and image, a concentration of socioeconomic activities may arise in and around the HST station. This transport system can, therefore, generate new economic gravity points in a city. New regional activities may settle here, but also activities moving from other parts of the urban region. Therefore, the HST normally brings about an *unbalanced* distribution of activities. Certain urban areas may be confronted with draining effects. As a result these areas may seriously deteriorate, and thereby decreasing the attractiveness and image of the whole urban region.

In order to realise an efficient use of transport infrastructure and lively urban areas a certain balanced spatial distribution of activities has to be striven for. Spatially-separated urban functions may cause inefficiently used transport systems whereby these systems are used only for certain limited periods of the day and are under-utilised during the rest of the time. For instance, a strict division of work and living areas in a metropolitan region almost inevitably leads to heavy one-way traffic flows between those areas during the rush hours. This often results in regular congestion because creating a new infrastructure to meet the very high demand is not economically feasible and/ or not desirable because of the negative effects on the quality of life.

By mixing activities in and distributing them among urban regions, a more balanced use of the transport system can be striven for. Then, creating new infrastructure and offering new public transport services will be more economically viable. Moreover, the accessibility of certain areas will improve, because exceptionally use of the system can be avoided. Therefore, a balanced spatial structure (the *harmonious city*) is typically an urban region in which one or more centres accommodate a mixture of activities, generating balanced traffic flows across space and through time.

In addition, such a combination of activities must be aimed for around HST stations in order to use the available secondary transport infrastructure in an efficient way. For instance, when an HST station accommodates mostly commuter trains in the morning and the evening, in the intermediary time other functions can be served. By, for instance, combining HST stations with shopping centres, the secondary transport infrastructure might be used in a more balanced way during the day.

A balanced spatial development around an HST station can strengthen both the transport function and the growth-pole function. The transport function is strengthened by a better spread of the demand for traffic over the day, and thus a more efficient use of the available modes. The growth-pole function is reinforced by the enhanced appeal of the urban region, which makes private and public actors more ready to invest. It is, therefore, in the interest of the urban region to strive for a certain balance with respect to the spatial distribution of activities.

It becomes more and more important to strive for sufficient liveliness in urban areas. Monofunctional areas, like office districts and residential areas, often seem to be abandoned during certain periods of the day. Streets and public spaces are empty, showing quite a desolate nature. At these periods, they lack sufficient liveliness to be considered as an attractive *urban area*. In general, in a lively urban area, people feel more comfortable to live, work and be in. Liveliness of an urban area means that:

1   there is a certain amount of people and traffic on the streets and in public spaces, without generating too much nuisance (activities and space);

2   there are almost always certain activities going on in the urban area. It is necessary to mix different urban functions in the area, to ensure liveliness during all parts of the day, week and year (activities and time);

3   there is variation in the elements of the built-up area. There is a wide differentiation of buildings and public spaces, making it an attractive area to live and work in for a wide group of people (activities and aesthetics).

The development of station grounds tends to be costly. Building on top of railway yards is expensive, because of, among other things, the need for noise- and vibration-proof constructions. That is why many investors, especially private ones, prefer to invest in office buildings, which often promise a better return (at least in the short term). The situation holds the threat of a development biased towards an oversupply of office buildings and consequently loss of attraction of the neighbourhood.

It is important to prevent overcrowding (and itsconsequent agglomeration disadvantages) in certain areas. When too many activities are concentrated in a HST station area, its accessibility may be threatened and relatively very high ground and rent prices may arise. The latter may imply that certain activities crowd out others, resulting in monofunctional areas.

The opposite of such an overload of activities is the draining away of urban elements from other areas. Districts that are faced with a relatively decreased accessibility may lose their attractiveness as business locations.

An outward movement of economic activities may result in a deterioration of such areas. They might become backward districts with relatively high unemployment and little possibility of recovery. These areas are often breeding grounds for all kinds of criminality. Ultimately, when no adequate solutions are found to prevent such a negative development, they might transform into so-called no-go areas, in which people do not feel safe and comfortable.

The government often has to play an active role to control the spatial distribution of activities in urban areas and specifically in HST station areas. If 'the market' only decides on the functions in HST station-areas, monofunctional areas could arise, because, for instance, offices promise the largest profits. However, in the long term, this might affect the quality of life, the accessibility and the liveliness of the urban areas involved in a negative way. The government can control this process by planning procedures, by construction authorisations, by raising buildings for public functions and by its transport policy (building infrastructure, tariff policy and public transport).

Criterion 5: Balanced Social Distribution of Effects

When an urban region is to be connected to the HST network radical adaptations are often necessary at and around the HST stopping-place. The positive and negative effects of these changes are normally not equally balanced among the population involved. Some will face special benefits, others only disadvantages. Inhabitants along the HST infrastructure, but residing far from the HST station, will particularly be confronted with nuisance; companies directly located at the stopping places will have particular advantages. In view of the relatively large input of public capital and the need to create sufficient social support, measures are necessary to bring about a balanced distribution of benefits and costs of the HST integration among the people involved.

Sufficient social support for the proposed adaptations have to be created. This applies especially to thosewho face almost entirely negative effects of the HST connection. Good communication has to take place concerning the benefits and desirability of the adaptations. Those concerned must have a say in the proposed changes. They must be able to declare their desires and troubles. With adequate communication, resistance against projects can be converted into support. Moreover, the opinion of the local population can affect the political support. Where there is excessive noise nuisance and/or decreases in the value of real estate a (financial) compensation arrangement might be desirable. When crowding-out of certain activities is desirable and/or inevitable, alternative locations for them should be offered.

Attention is also due to the interests of the travellers, an aspect that seems rather neglected in the implementation of the HST system. Since travellers do not in general get themselves organised, their interests are easy to overlook. In choosing HST trajectories, the decision-makers are inclined to heed the complaints of people living along the line more than the need to make the journey a pleasant experience for the passengers. Indeed, to judge from the obscure and dark pedestrian passages at some railway stations, the comfort of the passengers sometimes seems to be no more than a secondary concern. What they are entitled to is a safe, comfortable and appealing station environment which adds to the pleasure of their trip. That implies, among other things, avoidance of hazardous and dark tunnel passages for pedestrians and cyclists and the construction of safe traffic crossings.

Criterion 6: Organising Capacity

One condition for the successful implementation of the HST in the urban system is the creation of adequate organising capacity, to do justice as much as possible to the interests of the actors involved, and make optimum use of the available knowledge, labour and capital.

The achievement of optimum integration of an HST system in urban surroundings is complicated by the large number of actors involved, including the local authorities, the central government, railway companies, local transport companies, project developers, the entire population and the travellers. Their interests may converge as well as diverge. For instance, project developers and population groups may well have different concerns.

Even within organisations, different interests may play a role. For instance, the local government, responsible for the common concern of a balanced development of the urban region, frequently also acts as a commercial project developer. Within railway companies there may be a (potential) clash between, say, the transport function and the increasingly important function of real estate developer.

With the increasing competition between European urban areas it is necessary to take measures in time to be able to attract new economic activities around the HST station-areas. Therefore, an adequate vision and strategy have to be developed concerning the functions that could be accommodated at and around the HST station. Subsequently, this has to be translated into concrete policy measures, such as creating space for new activities.

In this respect, it is necessary that the actors involved recognise the importance of the common development of a vision and strategy. The absence of this may result in a situation where economic actors chose to locate in an other HST city or where the urban area is developed in an incoherent way. Examples of the latter are an excessive dominance of certain urban functions in the HST station area, for instance offices, or the lack of certain activities like restaurants and pubs.

To create sufficient organising capacity it is necessary that an actor leads the development process. Mostly, this will be the urban government, because many public functions are at stake, such as the organisation of public spaces and the configuration of public transport systems, and the city is the most appropriate level of scale. It might be desirable to develop the station area in cooperation with private actors, to raise additional financial funds and to have more market incentives. Their participation, therefore, may imply a more efficient and timely implementation of the necessary measures.

Structure of the Book

The criteria deduced and elaborated in this chapter constitute the framework of analysis of this research. In the following 14 chapters, the urban regions involved in this research are analysed with the help of this framework. All the case studies, therefore, have a clear structure: after a short introduction they include six sections in which their respective situations are analysed according to the criteria. The conclusions of the research follow the case studies. More information on the cities can be found in the annex, in which the *fiches* are integrated, produced by the representatives of the 14 Eurocities. Maps of the spatial situation of each urban region involved are also included in the annex.

1   The HST-integration in Amsterdam[1]

Introduction

Since 1996 Amsterdam has been connected to the HST network by a link with Brussels and Paris. Currently existing infrastructure is used, but by the year 2005 new dedicated infrastructure should be available. This will substantially reduce travel times from Amsterdam to Rotterdam, Antwerp, Brussels and Paris. In Amsterdam, the *Thalys* will probably provide alternating services, some to CS, the current main station, and some to a new station in the south of Amsterdam, *Amsterdam-Zuid*. Around this station a top location for offices in the Netherlands will be developed. The HST connection plays an important role in these plans: it will improve the attractiveness of the area.

Accessibility

External Accessibility

Amsterdam is currently connected to the HST network by a link with Brussels and Paris (the south link). The Dutch part of the track, however, uses conventional rail infrastructure. Thus, the HST cannot yet achieve high speeds. Dedicated rail infrastructure will be built, in two stages. The first stage, the track from the Dutch/Belgian border to Rotterdam, is expected to be completed around 2002; the second stage, from Rotterdam to Amsterdam, some years later. A second link (the east link), from Frankfurt to Amsterdam, is also planned, but that project is still in an early stage. Existing rail infrastructure will be upgraded in order to accommodate the HST. The upgrading will enable the HST to reach some 200 km/h. An important goal of this east link is the connection with the HST link Cologne-Frankfurt, which is expected to be available around the year 2000. Just as for Rotterdam, for Amsterdam the link with Germany is considered more important than the south link, because

Germany is by far the largest trading partner of the Netherlands. In the more remote future, a third link with Hamburg, Copenhagen and Berlin is envisaged. Berlin especially might be an important destination when it becomes the German government centre.

The south link stops at the international airport of Schiphol, some 15 km southwest of Amsterdam. The airport is an important intermodal hub, providing good connections with its hinterland. An important policy objective of connecting Schiphol to the HST is to realise a modal shift from air transport to the HST, for continental traffic as well as for feeder traffic of intercontinental flights. This modal shift is expected to be 1.65 million passengers in 2003 on the south link.[2]

The vision of the City of Amsterdam with regard to the HST is that the city should be connected to remain competitive in the international arena for the top segment of the offices market.[3] No major city development is expected on the grounds of the connection with the HST network alone. Rather, the HST connection is a necessary condition for Amsterdam to remain competitive as a major international location, but it is by no means sufficient. As far as the tourist market is concerned, a positive influence of the HST connection on the amount of tourists is expected, especially for American tourists on a 'Europe-in-one-week' tour.

The HST Stations

An important aspect of the HST connection of Amsterdam is the choice of stopping places. Schiphol is the first stop in the Amsterdam agglomeration. The second stop could be either the central station (CS), the current main station, or *Amsterdam-Zuid*, a station which currently handles limited amounts of passengers, but in time is expected to become the fifth largest railway station in the Netherlands. Both stations will be sufficiently equipped to accommodate the HST. The final decision on the HST routing has been postponed. In the end it will be left to the HST operator to decide which station will be used. The most commonly-held opinion is that in the beginning the focus will be on CS, and in a later stage *Amsterdam-Zuid* will become dominant, especially for the link to Germany (east link). For routing reasons, having three stops in the Amsterdam region is impossible. An option is to have the trains stop at *Amsterdam-Zuid* in business hours and to have the rest of the trains halt at central station, as they contain mostly tourists. A summary of the respective arguments for the choice of the HST station is given in Table 1.1.

Basically, two passenger segments can be distinguished: business travellers

Table 1.1   A comparison of two optional HST stations in the Amsterdam region

	CS	Amsterdam-Zuid
advantages	– best connection to urban transport system – best regional rail connections – appeal of monumental train station – closest to most tourist destinations	– expected booming offices area, which will generate business travellers – good accessibility by road – good location with respect to the HST network, especially for the East link
disadvantages	– relatively bad accessibility by road – few expansion possibilities – additional travel time due to illogical routing, especially for the East link	– accessibility by collective transport is weakly developed, especially in the short run – scarcity of available land, resulting in high land prices. This might result in the absence of train stalling capacity near the station

and tourists. The former are likely to favour *Amsterdam-Zuid*, the latter will, at least in the near future, prefer CS, as this station has the most sophisticated transport system into the city centre. An important issue in this respect is the construction of a north-south city railway link in Amsterdam. This link will connect *Amsterdam-Zuid* with the city centre as well as with North Amsterdam and CS. This link will thus greatly improve the position of *Amsterdam-Zuid* on the urban public transport system. A decision on the north-south link will be made by referendum. All inhabitants of Amsterdam may then decide whether or not they want this link. The expectation is that the referendum will approve the building of the link. Apart from this link, the municipal transport authority is rescheduling transport services in order to improve the accessibility of *Amsterdam-Zuid*.

Land Scarcity[4]

Another important issue related to the choice of the HST station, is the scarcity of land in *Amsterdam-Zuid*. This might lead to *crowding out* of activities which are normally required around a HST station. Three activities are mentioned: parking lots, a bus station and stalling capacity. The latter means capacity to stall trains outside the station, in order to clean and cater them. This activity should be close to the station, as a location far away increases the loop-time of the equipment, and thus increases costs, by up to Dfl 500 million, according to the operator. This factor might in the end become decisive for the operator in the choice of a HST station. For the city it would be more optimal if broader criteria, such as the economic effects, were assessed to choose an 'optimum' HST station. Therefore, the question of where to locate the stalling capacity should be handled with care.

Parking lots might be available only at very high prices, thus limiting the attractiveness of the HST station. Nevertheless, parking lots are available at *transferia*,[5] such as Amsterdam RAI and the Amsterdam ArenA. A bus station also claims its share of the scarce land. Thus, options to minimise the land requirements must be studied. Among other things, a system with a *people mover* to a distant bus station must be considered. Finally it might be added that, in Dutch tradition, accessibility by bike is explicitly taken into account in the planning of the new station's layout.

Integration of Transport Operators

There are different urban collective transport operators. One is the rail operator (NS), the other the urban public transport authority (GVB) which operates trams, buses and the city railway. Finally, there is a regional bus operator, the NZH. These three have joined hands in planning the future collective transport system in the Amsterdam region. They strive to achieve an optimum routing schedule for all transport modes, and a good service quality. Such integration of services could improve the position of collective transport in the Amsterdam region. Examples of integration include one ticket for a multi-modal journey and an integrated information system for routing options from origin to destination. In later stages one brand name might be adopted.

Economic Potential

The economic potential of the Amsterdam urban region is very high. It is a large capital in the proximity of an international airport, a seaport and an HST link. In addition, it benefits from Dutch macro advantages, such as favourable tax laws[6] and a relatively well-educated population, which speaks several languages. For these reasons, the fact that Amsterdam attracts proportionally more European head offices of international firms is hardly surprising. The city centre of Amsterdam is an important economic area, as well as a tourist destination. In paticular, financial services are of major importance. Furthermore, lawyers, consultants, architects, etc. are located in the city centre. Nevertheless, the importance of the economic function is diminishing, for reasons of limited accessibility and, more importantly, the lack of expansion possibilities for firms.[7] A shift of offices to *Amsterdam-Zuid* can be observed, a significant example being the ABN-AMRO bank.

Before the development of *Amsterdam-Zuid*, Amsterdam tried to develop an ambitious project for the north of the city centre, the IJ-banks, to stop the outflow of employment from the city centre and to attract new employment. This project failed, at least in its initial, ambitious goals. One of the main reasons for its failure was that the project was presented as one large unit. The private participants had to take a decision whether or not to agree on the total project. This would mean a strong commitment and much risk for private parties. For that reason they decided not to go along. Now the IJ-banks are developed in stages, and the residential function will be more dominant than in the original plans. Besides, the idea is now to attract small- and medium-scale business and cultural activities. This new orientation has proved successful.

Amsterdam-Zuid

After the initial failure of the waterfront project, *Amsterdam-Zuid* became the location where the city wanted to develop *the* new top-class location for offices. This location was already widely appreciated by the private sector, because of the excellent accessibility of the location, the availability of quality housing nearby and the proximity of Schiphol Airport. Thus, this project is not likely to fail through under-investment by the private sector, especially because no strict planning horizon is set. Rather, the planning allows flexible adaptation to market signals. That is the lesson drawn from the failure of the IJ-banks project. A wide coalition of interests has created a *integral plan.* Over the entire planning period, 20 years, 660,000 square meters of office space are planned. This plan strives for high quality, through a lot of greenery, no visible parking spots, an integral area layout and pleasant public places such as squares and the railway station. These attractive features might come under pressure in the implementation, however, as they do not generate direct revenue. The integral plan emphasises the need for good collective transport to keep the accessibility by road up to standard. Finally, the integral plan strives for a pluriform – or *harmonious* – area: apart from offices, more than 1,500 houses are planned, as well as leisure activities. Finally, it seems worth mentioning that the attractiveness of *Amsterdam-Zuid* depends in part on the policy concerning the expansion of Schiphol Airport. Two locations distant from Schiphol are being considered: one in the North Sea and one in the IJsselmeer. The latter option would place *Amsterdam-Zuid* even more central, and thus increase its attractiveness.

Quality of Life

The quality of urban life is an important policy objective of the City of Amsterdam. The use of cars in the city centre, a cause of discontent for inhabitants, will be restricted, and public transport promoted. This policy follows the outcome of a 1992 referendum which showed the preference of the Amsterdam population for a 'car-free' city centre. Thus, the number of parking lots in the streets will be decreased by some 30 per cent, and replaced on a large part by large scale multi-level parking facilities. By effective traffic management, providing car drivers with information about parking availability, driving and searching for a parking place can be reduced. Additonally, the urban transport system will be upgraded. A new north-south city railway link is expected and trams will increasingly use dedicated lanes and have traffic signal priority. The supply of leisure activities is broad and widely-appreciated, and quality housing is available. Thus, it comes as no surprise that Amsterdam is a favourable living location, resulting in high prices for housing. For these reasons, there is a shortage of housing facilities. This cannot be easily solved, as expansion options are limited by environmental constraints. In general, the quality of the living environment in Amsterdam is quite high and an asset in the international competition among cities for top-quality business.

Spatial Distribution of Effects

A large proportion of the jobs in Amsterdam are in the service sector, in such activities as commerce, banking, education, etc. The housing function in the city centre is mainly occupied by high-income residents. The city centre will remain a popular living location. An overly strong and unbalanced development of *Amsterdam-Zuid* might jeopardise the economic function of the city centre.

Amsterdam is trying to retain a substantial amount of economic activity in the centre in order to guarantee its pluriformity. Some tools are available to stimulate this. The most important is the price-instrument. Amsterdam tries to set the prices in the south area high in relation to the national price level, in order to attract new international companies instead of relocating companies. Furthermore, Amsterdam can influence the type of economic activities it attracts, because the city is the owner of the ground.

An important issue in this context is the relocation of the stock exchange. Owing to expansion requirements it cannot stay at its current location, the historical city centre. Thus, a new location has to be found. Although relocation in *Amsterdam-Zuid* would undoubtedly stimulate international investment, the city is hesitant to accommodate this move as it might result in a great shift of employment from the city centre, since a lot of related business is expected to follow the stock exchange. A similar shift was observed when the court moved to *Amsterdam-Zuid* and a lot of law firms followed. A location on the waterfront is now considered optimum for the exchange. A locational policy is followed with respect to Schiphol.

A lot of business activities wish to locate close to Schiphol. This is allowed only if these activities are considered *air-related*. Criteria for that status are not incontestable, but they can serve to influence which companies are allowed and which are not. The norms of air-relatedness for a location in Schiphol might be useful to avoid unnecessary competition between Schiphol and *Amsterdam-Zuid*, as Schiphol currently is the most expensive location in the Netherlands, a position *Amsterdam-Zuid* is aiming for. This coordination rather than competition should be possible, given the fact that Amsterdam is the largest shareholder of Schiphol.

Social Distribution of Effects

The direct benefits of the HST are enjoyed by travellers, either for tourist or business purposes. The majority of the population of Amsterdam will not benefit *directly* from the HST link. Obviously, indirectly all citizens benefit one way or another from a greater prosperity of Amsterdam. That message should be communicated, however, in order to get support for the HST connection. This is especially important if there are popular movements against such projects. In the case of the HST link that does not seem to be so. Some organisations in the vicinity of *Amsterdam-Zuid* have to be compensated, most importantly the sports clubs, which have to be offered new locations as their current location will be used for other purposes. These clubs show a cooperative spirit. Another class of affected persons are the inhabitants in the districts close to the HST station. They have shown some concern about parking problems in their neighbourhoods. Again, this group has shown no hostility towards the project as such. This cooperative spirit has not emerged spontaneously. The policy-makers have pursued an active policy to involve all kinds of interests in the decision-making process.

Organising Capacity

The administration of the City of Amsterdam is partly split up into district councils, which have their own planning policy. Also, a regional authority (ROA) has been set up, to govern the entire metropolitan region effectively. Thus, in the functional region of Amsterdam three public policy-making bodies exist. Apart from these bodies, other organisations – public as well as private – have an interest in the development in *Amsterdam-Zuid*, such as the national government and the provinces. The development of the new HST station cannot be analysed in isolation from the entire *Amsterdam-Zuid* project, as for instance, the layout of the infrastructure will greatly influence the shape of the area. In general, three different concepts for the construction of the infrastructure have been studied: *dijk, dek and dok.*

- *Dijk* (dyke): in this concept the bundle of infrastructure will be visible and dominant. This will result in a visual segregation between the two sides of the infrastructure bundle.
- *Dek* (deck): this concept, as does the *dijk* concept, envisages infrastructure on the ground level. In this case, however, a kind of extra level will be built above the infrastructure. This results in additional building space. The difference in height might be a problem, however.
- *Dok* (dock): this concept results in the construction of infrastructure underground. Thus, additional space comes available and there is no segregation of two sides. This option is the most costly – rough estimates indicate some Dfl 2 billion – but most promising as well.

The choice of any of these three concepts will severely influence HST-related matters directly. For that reason, an overview of the organising structure of the *Amsterdam-Zuid* project will be given. A coalition of public and private participants was formed to draw up an overall plan for the area. Participants were: the relevant public authorities of Amsterdam as well as three of its districts; the national rail company (NS); the national transport department, private parties such as the RAI congress centre and ABN-AMRO Bank; and other institutions located in south, such as the university and the World Trade Centre. This coalition was chaired by an outsider in policy-making but an insider in real estate, to keep in touch with the market. The coalition agreed on a integral plan. Although tensions between different interests might arise at a later stage, all participants are agreed on the basic goals of the project.

For the development of *Amsterdam-Zuid* some kind of development institution has to be created. A public-private partnership is considered an option, with broadly the same partners as the ones who drew up the integral plan. The national government may also participate as investor. For the government, this would be a new method of financing projects, as they are not to provide infrastructure without returns, but to participate as investors, aiming for a decent return. The fact that the government is willing to participate as a risk-taking investor will be an important signal to the market. Who will have the control of the HST station itself is still unclear, although it is most likely that the specialised subsidiary of the railway company will manage the station. For the HST specifically, the organising capacity to reach widely-approved decisions might be underdeveloped. A lobby organisation was set up in to assure Amsterdam's HST interests, with private as well as public participants. Its mission was successful, but it does not seek a major role in the decision-making process to come. The smooth rise and fall of this institution show the capacity to create successful ad hoc partnerships between private and public parties. For practical HST-related issues, such as the ownership of the new station and the station layout, the public organising capacity might be underdeveloped. Nevertheless, broad consensus seems to exist, so conflicts can be effectively resolved, as the common interests are considerable.

The Most Important Themes of the Amsterdam Case

Two Stations

In Amsterdam two stations – apart from Schiphol Airport – are considered possible HST stations. Both will be provided with sufficient infrastructure to accommodate the HST. For routing reasons it is impossible to stop at both stations, thus alternating services are likely. Amsterdam central station (CS), the current main station, is located in the north of the city centre. For most tourists this is the 'optimum' station, because of its location in the historical city. No major economic impact from the HST connection is expected here. The other station, *Amsterdam-Zuid*, will be developed in the south of Amsterdam, at an advantageous location in the HST network, especially with a view to the planned link with Germany. Probably, the CS will remain the main station in the coming years, especially for the south link to Paris, on which HST services are currently provided. In time the focus will shift to *Amsterdam-Zuid*, more conveniently situated for business travellers. An option could be to have the trains halt at *Amsterdam-Zuid* in business hours and the rest of the day at CS, to provide a good service for tourists. Near *Amsterdam-Zuid* a project to develop a top-class location for offices has been initiated. Because the HST connection is considered an important condition for the success of this ambitious project, the HST policy-making has been integrated into it. This has resulted in policy attention for the HST station in a wider context. No more than moderate political attention, however, is given to the effects of the HST as such. For this reason, plans for a well-functioning HST station have remained underdeveloped.

Land Scarcity

The new HST station is located in the middle of the new *Amsterdam-Zuid* project. As this project has only limited amounts of land available and aims to attract the top segment of the office market, land prices are high. Therefore the HST station's integration into a larger project tends to crowd out facilities normally available at a station, such as train stalling capacity, parking places and a bus-station. Without these facilities the internal accessibility of the station will suffer. Obviously, the absence of such facilities will severely influence the attractiveness of the HST station for passengers and the operator. There seems to be a conflict between the goal of maximising the number of passengers and that of maximally developing the business location *Amsterdam-Zuid*. This conflict has to be resolved, keeping in mind that in the end the HST operator decides where and when to halt the trains.

Spatial Distribution of Effects

The development of *Amsterdam-Zuid* will have major spatial consequences. The economic function of the city centre will come under pressure, as companies might want to move to south. The threat is recognised and market-oriented policies have been adopted to prevent the outflow of economic activity.

One measure is to develop high-quality accommodation only, so that the price mechanism will prevent a shift of companies from the centre to *Amsterdam-Zuid*. Prices will be too high for local companies, whereas international business can still be attracted, as the price level is only moderate by international standards. Besides, *Amsterdam-Zuid* sets out to attract large companies, whereas the centre of Amsterdam houses a lot of small-scale business. Finally, a new underground railway line from *Amsterdam-Zuid* to North Amsterdam through the city centre will be constructed. This line will improve the accessibility of the city centre and thus its attractiveness as a business location. Schiphol is a top-class business location near *Amsterdam-Zuid*, so competition between the two locations is likely. To avoid this, some coordination is striven for. Schiphol will accommodate air-related business and *Amsterdam-Zuid* will aim for other top-class business. This coordination can be realised, as Amsterdam is the largest shareholder of Schiphol and heavily involved in the *Amsterdam-Zuid* project as well.

Car Accessibility

Car accessibility of HST stations has proved to be an important theme in HST-related policy-making. This holds true for the Amsterdam case as well. Access by car to Amsterdam CS is relatively awkward. In the present situation only about one-tenth of the passengers arrives by car. This situation cannot easily be changed. However, Amsterdam CS is likely to become the tourist station and tourists are not as car-oriented as business travellers. In *Amsterdam-Zuid*, car accessibility is of greater importance, but the available parking capacity may be inadequate. Schiphol, close to Amsterdam, has very good parking facilities. Therefore, most regional passengers arriving by car might prefer Schiphol as the HST boarding station. *Amsterdam-Zuid* could serve as boarding station for business travellers from offices nearby at somewhat high parking tariffs. All three HST stations will have excellent accessibility by collective transport. Park-and-ride facilities, such as *transferia*, might reduce the need for parking capacity at the stations themselves. Finally, taxi cabs can resolve some of the parking problems. An attractive option might therefore be to sell HST tickets which include a taxi ride.

Notes

1   Coauthor: drs. P.W. de Langen, EURICUR.

2   According to a study by the Amsterdam Municipal Board of Urban Planning, 1994.
3   See, amongst others, a study by the NEI, 1992.
4   Land scarcity refers to *economic* scarcity: there is land available for building purposes, but the location close to the HST station is so attractive that there is much more demand for location in this areas than can be accommodated. Thus, land prices are high.
5   *Transferia* are locations with good accessibility by car, mostly located at the rim of the city, where travellers can park and change to collective transport into the city centre.
6   Tax laws for regional headquarters of foreign multinationals are quite favourable in the Netherlands compared with other countries on the continent.
7   As an indication, the following figures are illustrative: the current employment in the city centre is about 80,000, whereas it was about 150,000 some 20 years ago.

2 The HST-integration in Antwerp

Introduction

Since 1996, the high-speed *Thalys*-trains have stopped at Antwerp, for the time being at the peripheral station of Antwerp-Berchem. According to the plans, in the near future the HST will stop at the central station. To convert this head-end station into a through station, a tunnel will be built under the city. There is relatively little room around the CS to accommodate economic activities that could be attracted by the HST, nor has Antwerp as yet developed an explicit policy to draw socioeconomic profit from the HST integration. Because the city also lacks the administrative and financial means needed to evolve an energetic and decisive spatial-economic policy, it may miss out on advantageous development prospects. Another very pressing question related to the HST integration is to what degree the HST station needs to be accessible by car.

Accessibility

Access to Harbour and City

For external access to the Antwerp region, the available infrastructure capacity has to be shared by goods transport to Antwerp harbour and by passenger transport. That raises problems for road and rail infrastructure. The ring motorway around Antwerp is quite often congested. So, to keep the harbour accessible, measures are needed to stimulate the use of public transport and selective use of the car. The share of the railway in hinterland transport to and from the port is greater in Antwerp than in Rotterdam. However, rail capacity for the transportation of goods to and from the port is considered inadequate. Moreover, the trains pass through densely populated parts of the Antwerp agglomeration. The possibility is therefore considered of constructing a new

34

railway for goods transport that circumvents the populous areas and increases the rail capacity available for the port. The capacity thus vacated on the present rail infrastructure can then be used for passenger transport.

The HST Connection

Antwerp will be joined to the PBKA HST network. The Antwerp stop will lie between the Brussels and Rotterdam stopping places. From 2004 onward, two HSTs an hour are planned. At the moment Antwerp is called at (four times a day in both directions) by the *Thalys*, running between Paris-Nord and Amsterdam. It stops at Berchem, on the outskirts of Antwerp. Once the dedicated HST line is operational, the central station will be the HST station. The choice was between that and the Berchem location. The latter is more accessible by car and offers more space for large-scale development of economic activities than the CS. Nevertheless, in the end the CS has been preferred, the expected impetus for the revitalisation of the centre being a consideration. There is much degeneration and much vacant business accommodation, especially in the quarter northeast of the CS. The quarter numbers only 22,000 job opportunities to a population of over 60,000. A large-scale local social-economic revitalisation project was recently undertaken, financially supported by the European Union (in the framework of the URBAN Community Initiative). Another reason to opt for the CS was the appeal of the stately station building, a monument and showpiece of the city.

The connection to the HST line also works as a catalyst for the realisation of the north-south rail tunnel. For more than a quarter of a century plans have been made for a tunnel which should permit a through railway line through Antwerp. The present plans are to bore a tunnel at a depth of 18 metres beneath the HST station. On the minus-two level, platforms will be constructed for ongoing trains, including HSTs. They can then run unencumbered from south to north and back; for such trains, CS will no longer be a head-end station. On the minus-one level another four new platforms will be built, and on the plus-one level, six platforms will be retained (at the moment there are 10). The platforms on the plus-one and minus-one levels retain the character of a head-end station. With platforms on three levels, the capacity of the station can be substantially extended without violating the classical station building. The tunnel project requires an investment of 18,000 million BEF, of which 6,000 million will go to the renovation of the station. The building activities for the tunnel could be undertaken in 1998 and completed in 2005. About three-fifths of the investments will be financed by the central government. The remainder will come from, among other sources, European subsidies and loans from the NMBS/SNCB. The money flows will be coordinated through a financing company, *Financier TGV*. Not only Dutch destinations will profit from the new through rail connection: because regional trains will run on it as well, people living north of Antwerp will also be able to travel more quickly to the centre of Antwerp, and further to the south – an important aspect when it comes to strengthening the regional support for the construction of the tunnel. With respect to the economic exploitation of CS, the NMBS/SNCB operates via a real-estate subsidiary company, Eurostation.

Airports

For Antwerp the airports of Antwerp and Brussels are most relevant. The former has a limited regional function. This airport dispatched over 250,000 passengers in 1994. The principal destinations from Antwerp airport are London and Amsterdam. In due course, both destinations will be easily accessible by HST, the travel times then being, respectively, two hours 33 minutes and one hour 10 minutes. The expectation is that some demand for flights to London from Antwerp airport will remain. Companies in the Antwerp region in particular (the diamond sector for one) set great store on retaining the regional airport. To improve its performance, proposals have been made to lengthen the runway. However, there seems to be insufficient political and social support for such an undertaking, for one thing because the airport adjoins built-up residential areas. Brussels-Zaventem airport lies at about 45 km from the centre of Antwerp.

Pre-metro, the Preliminary City Railway

Antwerp exploits what is called here a pre-metro system. This public transport system runs in part underground and in part above ground, mostly on exclusive rolling stock consisting of somewhat superannuated tram carriages. There are three lines, which all share the section between the left Scheldt bank and the Opera. Two lines turn south past the CS, one to the Belgiëlei and one to the Mercatorstraat. In 1996 the third pre-metro line was opened; it runs past the CS to surface by the Sports Palace, on the northern side of Antwerp.

Accessibility of the CS

An important subject of discussion in Antwerp has been how far the CS, and hence the future HST station, has to be accessible by car. There is some tension between the ambition for optimum access to the city and that for an optimum quality of urban life. Both aims are highly relevant to the revitalisation of the inner city. Opinions diverge, however, about how to attain these aims. The choice of the CS as HST station reflects the concern for adequate access to the junction, of which access by car is an important part. Unlimited access of private cars to the centre is undesirable, however. For the sake of a high-grade living environment in the centre, the inconvenience caused by cars should be minimised. That is why attempts to make the centre more accessible should stress the role of the public transport. The present quality of secondary public transport in Antwerp is not up to par, however.

A (phased) upgrading of the secondary public transport system seems inevitable, therefore. Some important elements in that context are:

- the construction of more exclusive infrastructure for public transport, to raise the speed;
- adequate connections to other transport systems; in that respect P+R-systems on the outskirts of the town suggest themselves;
- the purchase of high-grade rolling stock. Some disadvantages of the present old stock are low comfort, low capacity and a lack of appeal in particular to potential new (HST) travellers.

The centre must be made easily but selectively accessible to cars. That means that those who are particularly partial to the car and are prepared to pay extra for its use (for instance, people travelling by HST for business reasons), must be permitted easy car access to the centre. Measures to that effect could be: traffic-guidance systems (dynamic signs pointing the way to car parks); pricing mechanisms on access roads; (protected) lanes for the exclusive use of target groups; parking facilities near the urban transport junction (CS) priced high enough to stimulate selective use.

There are plans to build two underground car parks in the immediate environment of the CS, with a total capacity of 1,250 cars. One of them is intended to be built south of the CS underneath a planned new square, the Kievitplein. It will be situated at the new southern entrance of the CS. The second one is proposed under the Astridplein adjoining the station. There does not seem to be much political support for this latter car park, in view of plans to make the Astridplein a traffic-free square, as well as drastically to cut down the car-traffic capacity on the Turnhoutsebaan leading to it. This road is intended to become an important public transport axis. It has to strengthen the presently weak east-west public transport relations and is therefore considered an essential precondition for the sound functioning of the CS as a transport junction. Access to the Kievitplein is better, since the Plantin and Moretus Lei will remain an important access road for cars. Hence there is more political support for the Kievitplein underground car park.

The structure of the public transport system is mostly radial: most lines start or end in the centre. The rail tunnel planned under the town will considerably extend the rail capacity near Antwerp. The possible construction of a new railway line for goods transport to the port will add to it, and bring the creation of a kind of RER-network in the region within reach. That high-quality network should first and foremost provide (relatively frequent) connections between city and region and between various locations in the ring of the urban region. The development of such a network belongs to the competence of the Flemish region. A new rail station will be built at the north side of the city. It could be used, for instance, by commuters going to Brussels, who at the moment has to cross the city by car.

Economic Potential[1]

The production structure of Antwerp is dominated by the port and a range of port-related industries and transport service activities. The port is the second in Europe in terms of transhipment (over 110 million tons a year), and grows rapidly (more than 14 million tons in five years). It defines itself more and more as a general-cargo port. The container sector is particularly fast-growing. Among the port-related industries, the flourishing chemical industry, the oil refineries and car assembly are of particular importance. Antwerp is the major international diamond centre. The diamond trade accounts for half of the world diamond trade and seven per cent of total Belgian exports. In addition, the tourist sector received a strong boost in 1993, when Antwerp was the cultural capital of Europe. The well-known pattern of a manufacturing sector declining in terms of employment and a growing service sector (except for transport) is confirmed in Antwerp.

The development of employment has varied with the international business cycle. The number of jobs declined by 15,000 (-5.3 per cent) between 1980 and 1984. A period of partial recovery (by 9,000 jobs) followed, which lasted until 1990. Since then, the number of jobs has once more declined by 4,000 to the 1982 level. From the point of view of the Antwerp city region, the situation appears to be less alarming. Since the early 1980s the decline of jobs in the city has been exceeded by the net growth of 23,000 jobs in the 38 towns of the Antwerp city region. There has been a shift of jobs from the central city to the ring towns, due to the lack of space in the central city, urban policy measures and the process of suburbanisation (Vranken en Abdeljelil, 1995).

Quality of Life

The choice of CS as the HST station is an opportunity to give the centre an economic boost. New economic activities may be attracted to the centre. The increasingly overcrowded motorways around the town provide one more reason for a high-quality railway station to become a significant location factor. The choice of CS could therefore work out positively on the urban quality of life. The economic impulse might restore degenerated neighbourhoods to new appeal. In addition, the rehabilitation could work as a magnet to the more affluent citizens who have left the town in the last few decades. However, the choice of CS could also have negative effects as the traffic generated by this transport junction could threaten the quality of life in the centre. To strive for selective car access to the centre seems indeed a necessary condition for its economic vitality.

Spatial Distribution of Activities

On the ground level of the CS there is space to develop commercial activities, shops in particular. In the environment of the station, but rather dispersed, there is quite a lot of vacant business accommodation. There is hardly any room for the large-scale activities that might be attracted by the HST station. Neither have any concrete suggestions been made about how to profit from the HST development. Admittedly, at a high level of abstraction, the conditions for making economic capital out of an HST connection have been investigated. One conclusion of that study is that it is essential for a city to anticipate how the power of such a junction can bring in new activity. By a wait-and-see attitude the town may miss out on valuable new economic prospects. Unfortunately, there has been no follow-up of this study to analyse the actual prospects in the inner City of Antwerp. The function of the station as a point of reference for new economic activities is thus unlikely to be sufficiently exploited.

The URBAN-project does not take the effects of the HST station into account. Chances are that economic activity attracted by the HST development will be unable to find sufficient space in the town quarter northeast of the CS. The URBAN-objectives may also frustrate potential effects of the HST station, for instance reserving sites exclusively for small-scale developments on behalf of the present inhabitants. The evolving competition between activities might well end up by profiting nobody, since it would obstruct the necessary revitalisation of the inner city.

Social Distribution of Effects

A theme for special attention is the social acceptance of an HST track through the densely populated centre of Antwerp. Especially in the Dam neighbourhood, where the railway will possibly surface, adverse effects may occur. Moreover, inhabitants of Berchem are at present inconvenienced by freight trains in particular. Berchem is one of the busiest junctions for goods trains in Europe. The trains skirt the built-up area, causing noise and hazards. Alternative lines for goods trains are being studied. It is, however, the quality of life in the centre that gives the most concern. As an HST station, the CS will attract extra car and other traffic, a threat to the quality of life in the centre. A situation could evolve in which the entire region profits from the improved accessibility, while the negative external effects are concentrated in the inner city.

Organising Capacity

The government body responsible for the rail infrastructure is the federal government. It is the most important financier of the rail tunnel through Antwerp. The Belgian government does not seem to bother about making capital out of the economic potential created in HST cities by its massive investment in infrastructure. The construction of the tunnel has to be approved by the Flemish region, the authority responsible for spatial planning and transport affairs in Flanders. The City of Antwerp, as advisor on the tunnel construction, is competent to set preconditions for the HST integration. The city itself does not contribute to the financing of the HST project.

The City of Antwerp is the proper authority to take additional measures towards optimum profit from the HST connection. Lack of consensus within the city corporation and lack of means to take adequate measures seem to be an obstruction, however. Besides, the administrative body responsible for economic policy (other than the port administration) seems rather too small to pursue an energetic and decisive economic strategy. That circumstance may well cause a lack of balance in the weigh-off of interests involved. Thus, regrettably, investment in the quality of internal accessibility and in locations appealing to new economic activities seems difficult to realise.

The Most Important Themes of the Antwerp Case

Economic Potential

The central station will be *the* HST station of Antwerp. That choice creates the opportunity to give the centre an economic boost, retain the monumental building as an attraction point of the city and accomplish the north-south rail connection that has been an ambition for some time. However, a lot of money will be invested in HST infrastructure in Antwerp without the promise of economic return. By present plans, an HST station may be realised with poor internal access and no space to accommodate the economic activities it might attract. A follow-up study to assess what type of economic activities can be drawn to the centre of Antwerp and how they could be accommodated in a balanced way in the immediate neighbourhood of the CS, is therefore urgently required.

The choice of CS will imply some necessary complementary measures, namely, to improve the internal accessibility, and the provision of space for HST-related economic activities. Failure to take these measures, from inability or otherwise, might in the end necessitate the appointment of a peripheral HST station, which would mean the waste of resources spent for the central HST station. In that connection, the founding of a specific (independent) organisation would perhaps be advisable, to be responsible for the development and exploitation of the HST station, comparable with the organisation of airports independently from the air-transport companies. For, indeed, there are quite important economic and transport-related interests at stake, which should be dealt with professionally.

Internal Accessibility

Examples of other HST stations in Europe demonstrate that a certain degree of car accessibility (connections and parking capacity) is a necessary condition for the junction's transport performance and attractiveness. However, improved car access to the centre of Antwerp is considered to threaten the quality of life and the performance of the (mostly surface) secondary public transport systems. Besides, the public transport system seems to lack what it takes to function as high-quality secondary transport to the HST. An analysis of the profile of expected HST travellers to and from Antwerp-CS recommends itself. Its results should serve as an important input for the reorganisation of the entire internal transport system (accessibility by car and public transport). An adequate traffic-control system in the inner city and improvement of the secondary public transport seem necessary from all points of view. To assess the parking capacity required near the CS, not only should the needs of train passengers be considered, but also those of surrounding services and facilities, such as hotel and congress facilities and the zoo. Needless to say, unlimited access of cars to the Antwerp inner city is undesirable. An adequate tariff system should ensure that only such car traffic for which high-grade access is essential will be permitted.

Organising Capacity

Complicated political structures (in Belgium as well as Antwerp) and a lack of financial means make it difficult to respond adequately to the new economic development prospects opened up by the HST. However, the economic situation in Antwerp necessitates cooperation of the relevant actors. From the urban regions of Bilbao, Newcastle and Liège we know that serious economic recession provides a strong impetus for actors to work together constructively and 'across-the-region' on a strategic plan to strengthen the regional economy. To prevent making the socioeconomic situation in the Antwerp region worse, a timely decisive policy to benefit from the HST integration is, therefore, necessary.

Note

1   The text of this section is based on Van den Berg et al., 1996.

3   The HST-integration in Brno

Introduction

At the moment, HST planning for the region of Brno is still mostly spatial planning. The main concern for Czechia is first to develop a good basic network of transport infrastructure. That calls for relatively large investment. To improve the Brno region's international accessibility is considered an important precondition for attracting new economic activity. In Brno, the move of the main station is being considered to facilitate the connection to the HST network and to create space for new urban developments.

Accessibility

Developing Rail Transport in Czechia

High speed is a relative notion. In general the assumption is warranted that, with the rise of a country's prosperity, the need for faster transport systems will increase (the social value of time rises with increasing prosperity). In Czechia, large-scale investment is now needed in all types of transport infrastructure, such as motorways, rail infrastructure and airports. The first concern is to build up an adequate basic network of transport infrastructure. The existing infrastructure will have to be upgraded step by step, in relation to and anticipation of the economic development of the country. For a long time, rather too little attention has been paid in Czechia to investment in the rail network. From 1989 onwards, several projects have been taken in hand to improve the rail network and make it ready for a speed of 160 km/h. The modernisation of the rail network is planned to be ready by 2007. Around 2000 tilting trains will be taken into operation. The travel time between Prague and Brno by train will then drop from three hours 15 minutes to two hours 15 minutes, and that between Brno and Vienna to about one hour 15 minutes. The improvement will permit better transport performances at acceptable investment costs. Currently, the construction of rail infrastructure for speeds up to 300 km/h is not under discussion. Such an advance would only be taken at the expense of the construction of other, more urgently needed infrastructure.

Developing the Rail Network around Brno

Brno lies at an important junction of transport infrastructure. The railway lines from Dresden and Prague to Vienna and from Nuremberg, Pilsen and Prague to Ostrava and Katowice pass through Brno. In the next century these sections will be gradually upgraded to high-speed lines permitting speeds of 300 km/h. Once *dedicated* HST infrastructure has been laid out between Prague and Brno, the travel time there and back can be reduced to just over an hour. A grave problem for Brno is how to justify the relatively high costs of investment in the HST network. To recover the investment within an acceptable term, daily passenger numbers of between 16,000 and 28,000 between Prague and Brno would be required. That figure is a multiple of the present transport flow between the two Czech cities. Internal air traffic between Prague and Brno is negligible, and, consequently, its substitution is hardly a consideration for deciding about the construction of the HST tracks. Therefore, the construction of the high-speed railway lines would have to be justified mostly by the expected rise of the international transport flows. Because Czechia lies centrally in Europe and is transversed by important transport corridors, the through HST lines are a European interest. In addition, internal demand for transport is expected to rise considerably as soon as there are adequate mutual transport connections.

Because of lack of resources, a number of desired investments in the rail network cannot now be carried through. There is a rather strong lobby in Czechia for the building of new roads. As a result, much of the national budget is indeed being spent on that form of transport infrastructure. Nevertheless, to reserve space at the present stage is essential to expedite the future development of the rail network. That explains why HST planning for Brno is currently mostly spatial planning.

Moving the Station

Brno is considering moving the central station about 600 metres, to allow for a more favourable urban development and a better connection to the international rail network. The space around the present station is too limited to permit expansion. In addition, the station and the related rail infrastructure obstruct the southward development of the urban centre. The expected connection to the European HST network and the related prospects of economic development are powerful motives to accelerate the reform of the municipal rail system. Timely anticipation of the new opportunities can yield an important comparative advantage with respect to other, competitive junctions, and is therefore of strategic importance to regional, and thus national, development.

A disadvantage of the rail layout in Brno is that in order to stop at Brno (at the new as well as the old station), trains from Prague to Vienna have to retrace part of the track, which means some loss of travel time. For the time being and at the speeds now envisaged for the rail network (up to 160 km/h) that need not be a serious problem. At a later stage, when speeds up to 300 km/h come into the picture, a new track might have to be laid out to avoid loss of travel time. To undertake that work now, in the present situation and given the relatively high investments needed, does not seem advisable. However, it is desirable to reserve the required space now.

Role of the Airport

At present, Brno airport plays only a marginal role in regular services (5,000 passengers in 1996). Most air transport served by Brno airport consists of charter services (115,000 passengers in 1996). Just two destinations are served by regular lines: Prague and Zurich. The airport is trying to increase their frequency. The extension of transport services hinges upon the market demand. For the time being, the airport has sufficient capacity to accommodate an extension of air traffic. The airport lies seven kilometres from the city. There is no direct rail service. A rail connection with the airport would be most profitable for charter traffic, which aims at a different target group than the regular services. Some charter passengers will probably choose the train for secondary transport if the quality is adequate. Brno airport will continue to be important as a feeder for the intercontinental airports of Zurich and Prague. The HST, on the contrary, will be particularly important for connections between Brno and the principal surrounding European cities. Both transport systems will indeed be significant for the city's international accessibility, but have no mutual complementary functions.

The Role of Other Transport Modes

In Brno, bus services currently play a major role in national and international traffic. In the future they are expected to be replaced by rail transport, as soon as the railway companies can offer a better product. Although the future main station of Brno will be further from the old centre, that will not make much difference in terms of internal access. Between the locations of the old and new stations, a new tram line (*Métro léger automatique*) is planned.

Economic Potential

Industrial activities constitute the basis of the regional economy. The economy of Czechia and of the region around Brno has long been dominated by industrial activities, notably machinery industry. The competitive advantage of the region is for the most part incorporated in the skills and relatively high productiveness of the workforce. The region is now trying to graft the present economic development on to the industrial basis by attracting related service activities. The industrial park is currently being restructured and revitalised. In addition, a technological park is being developed with links to the technical university, for which high-grade technological activities are being solicited. There is comparatively little unemployment in the region. The expectation is, however, that unemployment figures will rise with progressive economic liberalisation and under the increasing pressure on the profitability of economic activities. Improvement of international access is considered a major condition for the attraction of new economic activity. It will also open up better tourist prospects for the urban region.

Quality of Life

Because the chances of economic development hinge largely on the quality of the living environment, Brno has every reason to enter the European HST network in good time. The HST is a relatively environment-friendly mode which can replace part of the car and air traffic or at least prevent their unbridled growth. In that way, the HST can contribute a great deal to the quality of the living environment and to easy international access. Good-quality rail transport can also make bus transport, currently useful but relatively harmful to the environment, largely superfluous.

It is most relevant to know fairly soon how the plans for the new station will proceed. If the decision is delayed, investment in the surrounding station quarter is likely to stagnate. The building of the new station is supposed to give a welcome impetus to ameliorate the zone between the existing and the new station. This zone has fallen into serious decay, and delay of the decision about the building of the station would therefore be most ill-advised. It might undermine the confidence of potential investors and citizens in the future prospects of the urban region, and cause the loss of promising economic opportunities.

Spatial Distribution of Activities

Hopefully, with the construction of the new railway station, the development of a new urban zone on the south side of the old centre becomes possible. So far, the station and the related rail infrastructure have effectively blocked such development. Once that barrier has been lifted, the city can quite naturally expand towards the south. Care should be taken in planning the zone to prevent the formation of a new urban barrier. Efforts will have to be made carefully to integrate the new station and its surroundings in the environment. One suggestion is to construct part of the connecting infrastructure underground.

For the proposed development quarter, a mixture of activities is envisaged: houses, offices, and a variety of services. There is an area of over 1.2 million square metres available for development. The area will be developed in stages. The first stage, concerning mostly business functions, could be taken in hand regardless of the decision about the move of the station, but would be accelerated by that decision. At a later stage of development, the housing function will become more important.

Social Distribution of Effects

The new site of the station will be further from the old centre than the present one. The railway station could thus become less accessible to part of the population. Therefore, adequate collective transport to connect the new station to the old centre has to be provided. Because the much-decayed zone between the old and the new station site will be rehabilitated as the new station is developed, the urban living climate will be improved at the same time. The temporary building activity could cause some inconvenience, but residential buildings or cultural heritage need hardly be touched, and since, for the time being, no substantial infrastructural measures are necessary in the town, the negative effects for the citizens will be slight.

Organising Capacity

The present internal transport flows cannot justify the construction of the HST lines in Czechia; the European dimension is needed for a successful proposal. Therefore, the urban region of Brno has a great interest in exchanging information with other European cities and jointly putting pressure on the higher authorities to speed up the construction of the HST lines.

The move of the HST station seems of great strategic importance for the spatial-economic development prospects of the urban region. It could give a powerful positive boost to the attraction of new citizens and economic activity. The move of the railway station will also require substantial investments by national actors (the railway companies, among others). The profits expected from the planned development may seem insufficient to them to warrant the considerable investments needed. However, in the long term, the new development opportunities created and the enlargement of the regional market will be of great importance to the national actors as well. So in the long run, the interests of the urban and national actors are likely to converge.

The lack of regional government in Czechia, and in particular in the urban region of Brno, is seen as a serious obstacle to the development of a coherent regional policy, especially in the area of transport and physical planning. With an alert and decisive government layer with sufficient competencies, the problems concerned with secondary regional public transport and with the coordination of urban development with that of the airport could be taken in hand with more success.

The Most Important Themes of the Brno Case

Influence on Economic Development

Adequate international accessibility is an important precondition for the attraction of new internationally-oriented activity. The geographic situation of Brno at the crossing of important corridors, from Berlin and Prague to Bratislava and Budapest, and from Vienna to Warsaw, is a strategic one. Unfortunately, the present quality of its infrastructure is inadequate, especially in terms of international accessibility. Therefore, connection to the developing European high-speed railway network is a necessary condition for the city to attract new economic activity. It is not a sufficient condition, however. With important agglomerations such as Prague and Vienna close at hand, comparative advantages need to be offered to new companies. Such advantages could be a well-educated professional population and appealing levels of wages and productivity. Also, the quality of the living environment will be of increasing importance to attracting new activities. Therefore investment in the HST, a relatively environmentally-friendly transport mode, is of strategic interest to the urban economy of Brno.

Location of the HST Station

Brno is considering the construction of a new station that in future will serve as a HST stopping place, about 600 metres south of the present one. The present railway station offers no opportunity for spatial expansion and its available facilities are outdated. Its situation is an obstacle to the town's development towards the south. With the intended move, Brno hopes to create space for a mixture of new activities: business units, houses and services. The new station will be built along existing rail tracks, so that it does not call for substantial investment in new infrastructure. The building of the new station will mean an impetus to efforts to enhance the living environment between the old and the new station. The location of the new station will not unduly affect the travel times from Brno to other towns; only the service to Ostrava and Katowice will become faster. The final decision about the move of the railway station – approved in the master plan – must be confirmed quickly. To put it off would make the city's spatial-economic development uncertain, and make investors wary of putting their money into rehabilitating that degraded town quarter sufficiently to attract economic activity. In fact, pending the definitive choice of the new station's location, money is still being spent on the old one. However, it is not more effective to spend money on the old railway station, and since the upgrading of the old station might have a negative effect on the decision-making about the new one, the preferred development of the city might be in jeopardy. If Brno opts for the new station, it will put itself in the vanguard of Eastern Europe as to HST development. With an attractive station environment and easy internal access, Brno will fulfil an important precondition for making capital out of HST integration.

Relation with the Airport

At present, the city of Brno does not have a very good international accessibility. Brno airport provides only two regular services to Prague and Zurich, both at a very low frequency. The airport's most important function is currently the charter function. To increase the frequency of the regular services is considered the first logical step. At a later stage, the number of destinations can be increased. The regular services function as feeders for intercontinental flights from Prague and Zurich. Prague is far enough away for maintaining the airport to be relevant, especially to business travellers. The regional airport can certainly support efforts to attract new economic activity to the region. Connection to the HST system will not make the airport superfluous, for the airport will give the city access to intercontinental transport systems and to cities not (attractively) served by the HST. The HST, unlike air services, offers travellers centre-to-centre connections from one city to another. In that sense, the HST will be supplementary to the airport. Either transport system serves to improve the city's international accessibility, but they do not serve as feeders to each other's services. Therefore, there is no need to create an HST station at the airport of Brno. A good connection by regional railway would be desirable, however. Especially for charter transport, the regional train can be an important complementary transport mode.

4   The HST-integration in Brussels[1]

Introduction

Brussels lies very centrally at a junction of HST lines. The nodal function of Brussels will be strengthened further in the near future by the construction of new lines. The Brussels HST station is Brussels-Midi. Large-scale investment will be made in and around this modern station in the coming years in office accommodation, shopping functions and low-rent housing, in view of the important nodal function of the station. In the more remote future, Brussels *Schaerbeek-formation* in the northern part of the city is envisaged as the main station for HST connections.

Accessibility

External Accessibility

Brussels is connected to two HST lines: Amsterdam-Brussels-Paris (of which the section Amsterdam-Brussels still on existing track), and Brussels-London by the Channel tunnel. In the coming years, Brussels will become even more important as an HST junction, when the dedicated HST line Brussels-Antwerp-Rotterdam-Amsterdam will come into operation, as well as Brussels-Liège-Cologne. In Table 4.1 travel times by HST from Brussels to some major destinations are indicated. A line Brussels-Namur-Luxembourg-Metz-Strasbourg is also under consideration, but that will probably not be a dedicated HST line.

At the moment, Brussels-Midi in the southern part of Brussels is the central HST station, and according to the plans the future HST towards Amsterdam will also stop at Brussels-North. A weakness of Brussels-Midi is that it is a terminal station for trains from London. The Eurostar trains cannot continue from there. It would be more logical for Eurostar to run on to Amsterdam or

51

Table 4.1   Travel times from Brussels to different destinations by HST

Destination	1997	2002
Paris	2h03	1h22
Amsterdam	3h00	1h40
London	3h15	1h59

Cologne. The Belgian railways (NMBS) have drawn up plans to develop the more northern station *Schaerbeek-formation* into the principal HST junction, Midi being reduced to a secondary HST station where not all HSTs will stop. The main reason is that after the year 2010 Midi will probably not have sufficient capacity to accommodate all HST trains. The NMBS possess and control a large bit of land in *Schaerbeek-formation*, which they can develop themselves at relatively low cost. The NMBS, newly autonomous, have an interest in making the most of their properties. The regional government, the Brussels urban region, is strongly opposed to the development of *Schaerbeek-formation*, which it wants to be reserved for industrial purposes. The government fears a surplus of office locations in Brussels when Schaerbeek is developed. Another objection is the current absence of local and regional public transport at that location. The advent of an HST station would require high complementary investment to fill that lack.

Relation with the Airport

The international airport of Zaventem lies some 10 km to the northeast of Brussels. In 1996 the airport dispatched 13.6 million passengers and 464,000 tons of cargo. The annual growth of the number of passengers is between seven and 10 per cent. That spells serious capacity problems for the future. There is little space for expansion, and the accessibility of the airport will come under pressure. Concrete plans to expand airport capacity are not yet in sight. Another threat to the airport is that Air France has a checking counter at Brussels-Midi for Charles de Gaulle airport. When the line from Brussels to Paris is complete, it will take less than an hour to reach Paris-Roissy. Many travellers could switch to Roissy instead of flying by Zaventem.

Access over land to the airport is good, but can still be improved in some ways. At the moment, the airport can be accessed by a motorway or by a rail connection with the HST station Brussels-Midi, at a frequency of three trains an hour. In the near future, the airport and the Brussels region want to raise that frequency to between six and ten trains an hour, to keep the accessibility of the airport at par and achieve a change in modal split. To that end, adjustments in the rail infrastructure will be necessary. For the time being Zaventem is unlikely to get its own HST station. The present track proposals, which are at an advanced stage, do not, like earlier plans, consider the airport as a stopping place. Nevertheless, an HST stop at Zaventem would not be a bad option. The limits of the airport's capacity are in sight, and the HST can take over part of the European air traffic. The level of service of Zaventem would thus be raised. Connections to the line from Antwerp to Amsterdam and to Liège could transform the HST station into a strategic intermodal junction. The possible development of *Schaerbeek-formation* as the HST main station (at only a few kilometres from the airport) seems in that view suboptimum. The same is true of the North Station, which is also under consideration as an HST stop. Heavy investments would be necessary to make that station suitable for HSTs. Moreover, its connection with the airport is poor, although North lies nearer to Zaventem than the present main station Brussels-Midi.

Internal Accessibility

The Brussels-Midi HST station is easily accessible by public transport. Below the station is a stopping place of the underground city railway, and many regional trains stop there. To improve internal access even more, the regional government has drawn up an integral regional public-transport plan, which will make the centre of Brussels more accessible to citizens living within a radius of 30 km. The plan seeks to relieve the overburdened central railway axis Brussels-Midi-Central-North by virtually reserving it to HSTs, and channelling the local and regional trains along the western and eastern north-south tracks. The tracks and the stations are there, but need upgrading. On sections where there are no tracks, express buses will have to be put in. The decision to lead HST trains along the central north-south connection and the regional lines by the eastern and western branches implies that the central zone of Brussels will be less accessible to local train passengers. They will often need an extra change to the city railway or the express bus. Seen in that light, a more obvious solution seems to be to lead the HST trains from Brussels-Midi by Zaventem airport through the western or eastern corridor.

A serious problem in Brussels is the poor accessibility of the European Quarters by public transport. The exits from this area to the Brussels-Midi HST station and to the airport leave much to be desired, although the international institutions housed in that area make relatively frequent use of both HST and airport. The intention is, therefore, to improve the rail connection between Brussels-Midi and Zaventem. To that end a tunnel has to be cut, the costs of which amount to some 6,000 million BEF.

Car access to the present Midi main station is good. Access from the ring road around Brussels is easy and will be even better in the future. An advantage is that the peaks in HST travel come before the morning and after the evening rush hours. Most HST travellers who depart or arrive at Midi suffer little from congested roads. 2,500 new parking places are proposed around Midi, a number not considered very high. The HST station Euralille in Lille, where fewer travellers alight, boasts 6,000 parking places. Given the expected rise in HST ridership and the new lines to Liège-Cologne and possibly Luxembourg, the number of planned parking places does seem on the low side.

Economic Potential

The economy of Brussels is a strongly-based, modern service economy. Brussels is the seat of many European head offices and financial institutions; many European and other international government agencies are established there. The HST connections further strengthen the international profile of Brussels. The city is improving its international accessibility, an important location factor for companies and institutions operating on the international market. The zone around the present principal HST station, Brussels-Midi, is in that context being developed integrally with a view to its nodal function. The project Eurostation, a project of real-estate development with the railway company NMBS as greatest shareholder, aims at modernising the station and developing such HST-related functions as new office locations, congress centres, hotels and shops. The official start of the project was back in 1988, but only in 1996 was the actual implementation taken in hand. The main reason for the delay was that for years the division of responsibilities among different government agencies had remained obscure.

Quality of Life

One objective of the Eurostation project around Midi is to improve the living environment of the degraded neighbourhood around the station. A large area around the developing station grounds has been designated as a protected zone, out of bounds to offices. Moreover, the Eurostation project organisation has been committed by the regional government to contributing to the protection and renovation of the dilapidated houses in the environment of the new office complexes to be developed. The funding is expected to come from the exploitation of the office locations. In that way, economic and social impulses march in unison around Midi. A potential danger is that pressure will be brought to bear in the future to develop after all the zones now under protection. That could mean the loss of vital parts of the cultural heritage of this part of Brussels. Another aspect of the living conditions is that the Brussels region envisages an upgrading of public transport in the whole of Brussels. The improvement of public transport in combination with the HST connections will make the city more pleasant to live in. To that effect, the share of public transport versus that of the car will have to rise considerably.

Spatial Distribution of Activities

The area around Midi station will be developed into a prime office location, which should give a strong boost to the dilapidated and deprived town quarter. Midi is to become a Brussels growth pole. Moreover, it is to offer accommodation to a large congress centre and hotels. This implies that many existing economic and social activities that now exist in the area around Midi station will have to disappear. Many cafés and small shops will have to make way for the project developers. A weighty question for the (remote) future is how the area around Midi will develop if another station (*Schaerbeek-formation* or Zaventem Airport) were promoted to main HST station of Brussels. A possible new main station might well drain away the type of activities now being developed at Midi, which could spell disurbanisation of the area.

Social Distribution of Effects

The development of Midi has met with little social opposition, for one thing because a package deal commits the organisation of the Eurostation project to protect and rehabilitate the surrounding low-rent houses. However, during the last few years a large part of social life in the station's quarter has disappeared, caused by the massive expropriation of houses in the quarter. For this reason, many inhabitants havealready left the quarter. In the coming years, this process is expected to continue.

Organising Capacity

The organisation of large projects such as the development of an HST location or the reform of public-transport systems is a complex proposition in Brussels, because of the multitude of government agencies, semi-authorities and other parties involved. On the government level a great many agencies are active. First of all there is the federal government, which has control of Zaventem airport. Next, there is the Brussels region, in existence since 1988 when the new federal structure of Belgium was established. The Brussels region breaks down into 19 boroughs with their own burgermasters and a high degree of autonomy. In addition, Brussels has strong functional links with both Flanders and the Walloon region, both highly autonomous and fierce rivals.

Besides the great number of government agencies with often overlapping responsibilities and conflicting interests, there is a lack of leadership to break deadlocks. The federal structure of Belgium is such that the national government in many cases lacks the legitimacy and competencies to assume leadership. Within the Brussels region, the organisational problems are also serious. Troubles with coordination greatly delayed the developments around Midi-station. The creation of Eurostation coincided with the formation of the Brussels region, with the result that for a long time the respective responsibilities of Eurostation, the region and the borough to which the area belongs, remained obscure. Only recently does the deadlock seem to have been overcome. Another unanswered question is which station is to be the main station in the (far) future. Brussels region opts for Brussels-Midi, but the railway company NMBS prefer *Schaerbeek-formation*, where they have large properties, so that the running costs are low and no dispossession is needed. That seems a questionable reason to choose a location as HST station.

The cooperation between Brussels and Zaventem Airport is also beset with troubles, despite their mutual dependency. An important aspect is that the Brussels region has no authority whatever over the airport. The federal government is responsible for the development of the airport, but Zaventem is on Flemish territory. That gives Flanders great influence on its development, for Flanders is responsible for the physical planning and much of the infrastructure around the airport. The number of parties involved in the development of the airport in relation to Brussels is so great that to reach agreement about public transport connections, a possible HST connection and the expansion of the airport's capacity is a wearisome exercise. Some advance has been made: the federal government has united all parties to undertake a broad study of the future of the airport.

The Most Important Themes of the Brussels Case

Brussels as an Important European HST Junction

Brussels is already very central to the HST network, and will find its position further improved with the advent of new lines in the directions Liège-Cologne and Antwerp-Rotterdam-Amsterdam. Brussels thus occupies a prominent strategic position on the map of Europe. Given the city's great economic potential, Brussels is likely to profit from this position.

The Future Station

The question of which station will become the main HST station of Brussels has not been answered yet. At present, Brussels-Midi, situated in the southern part of the centre of Brussels, holds the position of main station, but its capacity is not expected to be large enough to accommodate the growing number of HSTs. The railway company NMBS is considering eventually developing the grounds of *Schaerbeek-formation* north of the centre of Brussels as an HST station. The main reason for the NMBS, now autonomous, to develop *Schaerbeek-formation* is the fact that it owns much land there. Considered from the viewpoint of an integral vision of the development of the Brussels agglomeration, this consideration does not seem to be adequate. Firstly, development of *Schaerbeek-formation* may lead to undesirable competition with locations in the centre of Brussels. Secondly, large investments would have to be made in additional secondary public transport. A more logical option might be to develop the airport as an HST station.

Relation with the Airport

The growth of Zaventem airport is obstructed by capacity and accessibility problems. Insufficient space is available for extending the airport's capacity. Good plans have been drawn up, however, for improving access to the airport by public transport by putting in a frequent train service between Brussels-Midi and the airport, and creating facilities for passengers to check in at the railway station. To solve the capacity problems of Zaventem, a structural solution would be to develop the airport into an HST stopping place. The HST could act as a feeder line to the intercontinental flights from Zaventem, and could also take over European destinations from the air services. The resulting synergy could improve the external accessibility of Brussels as a whole. The station at the airport is already suitable to accommodate HSTs, though admittedly considerable investments are needed to connect the station to the HST line to Liège-Cologne and Brussels-Antwerp-Amsterdam. At the moment, Zaventem airport does not feature in the plans as a potential stopping place for HSTs. The location of the airport outside the territory of the Brussels region is an awkward organisational and administrative problem. This hampers the adjustment of transport and spatial-planning policies, and thus the development of the airport into an HST station. Since the airport is situated in the functional region of the Brussels agglomeration, the parties involved should either coordinate or integrate their policies.

Development around Brussels-Midi

A large-scale project is in progress around the Brussels-Midi HST station. Offices, congress centres, hotels and shops have been planned in or near the station, and the functions to be developed are clearly related to the HST. The area has the potential to become an important growth pole. With the needs of citizens and the wish to preserve local cultural heritage in mind, a package deal has been concluded, by which the returns from the commercial exploitation of the area will be used to conserve and rehabilitate social housing. In the near future some resistance can be expected to the demolition of some 1,000 dwellings on behalf of the further development of the area around Brussels-Midi.

Organising Capacity

The organising capacity in Brussels seems to be suboptimal. A great many agents are involved in the development of such HST-related projects as the development of Brussels-Midi and the choice of the second HST station. The distribution of competencies among the agents is not always clear. The greatest problems spring, however, from the fierce rivalry between Flanders and the Walloon and Brussels regions, and the weak position of the federal government. Those factors have caused a general lack of leadership. In matters straddling regional borders, such as the development of Zaventem airport, this rivalry often makes for suboptimal decisions.

Note

1   Coauthor: drs W. Van Winden, EURICUR.

5　The HST-integration in Cologne

Introduction

This case study shows several elements that are of interest for the comparative analysis:

- Cologne is a fair example of the functioning of the German HST system, which with the French one dominates high-speed railway in Europe;
- in Cologne the HST is considered a powerful instrument to revitalise a city area;
- a multi-terminal HST station is planned in Cologne. The connection of two HST stations, located close to each other, generates space for infrastructure and related activities, and improves access by secondary transport systems;
- this case study shows that broad regional support for HST integration can be won by using the HST infrastructure flexibly;
- by involving many relevant actors in the decision-making, Cologne is trying to enlarge the social and political support for HST integration.

Accessibility

External Accessibility

The high-speed era opened on German railways in June 1991, when trains of the 'InterCity Express' type (ICE) began operating on the network at a maximum speed of 250 km/h. Since May 1995 these trains have been operating at a speed of 280 km/h. New high-speed lines have been built from Hannover to Würzburg and from Mannheim to Stuttgart; these lines make up about 20 per cent of the ICE-network, upgraded routes comprise the rest. The average distance between stops on the ICE network is 95 km (Jänsch, 1996). In the near future, six HST lines will connect Cologne with the main German and European cities:

1   the new Cologne-Rhine/Main line, connecting Cologne with Frankfurt. HST stations on this line are planned, among other places, at the airport of Cologne and in Siegburg (20 km from Cologne). Construction activities for this line have just begun and the services are expected to start in 2000. Travel time by train from Cologne to Frankfurt will reduce from two hours 15 minutes to 58 minutes. Given the growth of economic activities along this axis, this HST connection is considered of great importance for the economic potential of the Cologne region. The HST frequency will be five every hour on this line;

2   HSTs on the old Cologne-Frankfurt line will frequent Bonn and Koblenz, which are not served by the new Cologne-Rhine/Main line. One reason for building a new HST line on the right bank of the Rhine was that there are so many curves in the old line. To upgrade the old line to HST quality would have been too expensive. On this line, the HST frequency will be one every hour;

3   by 2005, the PBKA-network, connecting Paris, Brussels, Cologne and Amsterdam, is expected to be completed. Previous to that, HST rolling stock (the Thalys) will use the existing railroad tracks between the cities mentioned;

4   the Cologne-Dortmund-Hamburg line;

5   the Cologne-Dortmund-Hannover-Berlin line. These lines will be built at a later stage than the Cologne-Rhine/Main line;

6   the Cologne-Düsseldorf-Arnhem-Utrecht-Amsterdam line. This service will be carried out on existing tracks, which for a large part will be upgraded to HST quality.

Currently, there are ideas to extend the number of HST lines via Cologne to eight. An additional HST line for Cologne might be a connection via Eindhoven to Rotterdam. For the time being, this service might be run on existing tracks.

Given the large number of HST lines to be connected to Cologne, this city will achieve a vital position in the developing European HST network.

Travel times by train to major European destinations, such as Amsterdam, Brussels, Paris, Berlin and Milan, will be halved. The Cologne region will be an important junction in the HST network in the east-west as well as the north-south direction. Therefore, Cologne is expected to profit substantially from the new market opportunities offered through the European integration process. Besides the fact that the elimination of border barriers has enlarged its relevant market region, its economic potential will be further enhanced by the developing trans-European infrastructure networks, not least the HST network. However, the average speed of the HST services connecting Cologne is less than, for instance, those connecting Lyon, due to several stops in medium-sized cities.

Through the HST network the airports of Cologne/Bonn, Frankfurt and Düsseldorf will be connected. Therefore, a kind of multi-airport system might evolve, by which the scarce capacity of the airports can be allocated more efficiently and the flexibility and number of travel opportunities increases. The bypass HST line from Cologne to its airport will also be used by regional trains (*S-bahn* services).

HST Stations

Three HST stations are planned in the Cologne region: one at the airport and two in the city-centre, the central station (CS) and the Deutz/Messe station (DMS). It will be vital for their functioning that a high-grade transport link should be realised between the two central stations. Otherwise a situation similar to that in Paris might evolve, where the railway stations are poorly connected. When an adequate linkage has been realised, both stations can be considered to form one entity (a multi-terminal HST station). A similar situation exists at many airports, with even larger distances between the terminals. There are ideas for constructing a so-called 'people mover' between the two stations. On the right bank, this transport mode could be extended to halfway the *Messe* area. A procurement procedure has been started to select a group of investors and architects for the development of DMS.

The decision to develop DMS as well as CS as stopping places for the HST has been made mainly for the following reasons:

- in the medium term, space at the CS is expected to become short, and it may be difficult to accommodate the growing number of trains and related activities. Moreover, CS has poor car accessibility. Around DMS, on the contrary, there is sufficient space for extending the terminal, parking facilities and all kind of related activities. Besides, the parking facilities of the *Messe* can be combined with those of the HST station. DMS has also better access to the regional road infrastructure;

- the HST station DMS is considered a powerful instrument to develop the right bank of the city of Cologne, which suffers from deprivation and many other socioeconomic problems, such as a high unemployment rate.

The city of Cologne wants north-south HST services (from Frankfurt to Düsseldorf and Dortmund) to stop at DMS. These services can use a railroad track at a lower level than those crossing the Rhine. Should north-south HST services call at the CS, trains will have to go there and back (as at Lyon-Perrache) and through trains will lose travel time. Moreover, these trains have to cross the *Hohenzollern-Brücke*, the bridge connecting CS and DMS, which is a major bottleneck in the available rail infrastructure capacity. Every day 1,300 trains cross this bridge, which carries six railroad tracks. In principle, there is no space to enlarge the capacity of the bridge. Therefore, unnecessary train services on this track should be avoided.

Internal Accessibility

The level of public transport facilities at DMS is almost comparable with those of CS. Therefore, accessibility by public transport is not decisive for giving preference to one or the other station as an HST stopping-place. In the Cologne region, several projects to improve urban public transport are planned or have been carried out, such as the *Stadtbahn Mülheim,* between the Wiener Platz and the Frankfurter Straße, which will be completed in 1997. A new underground line is planned to connect the city centre on the left bank with the southern part of Cologne. The construction could start in 1998 and the investment will be about one billion DM. Furthermore, a new regional line (*S-bahn*) between Düren and Cologne is under construction. This line will connect with the airport and, therefore, will serve as feeder to the HST.

In comparison with other European cities, Cologne hardly suffers congestion on its car infrastructure. Much attention is paid to transfer points between individual and collective transport. At the moment there are about 10,000 park-and-ride locations in the Cologne region, and a decision has been made to double this number. An important regional transfer point is planned at the Cologne airport.

Economic Potential

Important pillars of the regional economy of Cologne are the media sector (WDR, RTL, VOX, VIVA and MediaPark), research institutes (universities), banks, insurance companies and industries, like Ford and Bayer. Other important sectors are chemistry, electrical engineering, precision mechanics and engine building. There is a transition process going on from a production economy to a service economy. This is noticeable in the changing nature of the economic activities as well as in internal developments within sectors and companies (contracting out of production activities and focusing on activities such as research, marketing and logistics).

The *Messe* of Cologne, the fair and exposition hall, is vital for the urban economy, generating employment and attracting visitors to the region. It has a dominant position in terms of international fairs and expositions in Germany as well as in the world. For the 1995–99 period, a 300 million DM investment has been planned to extend the *Messe* by 275,000 square metres. When there are large expositions the present DMS already faces congestion, and the continuing growth of the *Messe* thus also demands a reconstruction of DMS. The management of the *Messe* tries to encourage visitors to use public transport, on environmental as well as accessibility considerations. At the moment, expositions often start at 10.00 a.m. to prevent mixing up visitor traffic with the ordinary peak-hour traffic. The planned HST connections will be vital for the international accessibility of the *Messe*, especially in view of the direct rail connections with the three regional airports. Currently, there is only a connection by bus with the Cologne airport.

Quality of Life

The aim of the urban transport policy is to reduce car traffic and to promote more environment-protective transport modes. For the year 2000, the following modal split is expected if no adequate measures are taken: pedestrians 22 per cent, cyclists eight per cent, cars 55 per cent, public transport 15 per cent. However, the following modal split will be striven for: pedestrians 23 per cent, cyclists 11 per cent, cars 44 per cent, public transport 22 per cent. People increasingly prefer to take the train instead of the car at inter-urban distances between 100 and 500 km, as train services improve. The large number of park-and-ride facilities in the Cologne region is intended to stimulate that development.

Spatial Distribution of Activities

There is a clear difference in prosperity between the right and left banks of the city of Cologne. Sixty per cent of the population of the Cologne region live on the left bank. Industries, which were mainly situated on the right bank of the river Rhine, have declined. Consequently, the area suffers from relatively much unemployment and social decline. There is space available, often vacated industrial sites and railway yards, to develop new economic activities. The planned HST station at DMS is considered an important catalyst towards economic development. The entire area on the right bank could profit from the improved accessibility by car and train which this connection brings. The core activity of the new HST station site on the right bank will be the fair and exposition hall. The *Messe* is expected to stimulate the establishment of all kind of related activities, such as hotels, leisure, culture and sport facilities. The Cologne Arena, an accommodation for sport, music and culture, and the technical City Hall will be built in the direct vicinity of DMS. Moreover, a business park (Euro-Forum) which already houses several companies (among others information technology and telecommunication) is situated near the *Messe*.

Social Distribution of Effects

In Siegburg, a city with a population of 50,000, 20 km from Cologne, another HST station is planned to obtain a more balanced distribution of activities and, consequently, greater social and political support. Furthermore, the HST station at the airport can also be considered a regional one. On the new Cologne-Rhine/Main line, HST frequency will be five every hour. There will be alternating services: two HSTs will stop at Siegburg and two at the airport, while one HST will directly connect Cologne with Frankfurt. The interests of the different administrative entities are also taken into account: each involved *Land* will have its own HST station, at Montabaur in Rheinland-Pfalz and at Limburg in Hessen. Therefore, the intermediate areas will profit from the HST development. New residential areas can be developed in pleasant surroundings at relatively great distances from the large cities, but easily accessible. Therefore, not only the city of Cologne will profit from the new HST infrastructure, but also a large part of the region. Thanks to these plans, much social support for the HST development has been won in the Cologne region.

Organising Capacity

In 1987 the *Arbeitskreis PBKA* was set up, and in 1994 the *Arbeitskreis Köln-Rhein/Main*. In these organisations the following actors are voluntary participants: the relevant cities and *Kreise*, airports, ministries of transport (of the *Landesregierungen*), the railway industry (for instance Siemens), trade unions, chambers of commerce, the cooperating international railways and the *Deutsche Bahn A.G.* The city of Cologne chairs both working groups, which have meetings twice a year. The cathedral city has played an important role in getting together the different national railway companies, among others those of Belgium and Germany. The setting up of the *Arbeitskreises* was considered the best opportunity of getting the relevant actors together.

According to the discussion partners in Cologne, the time is right to develop DMS as an HST station, with all its related activities. At the moment, the development of railway sites is getting full attention. Therefore, it is relatively easy to find actors prepared to participate in this development. This attention is expected to fade in one or two decades. By that time, finding of investors for the development of the HST site may be more difficult and the economic spin-off will be smaller. Until now, the city of Cologne and DB have not been in full agreement about the division of functions between CS and DMS. DB considers CS the most important HST station and expects DMS to have only a marginal function in HST traffic. A gradual change is noticeable, however: DB increasingly tends to consider DMS an important HST stop.

The Most Important Themes of the Cologne Case

Development of a New City Area using the HST Station as an Instrument

According to the proposal of the city of Cologne, two HST stations in the centre of the city, the old central station (HBF) and Deutz/Messe (DMS), are discussed. With a view to the many HST lines that are to meet at Cologne, the most logical development seems to be to exploit both stations as HST stopping places. The Central Station will (in the course of time) lack sufficient capacity, so that to spread the transport flows over several terminals is an apt solution. Besides, it would be a pity to lose the precious time saved by the new HST lines by making north-south connections call at the CS. Moreover, the DMS is considered a powerful instrument to boost the development of the socio-economically lagging right bank. There is sufficient space around DMS for extending the terminal, parking facilities and all kind of related activities. Besides, the parking facilities of the *Messe* and the Arena can be combined with those of the HST station, through which this would probably become the HST station with the largest parking capacity in Europe. DMS also has better access to the regional road infrastructure than the central station.

Providing there is a good mutual interconnection, both stations might function as one entity. A comparison can be made with airports with more than one terminal. To the customers, the stations will have to be presented as an entity: for instance the central station with an east and a west terminal. Travellers will be readier to accept the concept if, in their perception, the HST station is accommodated at one place. That perception is important to maximise the HST effect of attracting new HST-related activities. There are some who fear that the development of two HST stations close together will lead to a kind of Parisian situation, with troublesome transfers between head-end stations. However, such a situation can be avoided by providing easy, fast and comfortable transfers. For Cologne, a type of automatic people mover would fit the bill. Irrespective of the present transport flows between the terminals, a high-grade connection seems a necessary condition for HST station to perform adequately as a multi-terminal. Moreover, a good connection may create synergetic effects. Thus CS might profit from improved car access to DMS, while DMS might benefit from the better link with the old city centre. Paris, just quoted as a bad example, may also show ways of linking stations that are worth considering, such as the pedestrian tunnel planned between Gare d'Est and Gare du Nord, and the automatic footbridge that is to connect Gare de Lyon with Gare d'Austerlitz.

Enlarging Support for the HST Development

The Cologne case shows some measures to gain support for the HST development in the region. The most striking measure is the planning of the regional HST stations. At 20 km from Cologne, in the city of Siegburg, and at the Cologne-airport, HST stations are planned at which some (not all) HST services will call. Each *Land* that is crossed by the new Cologne-Rhine/Main line will have its own HST station. These measures have made the decision-making process around the HST infrastructure easier and shorter. Agreement about the plans could be reached sooner because of less social and political resistance. A disadvantage of the measures may be that the quality of the HST system is affected, since added stops might slow down the average speed of the HST services. The city of Cologne initiated the establishment of

Arbeitskreise ('PBKA' and 'Cologne-Rhein/Main') to stimulate the support for the HST and to solve common problems. Actors could declare their preferences and influence the decision process. Collective operating and a shared vision and strategy concerning the HST integration in Cologne stimulate efficient and powerful decision-making. Moreover, the *Arbeitskreis* has proved to be a good instrument for a collective lobby for new HST tracks.

6   The HST-integration in Geneva

Introduction

This case study analyses how the introduction of the HST (high-speed train) affects the Geneva region. The basis of the analysis is the monograph actors from the Geneva region had written for the first stage of the Eurocities-TGV research. This monograph has been subjected to the criteria deduced in the theoretical introduction to the second stage of this research. For the purpose of this analysis discussions have been held with relevant actors from the Geneva region (see the list of discussion partners). Additional information and literature have also been used (see list of references). Specific fields of interest of the Geneva case are:

- organisational problems in border areas;
- the relationship between the development stage of the HST network and the choice of HST stations.

Accessibility

External Accessibility

Since 1981, Geneva has been served by HSTs from Paris. These trains stop at the central station of Geneva, Cornavin. These HSTs use conventional tracks from Mâcon to Geneva, and *dedicated* HST lines elsewhere. To travel by HST from Paris to Geneva, a distance of 550 km, takes three hours 29 minutes. In 1993 800,000 passengers used this service, which runs five times daily. In addition, there is a daily HST connection with Montpellier.

Two new HST lines to Geneva are under study:

1   the *Léman-Mont-Blanc* line. This line runs from Bourg en Bresse to Mâcon,

where it will join the existing Paris-Lyon HST line. This connection will reduce travel time from Geneva to Paris from three hours 29 minutes to two hours 15 minutes, to Lyon from one hour 48 minutes to one hour and to Marseilles from four hours 44 minutes to two hours 25 minutes;

2   the *Sillon-Alpin* line. This line runs via Annecy to Chambéry and will be a connection of Geneva to the planned HST line from Lyon to Turin. This connection will reduce travel time from Geneva to Paris from three hours 29 minutes to two hours 45 minutes, to Lyon from one hour 48 minutes to one hour and to Marseilles from four hours 44 minutes to two hours 16 minutes

For the decisions around the planned HST lines to their region, Geneva completely depends on France, since the lines run nearly entirely on French territory. It is therefore of the utmost importance to find solutions that are mutually advantageous.

The essential condition for France is that the Lyon-Turin connection becomes a major link in the HST network. The investment will be relatively high, for one thing because several tunnels will have to be constructed. Because it is considered an important European connection the EU will contribute to the financing of it. To connect Geneva through the Sillon-Alpin line is for France the most attractive alternative, because it implies a more frequent use of the Lyon-Turin connection, making it more and sooner profitable.

Within Switzerland, actors are not in agreement about the HST network to be constructed. Basel and Geneva are the main nodes for connecting Switzerland to the European HST network. In official Swiss documents the Léman-Mont-Blanc line is recorded as Geneva's (only) connection to the European network. This line will save Switzerland more travel time than the Sillon-Alpin alternative. How to finance it is not yet clear. Within Switzerland there are two more or less competitive projects: the Léman-Mont-Blanc line and the Dijon-Lausanne line. The latter would have to be upgraded to HST level. The fear in Switzerland is that construction of the Léman-Mont-Blanc line will reduce the Dijon-Lausanne line to a secondary one, thus diminishing its expected yields.

Which connection is the optimum one for Geneva depends on the preferred spatial-economic development. Strategic goals of Geneva are (in order of priority):

1   to improve its international function as the domicile of international organisations;

2   to improve the relationship with the most important Swiss urban regions, such as Lausanne, Bern en Zurich (with the Rail 2000 project);

3   to improve the relationship with Lyon and further to southwest Europe;

4   to improve the Sillon-Alpin axis (which would benefit the airport, because an important part of its catchment area lies along this axis);

5   to improve the relationship with Milan;

6   to improve the relationship with Turin.

The Sillon-Alpin line is preferable for goals 4 and 6. The Léman-Mont-Blanc line might be more advantageous for the first goal, because it produces faster connections with Paris and London. For 2, 3 and 5 the choice is immaterial. Therefore, from the consideration of the alternative spatial developments, the Léman-Mont Blanc-line seems preferable. In the long term, it seems to be essential for Geneva to be linked to the Léman-Mont-Blanc as well as the Sillon-Alpin line, lest Geneva become a dead end of the HST network. The development of exploiting tilting trains (*trains pendulaires*) on conventional tracks offers additional possibilities for Geneva to be connected to the European HST network. For Geneva, the aim is to constitute a junction in the European HST network and an interface between the Swiss and the French network.

Internal Accessibility

The main problem of the HST integration in Geneva is where to locate the terminals. HST stations are looked upon as the main development poles of the urban region. At present, HST trains stop at the Cornavin station. The railway station at the airport and the French station Annemasse are considered (complementary) alternatives.

1   The Cornavin station will remain the principal stopping place for HSTs, for the time being. However, that might change in view of the expected lack of space at this location, its relatively poor car-accessibility and the desired peripheral spatial-economic developments of the Geneva region.

Stopping at the Cornavin station does serve one of the major aims of the European HST network: to provide fast heart-to-heart links between the major European metropolises. For Geneva, the HST is to serve as a catalyst for better integration of the central station in the urban structure. At the moment, it rather separates different parts of the city. To connect the different parts, Cornavin has to be firmly integrated in the urban fabric (from *coupure* to *couture*).

2   The airport railway station, in operation since 1987, is used mainly as a complement to air transport. It is hardly if at all used by people living in the vicinity of the airport. At the moment, HSTs do not call at the airport, because the railroad track lacks a certain necessary part. The airport is located close to the French border. The business and facility park related to the airport, the *Rectangle d'Or*, might be extended onto French territory.

3   The Annemasse station is located on French territory, peripheral to both Geneva and the municipality of Annemasse. It is used mainly by French people. The station accommodates services to Evian-les-Bains, Chamonix, Annecy and Bellegarde. There are plans for a light-rail connection between Annemasse and the Cornavin-station (and further to Pays de Gex), which could be realised within eight or 10 years. There is sufficient space for development around this station. Given the limited size of the social, economic and transport activities in its direct vicinity, this location seems to lack potential. There is a clear difference between French and Swiss city planning around stations. Switzerland strives for a high building density, but France does not. Indeed, around the Annemasse station the building density is low. The Annemasse-station is regarded as an important frontier-crossing development pool. On the Swiss side of the station the development of some new neighbourhoods is foreseen. A great disadvantage is that through trains and important connections to the other Swiss cities and to Milan do not call at the Annemasse-station.

Economic Potential

Because of the frontier barriers between Switzerland and the states of the European Union, Geneva faces relatively high transaction costs within and outside its functional urban region. Moreover, its competitive position is worsened by the relatively expensive Swiss franc. To maintain and improve its international function is one of the spearheads of the economic policy of Geneva. Geneva houses about 200 international governmental and non-governmental organisations, such as the Office of the United Nations, the International Committee of the Red Cross and the CERN (*le Centre Européen de Recherches Nucléaires*). Ten per cent of the employment in Geneva is related to these organisations (26,000 jobs). Furthermore, there are more than 250 multinational companies in the region, generating 20,000 jobs. For those organisations an adequate multimodal accessibility is essential. The airport in particular plays an important role in that respect as the international organisations located in Geneva often operate on a global scale. The tertiary sector is dominant in Geneva; four-fifths of the employment of the Geneva-canton and 87 per cent of the city's is accounted for by this sector. The bank, insurance, congress and hotel sector and urban tourism are especially important. To promote urban tourism, adequate international accessibility of the city centre is vital. The HST connection can play a very important role in this respect.

Quality of Life

Switzerland more or less sets the trend in providing a high-quality environment. It helps Geneva to attract economic activities, since pleasant surroundings are more and more becoming an essential precondition for economic growth. This goes especially for the attraction of international organisations and the strengthening of urban tourism. Environment measures imposed by the federal government restrict especially car traffic in the city centre. On the one hand, this threatens the car-accessibility of the Cornavin station. On the other hand, it makes investment in the urban collective transport system easier to realise. This applies, for instance, to the plans for the construction of the new light-railway connection.

Spatial Distribution of Activities

The regional policy of Geneva is based on two principles:

1   to establish complementarity between Geneva and the (French and Swiss) regional secondary centres, such as Nyon, Annemasse and Ferney-Voltaire;

2 to promote a sound transfrontier *esprit* between Geneva and the *départements* of l'Ain and the Haute-Savoie.

In respect of 1), one effect of the HST is an improved relationship between the city and the region. The introduction of the HST would indeed be an incentive to improving the mutual traffic links, of which the planned light-rail train between Annemasse, Cornavin, the airport and the *Pays de Gex* is the most important element. This transport mode will serve as the backbone of the public transport system. The light-rail train also has to serve as the linking element in the urban region; it has to prevent separation of different city parts once they are connected to the HST system.[1] Besides, upgraded urban collective transport systems may help to curb (the growth of) individual traffic (especially cars). As fas as Geneva is concerned, it is advisable to further the development of the urban periphery: the city must, so to speak, unfold outward. An HST station at the airport or at Annemasse, located more or less peripherally, could function as a catalyst to that end.

As far as 2) – the improvement of the transfrontier relationships – is concerned the functional-economic region of Geneva exceeds the borders of Switzerland (95 per cent of the border of the canton of Geneva runs along French territory). Therefore, to maintain structural relations with relevant French actors is essential for generating structural economic growth in the Geneva region. An important organisation in that respect is the Comité Régional Franco-Genevois (CRFG). Transfrontier cooperation is hindered by Switzerland's not being a member state of the European Union, which entails additional transaction costs due to frontier barriers. Other negative effects of the border location of Geneva are unbalanced development of the urban area, unbalanced fiscal financial flows and increasing commuter traffic.

Social Distribution of Effects

Since, it is quite difficult to get sufficient social support for dramatic changes of the urban structure, the substantial reconstruction of the Cornavin area is likely to meet with some social resistance. Under the circumstances, Geneva should try for a balanced division of benefits and costs between the French and Swiss parts of the region. If the connection of Geneva generated positive effects for the French part, the HST infrastructure to France would be easier to realise.

Organising Capacity

The canton of Geneva is the principal actor in the decision-making around the HST integration in the Geneva region. The municipalities play a secondary role. At the moment, the directly involved parties have no major differences of opinion concerning the HST integration. However, differences might evolve once the concrete project proposals are presented, because dramatic changes of the urban structure are unlikely to find sufficient support. Decision-making in Switzerland is often slowed down by the decentralised administrative structure. With many actors eager to declare their preferences, the complexity of decision-making tends to hold up the process. Moreover, it is mostly impossible to concentrate on just one project. To generate sufficient social and political support for new projects the means have to be distributed among a multitude of projects and regions (a situation that is more or less comparable with the Dutch one). On the other hand, those very circumstances might facilitate the decision-making around the Léman-Mont-Blanc line, in addition to the Dijon-Lausanne connection. The Swiss tend to resent powerful leadership, which they think is contrary to their administrative culture. Still, leadership is often a vital precondition for large-scale projects to be accomplished.

The Most Important Themes of the Geneva Case

Organisational Problems in Border Areas

Like Strasbourg, Lyon and Turin, Geneva is peripheral to its own country. The increased internationalisation of economies offers such cities new development opportunities, because they are more central to their new relevant regions. However, to realise new transport links they depend on sound cooperation with the neighbouring countries. Important international corridors often lack adequate infrastructure, in many border regions there are infrastructural bottlenecks, while national networks tend to lack proper connection. These deficiencies are illustrated clearly by the configuration of many national road networks. Even in the most developed parts of the European Union, highways often become secondary roads as they approach national borders. For peripheral urban regions to realise new infrastructure, they need not only to draw up adequate strategies for communication with their own national governments, but also to establish and maintain sound relations with the relevant governmental bodies in the neighbouring countries. That necessity complicates the realising of large-scale projects and demands a powerful organising capacity. For Geneva, it is important to constitute an interface between the Swiss and the French rail network. In the short term, the dependency of Geneva on France and the decreasing investments in new HST infrastructure in this country might necessitate focusing on the realising of high grade rail infrastructure within Switzerland.

Choice of HST Stations

Given the relative compactness of the canton of Geneva it seems advisable to keep the number of HST stopping places as low as possible. More HST stops imply more investment in accessibility and in the accommodation of HST related activities. A station's accessibility refers to access by car (access roads and parking facilities) and collective transport (trams, buses, etc., but also secondary regional and national trains). To warrant duplication of such investment, a town must have a certain critical size, which Geneva does not have. Besides, concentration of the HST stops increases the 'HST effect': the attraction of new economic activities (among which hotels and office accommodation).

In Geneva, three HST stopping places are being considered: the Cornavin station, the Annemasse station and the international airport. The Annemasse station does not seem an obvious choice. The Annemasse station is unfavourably situated in respect of many through HST lines, Milan, and the major Swiss towns. Moreover, economic and social activities around the Annemasse station are few and far between. The required investments for developing this area are probably not warranted, considering the less-than-optimal location of the station.

A staged development of the HST stations seems advisable. In the first instance, the continuation of the centrally situated Cornavin station being the most important HST station is the most plausible. It would reinforce the present international and tourist function of Geneva. Moreover, Cornavin currently boasts the best connection to important HST lines, regional and national rail sections and complementary public-transport services. Disadvantages of the Cornavin location are the relatively poor car access and the lack of space. Selective car access to the Cornavin station by means of adequate pricing (optimum access for those willing to pay for it) seems necessary, therefore. To that effect, measures comparable to those required in Antwerp will have to be taken. Because of lack of development space in the immediate surroundings of the Cornavin station, the 'HST effect' will have to be accommodated at some distance. That makes high-grade collective public transport from that station, such as the planned new tram line, all the more urgent. It is advisable to create an independent organisation for the development and the exploitation of the HST station, in order to guarantee and retain a high quality of accessibility and facilities at the station and to attract HST-related activities.

In the long term an HST connection to the airport seems advisable. The airport location of Geneva has more spatial development opportunities and a better accessibility by car than the Cornavin station. New businesses can be accommodated on the French, as well as the Swiss, side. There seems to be sufficient (potential for) intercontinental flights to legitimate a high grade connection between the airport and the HST system. In the long term, considered the expected substantial growth of both the air transport and the HST system, it might be necessary to combine both systems and elements of the system in order to benefit of synergetic effects and economies of scale. Therefore, a necessary condition for a sound development of the HST station at the airports might be a closer cooperation with Lyon-Satolas. Both junctions can be considered as two complementary elements of a system that guarantees an adequate international accessibility of the region. A high-grade interconnection by means of the HST system would increase the accessibility and hence the attractiveness of the region. In the long term, both airports could develop certain specialist international services, which might be supplementary to each other. By this means, the efficiency and effectiveness of the total transport system in the region could be increased.

Maintaining the Cornavin station is of special importance for the urban-tourism function of Geneva. If the airport were eventually to become the most important HST stop, the HST could go on to Cornavin after stopping at the airport. That addition to the service would not slow down the HST service from Geneva airport, then the most important HST station. The eventual choice of the airport for the main HST station would necessitate extending the volume of regional and national train traffic and complementary public transport to that junction.

Note

1   Comparable with the planned rail link between Lyon-centre and Lyon-Satolas.

7   The HST-integration in Liège

Introduction

At present, Thalys-trains stop at Liège. Early in the next century, a largely dedicated HST track is to be completed between Brussels and Cologne, permitting high-quality HST services through Liège. A new HST station with excellent car accessibility will be built. Along with the building of the new station, the surrounding neighbourhood will be reconstructed, to accommodate new HST-related activities. The HST is supposed to play an important role in the revitalisation of Liège's urban economy.

Accessibility

External Accessibility

Liège will be on the HST line Brussels-Aachen-Cologne. To limit costs, this line will make maximum use of existing infrastructure. Of the 152 km of railway connecting Brussels with Aachen, two sections, with a total length of 84 km, will be newly constructed. To the east of Liège, a six km-long tunnel will be dug for the HST. In the future, the TGV-Est, from Paris by Strasbourg to Frankfurt, will be a heavy competitor for services from France to Germany. Estimates set the catchment area (*zone d'influence*) of the HST station at Liège at 2.3 million people for the destination Cologne, 2.9 million for Paris, and 5.9 million for London. At the moment, the Strasbourg population is included in the catchment area for the destination London. Of course, that will change once the TGV-Est is complete, when Strasbourg will also take over part of Liège's catchment area.

Currently, the Thalys calls at Liège twice a day in both directions of the Paris-Brussels-Liège section. The travel time to Paris, via Brussels, is now three hours 15 minutes, and will drop to two hours 10 minutes when the final HST section is complete. The travel time between Liège and Brussels will then be reduced from one hour to 38 minutes. The present schedule allows a trip from Liège to Paris and back to be made in one day. In December 1997 the service will be continued to Aachen and Cologne. Passengers will then travel from Liège to Cologne in 58 minutes. Although Liège and Aachen are only 50 km apart, the HST will stop at both cities. At the moment the principal rail destinations from Liège are Brussels (accounting for 31 per cent of train passengers), Namur (22 per cent) and Aachen (20 per cent).

Choosing the Location for the HST Station

Liège had a choice between a central and a peripheral location for the new station. Those responsible were influenced mostly by the way such choices are made in France. The prominent success factors of the French TGV seem to be the high commercial speed and the possibility of penetrating into the town centres. In France there are 130 HST stations, most of which are situated in the urban centres. There are only eight HST stations outside city centres: Maçon, Vendôme, Massy, Roissy-Charles de Gaulle, EuroDisney, Lyon-Satolas, Moisenay, and the 'Chunnel' terminal. There is mostly a special reason for preferring an outside location, such as the entrance to the Channel Tunnel. At any rate there are in Paris, along the *grand contournement*, three HST stations (Massy, Roissy, and EuroDisney). Two of the peripheral HST stations, namely Satolas and Moisenay, have so far failed to attract many passengers.

In Liège there was no particular reason to build an HST station outside the agglomeration, so, as in most French towns, a city location was preferred. The importance of integrating the HST in the existing rail network has been a consideration, since the presence of connecting lines enhances the value of the total HST product. The choice of a location other than the present main Guillemins station as stopping place for high-speed trains would imply the creation of a second junction for additional transport. For such an investment to be profitable, a certain critical mass of economic and transport activities is required. Liège seems to lack that critical mass. Yet another consideration is that to promote the more or less centrally situated Guillemins station to HST status will hopefully give the town an economic impulse, whereas a peripheral station would stimulate the move of activities from the centre to the periphery.

Erection of a New Station Building

The Guillemins station will be moved 200 metres towards the river Maas. Unlike the present building, the new one will be accessible from two sides: as well as a front entrance there will be one at the back, where a new multistorey car park for 800 cars will be built backing onto the hill. This garage will serve not only the HST stop but also various urban functions. There will be a direct access road from the new motorway connection E25/E40 that will be in operation by 2000. In addition, the access track to the station will be adjusted to allow trains to approach the station at a higher speed (100 km/h instead of 40 km/h). The new HST station is designed by the Spanish architect Calatrava, who was also the designer of the HST station of Lyon-Satolas. The costs of the station project are estimated at a total of BEF 2,500 million, and will be supported in full by the federal government. The works at the station are to be undertaken in 1998 and come into operation in 2002.

The station will have the following functions:

1   transport function. The station is first of all an important bimodal transport junction, offering transfer from train to car and back. So, the various services on offer have to do mainly with transport, such as the sale of rail and bus tickets and the renting of cars. In addition, there will be derived services, such as tourist and hotel information;

2   commercial function. Because the HST station is a place where many people pass every day (and mostly have to wait a while), there is a great potential demand for various goods and services. Accordingly, space will be made available for sundry commercial activities, such as banks, communication provisions (post office, etc.), catering services and small shops. The general opinion is, however, that the commercial function must not be allowed to dominate the station.

As well as its transport and commercial functions, the station has image-building and social functions. The HST station should have appeal and enhance the city's image. It is also a high-grade public space where people have a chance to meet.

Bierset Airport

Liège has a small airport called Bierset. It is used for freight flights, a few tourist charters, and military flights. Attempts are being made to extend the freight function. Night flights from Liège are permitted. Therefore, the airport has been chosen for a TNT hub. That integrator used to centralise its services from Cologne airport. At the moment, a sorting centre for TNT is under construction near Bierset. Moreover, with the help of European subsidies

(Liège is an Objective-2 region) investments have been made in new buildings near the airport. A railway station for goods, where high-speed freight trains could stop in the future, has been planned.

Internal Accessibility

To widen the catchment area of the HST station, good secondary connections in the Euregion and the agglomeration are required. Additional public-transport services must not lose the costly HST time gains. Within the Euregion adequate additional rail services would have to be provided to, among others, the following towns: Hasselt-Genk (Belgium), Maastricht (Netherlands), Heerlen (Netherlands), and Eupen (Belgium). These connections could be arranged either by intensifying the present IC services, or by developing an RER system. There seem to be organisational obstacles, however. Within the Euregion, three different railway companies are responsible for improving the rail services: the SNCB/NMBS, the DB and the NS. These organisations may be inclined to give priority to harmonising inland train services rather than transport relations in the frontier region. Another obstacle is formed by the relatively wide cultural differences between the sub-regions.

In the Liège agglomeration there is no urban rail transport, nor are there any plans to provide it. Because the town is small and financially rather weak, the construction of a light-railway network is not considered a realistic proposition. Secondary public transport services from the station are thus exclusively provided by buses. The regional public transport company has not yet made any plans to adjust its services with a view to the HST integration. Only a marginal rise in ridership is expected from the HST connection. Those travelling by HST for business are unlikely to get on the bus, but commuters may. Probably there is a potential need for high-grade secondary collective transport from the HST station to the centre. That will have to be provided mainly by taxis and (mini-) buses. The main concern is not to squander the precious time gained by the HST. To that end, the availability of exclusive lanes for secondary collective transport in certain parts of the centre seems advisable. Because of the lack of good rail connections in the Euregion and of an urban rail system, easy car access to the HST station of Liège is essential.

Economic Potential

Industrial activities were important to the economy of the Liège region in the period from 1850 to 1970. After the closure of several mines and a heavy crisis in the metal industry at the end of the 1970s, the regional economy fell into a downward spiral. New economic activities had to be attracted to combat the relatively high unemployment figures. At the moment, the employment rate is 12.7 per cent.

Liège finds itself in the transition from urban disurbanisation to reurbanisation (see Van den Berg, 1987). After a stretch of time in which economic activities and inhabitants of the agglomeration tended to move to the periphery, the municipal government has made explicit efforts to stimulate the growth of population and economic activities in the centre. Unfortunately, the city of Liège lacks appeal as a residential and business location, for which, among other things, the past dominance of industrial activities and the fact that a busy motorway cuts through the town are to blame.

Quality of Life

The HST is supposed greatly to improve the image of the city, and to attract new inhabitants and new economic activities to it. The planned HST connection has stimulated the revitalising of the town, and inspired the citizens with hope for a better and more enjoyable living environment. That is one reason why there is much support for the HST development. In addition, a new motorway circumventing Liège is to divert part of the through-traffic now passing through the centre. The idea is to make Liège first and foremost a good place to live in. To keep the present inhabitants happy and attract new ones, the quality of the living environment must be raised. In that way, the essential basis is laid to support new economic activities.

Spatial Distribution of Activities

The Old Station Quarter

The Rue de Guillemins, the street confronting the present Guillemins station, houses many retail and catering businesses. Since the economic recession and the opening of a large-scale peripheral shopping mall, many businesses in the Rue de Guillemins have failed. The present shopkeepers in this street are afraid that the advent of a new shopping centre near the future HST station will mean the end of business in the Rue the Guillemins. The expectation is that the most dynamic actors of the Rue de Guillemins will move to the new shopping mall by the station. Unless the vacated premises are given a new function, degeneration of the street is unavoidable. A residential function seems the most logical.

The New Station Quarter

Since the early 1980s, the proposed new station quarter has accommodated the *centre administratif* of the Ministry of Finance. However, there is still room for much development in this quarter. The original buildings were demolished at an earlier stage, when a more ambitious development around the *centre administratif* was envisaged. The area to be developed covers several hectares. In about 20 years, some 100,000 square metres of new buildings have to be created. At the moment, there are plans to build three large complexes in this quarter. In addition, the living environment will be enlivened by a new public park. By the present plans, several buildings in the zone confronting the station will have to be demolished. In the new station quarter, the development of 10,000 square metres of new shopping space is foreseen.

Presumably demand on the real estate market will be sufficient to support the development of the new station quarter. By 2002, travel between Liège and Brussels will take 30 minutes, more than half an hour less than at present. Liège will then be able to vie with Brussels for new economic activities. Establishment in Liège will probably be cheaper than in Brussels. Space is held available near the new HST station to create conditions conducive to new economic growth. As a matter of fact, the development company (*promoteur*) of the new station quarter and of the Place Saint-Lambert[1] is also active in Brussels. The town government has set certain criteria with respect to the proportion of commercial activities, offices, etc. in the quarter concerned. Around the station, activities can be accommodated related to the 24-hour economy, on behalf of that part of the population that has little time to spare. It is they who will be the principal users of the HST and the complementary services. To save time, these services need to be concentrated at one location. Communication services, banks, shops for daily necessities, cinemas and sports facilities (such as fitness rooms) come to mind.

Palais des Congrès

The Congress Palace is situated quite close to the future HST station. The HST connection is expected to have a positive effect on the functioning of the

Congress Palace. The proportion of international manifestations, still small at the moment, is hoped to be raised with better international access. On the one hand, the relevant region of the congress centre will be extended by the HST connection; on the other, the competition with other cities/congress centres will become keener. At any rate, a city like Maastricht, that boasts an international congress centre but lacks an HST connection, is undoubtedly at a disadvantage in the competition.

Social Distribution of Effects

Minimising the Traffic Nuisance

In front of the new station, a station square accommodating, among other things, a bus station, needs to be developed. Two access roads to the station will be constructed (probably both one-way roads), leading to a kind of oval roundabout by the Maas. The citizens living in the neighbourhood in front of the new HST station are concerned about the additional traffic the station will attract. The city has drawn up a traffic circulation plan, but the inhabitants do not think it does justice to their ideas. They believe that extra traffic measures are needed to prevent nuisance. Certain roads in that neighbourhood may have to be closed to through-traffic.

Economic Value of Houses

With increasing road transport congestion and plans to raise the capacity of the road infrastructure substantially finding little support, rail transport is expected to gain importance. As a result, more and more people will want to live close to the station. One question arising in the context of the reorganised new station quarter is whether present inhabitants should have first option for the new houses. The plots involved have a relatively high market value, and the city has an interest in demanding market-oriented prices in order to make capital out of the 'HST effect'. To realise only council housing on the vacated premises would mean a waste of capital. The additional revenues that can be raised here can be spent on the revitalisation of the town, and thus the general welfare. Some of the present inhabitants will therefore probably have to move out, but they must be offered acceptable alternatives.

Organising Capacity

In Belgium, choices relating to HST infrastructure and its financing are made on the federal level. The regional and lower authorities do not contribute to the financing of the HST infrastructure. To limit the investment costs, Belgium has chosen merely to improve certain stretches instead of laying out dedicated HST infrastructure. That applies, for instance, to the sections between Antwerp and Brussels and between Brussels and Louvain. However, decisions about spatial planning are made on the regional level. Therefore, the Walloon region has to approve any building applications for the HST tracks.

On behalf of the development of the new HST station complex in Liège, a specific public-private organisation, called Euroliège, was founded in 1993. It is three-quarters the offspring of the SNCB and one-quarter of the Société de Développement de Liège-Guillemins. The actors involved are satisfied about the working of Euroliège. In fact, the city of Liège is not represented in Euroliège.

The Most Important Themes of the Liège Case

Instrument for the Revitalisation of the Agglomeration

The HST is regarded in Liège as an important instrument for the revitalisation of the agglomeration. It is expected to speed up the transformation of the urban economy into a service economy. In that context, the building of a new, appealing HST station in Liège stands as a symbol of the renovation of the town. The HST is hoped considerably to enhance the image of the town as a residential city where the living is good, and as a promising location for business enterprise. In Liège, substantial measures are taken to profit from the 'HST effect'. For example, several buildings in the neighbourhood in front of the new HST station will be demolished to make room for a new station square and new HST-related activities. For one thing, a new shopping precinct will be built near the HST station. The centre of gravity of commercial activities will thus move from the old to the new station quarter. For another, high-quality houses will arise in the new station zone. The situation of Liège is in some aspects like that of Liège shopping centre with excellent access by car, are aspects common to both cases.

Need for Upgrading the Regional Secondary Collective Transport

For Liège the essential concern is to extend its relevant catchment area beyond its urban region, which is probably too small for a profitable exploitation of the HST station and its related activities. Some measures to that effect would be the pursuit of an explicit marketing strategy to reduce psychical distances and the creation of easy access to the station to reduce physical distances. The marketing strategy would be to put forward the HST station as a natural traffic junction for the entire Euregion rather than just the Liège urban region. What matters is to pinpoint the station on the mental map potential travellers have of the junction. They should anyhow consider Euroliège as they plan their travel routes.

Travellers should have easy access to the station by private cars or collective transport. A multistorey car park planned near the new HST station with direct access from and to a new section of motorway will offer excellent provision for private cars. However, the access by secondary rail transport leaves much to be desired. Admittedly, at present relatively few passengers make use of public regional transport, which is in part due to its inadequate speed, frequency and comfort. On the other hand, the present volume of the transport flows does not seem to require early improvement. The question that arises is how to break that vicious circle.

A further problem is that rail services in this Euregion are anyhow difficult to improve, for one thing because they are exploited by different national railway companies, and for another because they cross culturally very diverging sub-areas. The possibility of new actors entering the rail market in the near future seems to open new prospects. To help break the vicious circle, incentive subsidies could be held out to actors offering (better) regional collective transport. That could be done through the cities involved, but also by the European Union (for instance as a means to stimulate cooperativeness in the Euregion).

Note

1   Place Saint-Lambert is another important development pool of the town. It is an outstanding historical centre and is now being completely redeveloped.

8   The HST-integration in Lille

Introduction

The decisions to construct the Channel Tunnel and plan a major HST junction near Lille have been of fundamental significance for that city's economic future. Easier international access by the HST has enhanced the image of the urban region. To make economic capital out of it, Lille has undertaken various, more or less cohering, urban projects. The question remains, however, whether Lille has indeed sufficient economic potential to make effective use of its improved accessibility.

Accessibility

Connection to the HST Network

Lille is situated at a significant junction of international HST lines. HSTs from England through the 'Chunnel' pass through Lille to continue either southward to Paris or northward to Brussels. However, the town is somewhat unfortunately placed in respect of the HST connections between Brussels and Paris. A stop at Lille implies a loss of 15–20 minutes' travel time. Actually, the Thalys between Amsterdam and Paris passes Lille by. The construction of the *contournement* around Paris has been essential to Lille inasmuch as it permits very fast travel between Lille and other cities in the province, such as Lyon and Montpellier, without losing time near Paris. Lille has thus become a vital hub in interconnected Eurostar and province-province services. Brussels, on the other hand, is an important hub for the interconnection between the Eurostar and the Thalys. By the end of 1997, the HST line from France to Brussels will be complete, and the travel time between Lille and Brussels will then be reduced from the present one hour 10 minutes to 38 minutes.

At the moment, HSTs depart from Lille in both directions, seven to Lyon and 18 to Paris (to be extended to 24). Completion of the HST line between the 'Chunnel' and London is foreseen for 2006. It will then be possible to get from Lille to London in one hour (against two hours at present), and from Paris to London in two hours. No direct HSTs are as yet foreseen from Lille to Amsterdam or Cologne; changing at Brussels will remain necessary.

From Paris, HST lines run to various places in the region around Lille, which boasts some 15 HST stopping places. The shape of the network bespeaks the dominant position of Paris: while Paris maintains relations with the secondary towns, the socioeconomic relations among the secondary towns themselves are unsatisfactory. A hub-and-spoke structure of (regional) trains to the places in the region, with Lille as the hub, would be more logical, but since it does not exist, hardly any HST passengers continue their journey from Lille by train.

HST Stations

There are in Lille two HST stations: the old central station *Gare de Flandres* (a head-end station) and the new *Gare Europe*. The distance between them is some 800 metres. Between the stations a multifunctional complex has arisen, comprising among other things a large shopping centre, an hotel, offices and houses. *Gare de Flandres* is the stopping place for conventional train services and HSTs to and from Paris; *Gare Europe serves* the *Eurostar* and the HSTs to the province. Some 100 HSTs call at Gare Europe at daily. The decision to build two stations was made largely to save costs. To accommodate the HST connection, a new station had to be provided for through trains, but to concentrate all trains at one station – and consequently to abandon *Gare de Flandres* – would have necessitated costly infrastructural adjustments. A great drawback of the present constellation is the awkward connection between the two stations, in particular for passengers carrying luggage. The space available for commercial activities at *Gare Europe* is not yet fully occupied. Measures are being taken to make the station more convenient. There is some anxiety that the capacity of *Gare Europe* will be inadequate to cope with the new important HST connections planned to be ready by the end of the next decade.

Internal Accessibility

Present interaction between the two HST stations is at a low level. The quality of the mutual connection is considered inadequate. Infrastructural measures and clearer signs to direct passengers might improve the situation. A *passerelle* is planned to reduce the walking distance between the stations. Signs that catch the eye of HST passengers might guide them to the underground railway.

Another suggestion is to run an (electrical mini-) shuttle bus between the stations. A promise of free travel for HST passengers might induce them to use some form of public transport instead of resorting to cars for their secondary travel. From the centre of Lille, tram and underground city railway are quite capable of handling feeder transport to the HST .

At present, only a marginal proportion of passengers is travelling by train from the region to Gare Europe: only five to 10 per cent of all passengers passing through that station. That may be due to the fact that many places in the region are already served by HSTs from Paris, and to the poor quality of the regional train services, the suboptimum connection between the two stations, and the easy car access to Gare Europe. There might nevertheless be a potential demand for secondary traffic by train. To widen the catchment area of the HST stations (especially in the direction of southern Belgium), the quality of regional train services to such towns as Courtrai, Roubaix and Ghent needs improvement. Moreover, if other parts of the region are to profit from the improved external accessibility and the related economic effects, the region's internal accessibility by collective transport must be upgraded.

Currently, the car is by far the most important secondary transport mode for the HST. The parking capacity near Gare de Flandres is limited and mostly fully occupied. Parking is relatively abundant near Lille-Europe and Euralille, but the extra traffic it attracts threatens to block access to these HST stations. Additional measures to guarantee easy access to the HST stations are therefore indicated. One such measure could be a toll system on the *périphérique,* which would accomplish selective access to the station to those prepared to pay for the privilege. Another possibility would be to stimulate taxi transport, for instance by permitting more competition, reserving lanes for taxis, offering combined tickets for HST and taxi, and selling train tickets in the taxicabs.

Airport

From Lille there is an excellent HST service to Charles de Gaulle Airport, bridging the distance in about 50 minutes. Moreover, air passengers can check in for flights from Charles de Gaulle at Gare Europe. Lille Airport does not yet have a rail connection of its own, although it lies close to the junction of the HST lines Lille-'Chunnel' and Paris-Brussels, and has a conventional railway line running alongside. The airport authorities would like to get a good rail connection with Euralille by a branch line. The airport managers are trying to detract certain functions, in particular charter flights, from the Paris airports, which are approaching their saturation point. Now charters are complementary to the HST, unlike scheduled flights, which, especially in France, compete with HST services. So, if charter flights could be diverted to Lille airport, a rail service between the airport and the HST station would become attractive to the SNCF.

Economic Potential

The economy of the urban region of Lille is largely based on industrial activity. The service sector is only moderately developed. The closure and reorganisation of many industries has caused a lot of unemployment (13 per cent). No real core competencies can be identified in Lille, nor does it have distinct comparative advantages in certain sectors. To broaden its economic basis, Lille is trying to attract more service activities. The HST connection is cast in the role of an important catalyst.

Of all European GNP, about five per cent is generated in the Paris region, five in the London region, and another five in the Ruhr area, against no more than one per cent in the region Nord Pas de Calais. So, economically the region is rather insignificant. That makes it hard to keep and attract high-skilled citizens. At the moment, about two-fifths of qualified youngsters from the region find a job in Paris. With better international access and progressive European integration, these young people might even spread their wings to the London region or the Ruhr area. Improved accessibility could thus have a draining effect, and the central role now envisaged for Lille would work out negatively rather than positively. What the region needs is to strengthen its economic potential. To make real capital out of its nodal position, Lille needs substantial endogenous development. The question is then what functions could serve as motors for Lille? Some sectors that seem promising for the region are industry-based services, urban tourism and medical activities. Lille wishes to orient in particular to northern Europe (Benelux and Germany). In view of its well-developed industries, the region seeks cooperation with comparable regions of complementary activity, such as the Ruhr area and the Randstad. A point to consider is that the housing stock in Lille lacks diversity. To attract and keep a qualified workforce, investment in the gradual rehabilitation of the housing stock is necessary.

Urban tourism is greatly underdeveloped in the Lille region. The HST connection and the development of Euralille have boosted the number of travellers visiting the centre of Lille. The city has an attractive historical centre, with various (potential) tourist attractions, such as the Citadel and the Palais des Beaux Arts. In addition, the industrial history of the region might be a good theme for attracting visitors (organisation of museums and expositions on that theme). Lille still lacks a major cultural attraction with sufficient (European) appeal. One discussion partner suggested a permanent exposition showing the history and change of the European towns. Urban tourism could also be promoted by offering packages, for instance permitting Asiatic and American tourists to visit Paris, London and Brussels. To that end, the (social) infrastructure would have to be enriched with hotels and a rail connection with the airport. Adequate marketing of the appealing elements present in the region, and organising capacity, are necessary conditions.

Quality of Life

One object of the Euralille project is to shift part of the *périphérique* so that this motorway no longer cuts off the Palais de Congrès and other buildings from the rest of the city. Lille will thus be relieved of one of the present two infrastructural barriers. The construction of the motorway has been strongly stimulated by the national government as a means to facilitate access to the HST stations and thus raise their profitability. However, the motorway project is hardly conducive to a pleasant urban living environment. Major flyovers projected high above surface level will traverse the centre of the city, polluting the horizon and creating a lot of noise. Locally, the present choice is not considered a good solution, since it does not adequately cope with the awkward division of the city. A (more expensive) subterranean connection would have been preferred. Actually, the construction of a genuine *périphérique* east of the entire Lille-Roubaix agglomeration is also under consideration.

Spatial Distribution of Activities

Euralille

Efforts to attract new activity to the Euralille office buildings have not yet been very successful. As well as a number of companies from elsewhere in the region, some 15 companies have settled here that are new to Lille, five of them from abroad. They are mostly banks and financial institutions and companies engaged in informatics and communication technology. The interest of international business for Euralille is less than had been expected on the strength of its international status. Of two envisaged developments, the following can be said:

1 regional companies were expected to establish themselves by the HST station in order to penetrate new markets in Paris, Brussels or London. That hope has not been fully realised. Perhaps the target companies have not discerned enough few new market prospects and/or have too little international orientation;

2 another hope was to attract (foreign) companies active on international markets. The response has been disappointing. Perhaps Lille lacks the economic potential to attract new activity.

That some offices at Euralille are still standing vacant makes it hard to find investors in new, already planned, office buildings. There is sufficient demand, however, for the residential accommodations, of which student's apartments. The commercial activities of Euralille are prospering. Customers, of which quite a few are from Belgium, are drawn from an area of 30 km around Lille. Euralille has also created a rise in the number of visitors to the old centre. Most shops established in Euralille are ordinary rather than select, the superior shops having stayed in the old centre.

The *schéma directeur* for the Lille region was published after Euralille had been realised. Previously, there was no proper integral vision of the preferable development of the Euralille-area. Fragmentation and lack of coherence among the elements are the consequences. So far, Euralille has produced some 2,800 job opportunities. Several parts of Euralille, among them a four-star hotel, still have to be built. The expectation is that investors in the hotel will be found, because Lille is short of good hotel accommodation. Connection to the HST network does not directly increase the demand for hotel rooms, however. Experiences in Lyon have indeed shown that the connection to the HST network has even led to less hotel use. So, to justify investment in a luxury hotel, additional visitors would have to be drawn to Lille by other elements attractive enough to make them stay the night.

Social Distribution of Effects

The expected positive influence on the social-economic development helped to create sufficient support among the local population for the drastic changes foreseen in and around the HST stations. There was some anxiety that the major shopping centre at Euralille would drain many shops from the old centre, but that fear has proved unfounded. The Euralille shopping mall plays a complementary role to the old centre. It draws visitors from the entire region and has indeed stimulated their interest in the old centre. Regrettably, quite a lot of private cars are attracted as well, to the detriment of the living environment in the city centre. Therefore, to stimulate the use and improve the quality of regional collective transport is highly desirable.

Organising Capacity

A number of related activities have sprung up near Lille's HST junction. Their rapid development is due, among other things, to the general feeling that the urban region stood a good chance of an upward economic surge. The momentum has been used with energy and enthusiasm. Now that some time has past, the important thing is to maintain the momentum. The project is not yet complete. Investors have to be found soon for several elements still awaiting realisation to consolidate the gain of status and obtain the confidence of economic actors. If grounds around Euralille are left vacant, without substantial building activities going on, confidence might subside fast. For one thing because of the disappointing results regarding office activities, investors tend to be wary. There seems to be little trust in the region's economic prospects. Therefore, it is imperative to find a motor capable of reactivating the Euralille momentum. A good strategy has to be drawn up for a strong endogenous economic development of the region, effectively pushing the economy of Lille into an upward spiral.

The Most Important Themes of the Lille Case

Economic Effects

Energetic efforts have been made in Lille to accommodate the expected HST effects. Because of lack of interest among private investors in follow-up projects, developments related to the HST station seem to stagnate somewhat. What seems important now is to set into motion the endogenous economic processes needed to give economic actors sufficient confidence in the potential of the Lille region. The momentum achieved after the strategic decision to situate the crossing of two highly important HST lines at Lille needs consolidation. Economic progress can be promoted by forming strategic networks with more or less complementary urban regions. The Brussels-Antwerp-Ghent region, the Randstad, and the Ruhr Area suggest themselves. Good HST lines to these regions in particular are therefore wanted. The completion of the HST line to Brussels by the end of 1997 counts as a crucial step in that process.

Three successive strategies for the Lille region can be distinguished:

1 Lille as a European junction of important traffic flows. The decision to lead the HST line to the Channel Tunnel through Lille has been fundamental to the town's status as an international nodal point;

2 Lille as a European junction generating the value added related to the transport flows. This strategy envisages the supply of services at and around the transport junction, so that the urban region can make economic capital out of the transport flows. This strategy has been translated into the Euralille-development and in the building of houses, business companies and commercial activities near the HST station;

3 the development of a European metropolis, whose good international accessibility and enhanced image will act as a catalyst on the economic activities in the entire urban region. For this strategy, the presence of sufficient economic potential within the urban region is essential. A certain endogenous economic progress is needed to profit from the improved accessibility and status. If economic potential is lacking, complementary measures are needed to achieve an upward economic spiral. It may then be necessary for the higher authorities, that is, the French and European governments, to adopt a policy of (financial) support.

External Accessibility

Lille has an unfavourable position in respect of the Amsterdam-Paris HST line. A stop at Lille implies a 15–20 minutes' loss in travel time. Currently, the Thalys does indeed not stop at Lille. It shows how important the planning of an HST junction is in respect of an HST line. That is a point of great concern for those cities for which the precise course of the HST lines has still to be laid out. For Strasbourg, for example, the situation of the present central station in respect of the Rhine-Rhône line is suboptimum. An additional HST station would be one solution; another would be to adjust the infrastructure such as to provide the main station with a through line to serve the HST.

By coupling Lille airport to the rail network, it could develop into an alternative for the Paris airports nearing capacity. It might also stimulate the region's tourist function. By offering tourists from, say, Asia and North America packages including visits to London, Brussels, Paris and Amsterdam, Lille can make capital out of its good international accessibility. Lille could also make better use of its own tourist potential (among other things, the appealing historical city centre), profiting from the enhanced image of the region.

Internal Accessibility

At the moment, there is insufficient cohesion between the various elements of Euralille. Primarily a solution will have to be found to harmonise the present HST stations. A suggestion is to present the station as a single entity, providing better connections through a *passerelle* and/or minibus (to upgrade the psychological and physical mutual access). Better indications of the services available (especially the underground railway) could stimulate the use of regional trains as secondary transport to the HST, and thus enhance the role of a junction where several types of collective transport meet. Combined tickets for the various types of collective transport could serve to that end.

Euralille and the HST station have increased the need for easier car access to the centre. On the other hand, the additional traffic induced by Euralille may become a threat to the accessibility of the HST station, since different target groups are involved. Access by car is on the whole adequate, with the exception of the Gare de Flandres. A weak link is access from the region by collective transport. It causes the majority of visitors from the region to resort to the motorcar. To make the urban region more attractive, investment in better public transport between Lille and the surrounding region is essential.

9   The HST-integration in Lyon

Introduction

Lyon is a junction in the first French HST line. At the moment, the town has three HST stations: the old central station Perrache, the new centrally situated HST junction Part-Dieu, and the peripheral multi-modal junction Satolas. In Lyon, most attention is currently focused on Satolas. In spite of splendid development prospects, this HST station is still under-utilised. The idea is for the HST station to support the growth of the airport, because it improves access to it and thus widens its catchment area. The HST network enables travellers from Lyon to reach the major metropolises of Europe at all points of the compass within three and a half hours. The Lyon region will thus gain excellent access by road, rail and air. Since it also boasts a diversified economic basis and pleasant surroundings, the region has quite promising growth perspectives.

Accessibility

External Accessibility

The first French HST line between Paris and Lyon came into use in 1982. The effect on the number of moves and the modal split between the two cities was great. Between 1980 and 1985 the number of moves on the Paris-Lyon axis rose by 56 per cent. The number of passengers per train rose by 151 per cent; the number of passengers per aeroplane declined by 46 per cent. Next to the existing Paris-Lyon HST link, three new lines with dedicated HST infrastructure are planned:

1   the *TGV Méditerranée*. This is the line that runs from Lyon to Marseilles and on to Montpellier, Nice and Barcelona. The opening of the service between Lyon and Marseilles is envisaged for 1999. It will cut the travel time between the two towns from two hours 40 minutes to just over an hour;

2   the *TGV Lyon-Turin*. This HST line will be combined with a line for goods trains, so that the required investment costs can be shared. The costs are pushed up by the necessity of cutting a 51-km long tunnel. The combination will also accelerate the realisation, because the political wind stands fair for the building of rail infrastructure for goods transport. The work will be accomplished in stages, the first part to be ready by 2007;

3   the *TGV Rhine-Rhône*. This is the HST line from Lyon to the Ruhr Area by Strasbourg. The time schedule for this line has not yet been drawn up.

In 1997 a new (national) *schéma directeur* for the construction of HST lines will be published. What with the losses sustained by the SNCF and the need for economies on the national level (mostly to satisfy the EMU criteria), some of the HST projects will be delayed. The *schéma directeur* is to indicate which HST lines will have priority and which will be put off till later. The SNCF is also considering the possibility of raising the return on the investments by admitting other types of train (regional and national) to the HST infrastructure. To that end, experiments are being made on the line between Lyon and Paris. The introduction of tilting trains on conventional infrastructure is another endeavour to raise the quality of rail transport at lower cost than would be involved in the construction of dedicated HST infrastructure.

The HST Stations

The Perrache HST station was the main station of Lyon until the 1980s. Perrache lies centrally in the peninsula and is eminently accessible by public transport. It also has a direct connection with the parallel motorway. Perrache has been reduced to a secondary function, especially for long-distance services. As a stopping place for high-speed trains it has the disadvantage of being constructed as a head-end station, accommodating no westward HST services. Only non-through-HSTs stop at Perrache. Because the available capacity is approaching saturation, in due time sizable investments will become necessary in the adjoining rail infrastructure, especially westwards.

Part-Dieu, in use since 1983, currently counts as Lyon's principal railway station. It has profited from the relatively fast development of the surrounding urban area and the adjoining HST network. In 1984, 27,000 passengers used Part-Dieu; in 1992 their number had risen to 37,000. In the same period, the number of passengers at Perrache fell from 26,500 to 24,000. Like Perrache, Part-Dieu suffers from congestion on the connecting rail infrastructure. The complementary public transport networks of Part-Dieu are considered insufficient to cope with the increasing transport flows.

Satolas is the only French airport besides Paris-Charles-de-Gaulle with a direct connection to the HST network. The HST station was opened in 1994 and lies on the *contournement* line of Lyon. The station has largely been financed by the region. The multi-modal junction 25 km east of Lyon is not yet connected to the conventional rail network. The *contournement* accommodates mostly through-HSTs running north-south and back. Every day, about 34 HSTs pass Satolas (and Lyon) without stopping; only 10 or 11 actually call at Satolas. Three strategic development targets have been drawn up for Satolas: i) development into junction-cum-industrial estate; ii) development into HST-HST hub; and iii) development into bimodal hub (HST aeroplane transfer point).

The reason why SNCF allows only a limited number of HSTs to stop at Satolas is that the expected number of passengers to be served at this junction is too small to warrant a loss of seven minutes' travel time. The smallness of the Satolas catchment area of Satolas is due to several factors:

- there is no rail connection between the centre of Lyon and Satolas. The connection would demand an investment of 2,000–3,000 million FF. However, the present number of travellers on this transport section, some 1,000 a day, is considered insufficient to warrant the investment. At the moment a shuttle bus runs between Lyon and Satolas at a frequency of three per hour. In the coming decade, Satolas is to be integrated into the regional rail network. In spite of its high costs, there is broad consensus about the necessity of that project. The regionalisation of the railways, through which the regions will take over the control of the regional rail transport from the state, is important in that connection. The expectation is that the region will give high priority to the connection of Satolas with the regional rail network;
- the number of flights through Satolas is still limited, with hardly any intercontinental flights. Yet it is precisely for such flights that the HST can fulfil a complementary function. The further liberalisation of European air space will probably engender a rising number of flights to and from Satolas. The terminal capacity of the airport will have to be enlarged to accommodate the increased passenger flows, an operation that involves an estimated investment of some 4,000 million FF. In its *schéma directeur* the national government has recognised the strategic importance of continued growth of the multi-modal junction Satolas. An important factor

in that connection is the saturation of the Paris airports;
- that Satolas lies outside the jurisdiction of the Communauté Urbaine de Lyon is an obstacle to, among other things, the harmonisation of transport and spatial planning between Lyon and Satolas;
- at present, too few HST lines meet at Lyon. Once other HST lines, such as the TGV-Méditerranée, the TGV Lyon-Turin and the TGV Rhine-Rhône, are in operation, the need to make use of the multi-modal junction Satolas will be greater.

Economic Potential[1]

Measured by its contribution to French gross national product, Lyon is the second economic centre, behind Paris. The production structure is differentiated and comprises a relatively large proportion of knowledge-intensive (growth) sectors. More than 3,200 companies can be called 'high-tech'. In addition there are still quite a few traditional industries, such as textile, machine construction, electronics and the lorry and coach factory of Renault (RVI), Lyon's largest employer. Other major employers are Rhône-Poulenc (chemicals), Société Lyonnaise de Transports, Carrefour (retail trade), Atochem (chemicals), Ciapem (electronics), Framatome (nuclear energy) and Crédit Lyonnais (bank).

Because of its geographical situation for one thing, Lyon has traditionally been a market centre, where various supra-regional service activities have flourished. Within France, Lyon counts as a financial centre. Some 60 banks have establishments here. Its interest as such has decreased, however, after the closure of the Exchange in January 1992. That only relatively few decision centres (headquarters of large institutions or business companies) have settled in Lyon is felt as a serious lack. Among the high-grade industrial sectors, the 'medical complex' is important. This complex comprises R&D establishments of many public institutions and private businesses, production units of pharmaceutical, medical-technical companies, a major medical faculty, and a range of hospitals. Lyon rightfully defines itself as a *métropole de la santé*.

The restructuring in the traditional industrial sectors has had great influence on the development of employment. In Grand Lyon, nearly 37,000 out of 137,000 jobs in industry were lost between 1982 and 1993. By contrast, the tertiary sector gained 45,000 jobs. Since 1990 especially, employment has declined, the reason being that the growth in services no longer makes up for the decline in industry. In 1990, the percentage of unemployed was 9.3 in

Grand Lyon (49,600) and 9.2 in the City of Lyon (18,000). In 1982 the figures were more favourable: 41,000 in Grand Lyon and 15,000 in Lyon. The central city and the region differ little in terms of unemployment, which is due to the suburbanisation process, which, compared to many other western European metropolises, is not very selective. Indeed, the proportion of foreigners (especially North Africans) is greater in the suburban ring than in the City of Lyon itself.

Quality of Life

The conditions in the Part-Dieu district no longer meet modern demands for harmonious urban development. For one thing, car traffic is too dominant; for another, the station is poorly integrated into the urban structure. Among the projects now in progress to ameliorate the situation are efforts to upgrade public transport within and to this district. At present, Lyon is still cut through by a motorway, which runs past the Perrache HST station. The congestion on the motorways around Lyon urges an early construction of the planned motorways west of Lyon and east of Satolas. Once the new western ring motorway is complete, the one now cutting through the centre past Perrache station can be reconstructed into a normal thoroughfare. The southern part of the peninsula can then be upgraded and the quality of the living environment in the centre raised. This is regarded as one of the most important changes in the town, and as such, is given priority.

Spatial Distribution of Activities

Until now, there have been hardly any economic relations between secondary French towns, such as Grenoble and Lyon. The economic activities of such towns were mostly Paris-oriented. Relations among secondary French towns are now gradually evolving, a development that will have to be sustained by the upgrading of collective regional transport. In that train of thought, the HST network, bringing neighbouring cities such as Marseilles, Turin and Montpellier within reach in less than an hour and a half, will strengthen the economic and social relations with those towns. As the situation is now, because of the lack of a direct air link between Lyon and Turin, travellers get from Paris to Turin more quickly than from Lyon to Turin. That will change with the realisation of the Lyon-Turin HST service.

Within the City of Lyon there are two economic centres: Part-Dieu and the Peninsula. Part-Dieu has hardly begun to attract international business companies. A rail connection with Satolas multi-modal junction could stimulate the development of both Part-Dieu and Satolas. Grand-Est, comprising Satolas Airport, is a fast-developing area within the region. Here, outside the metropolis itself, are found the most promising economic development poles of Lyon urban region: *la plaine de l'Ain* and the *ville nouvelle de l'Isle d'Abeau*. There is some concern that further development of Grand-Est will drain away activities from the centre of Lyon. For a balanced spatial planning it might be preferable for both areas to come under the same administrative authority.

Social Distribution of Effects

Satolas airport causes little nuisance because of its fortunate geographical position in respect of residential areas. Therefore, night flights are permitted from Satolas. Between 40 and 45 flights are carried out every night. Several integrators, such as DHL and UPS, avail themselves of the night-flight possibilities. Some night flights could be replaced with high-speed rail services. Already the schedule counts three HSTs a night from Satolas on behalf of French Mail.

Organising Capacity

Satolas lies outside the territory of the Communauté Urbaine de Lyon, on the border of the Rhône and Isère departments and near that of l'Ain. Forty-eight per cent of passengers at Satolas come from or are going to the area of *la Grande Lyon*. Several actors urge expansion of the Communauté Urbaine de Lyon territory to bring the airport within its district. That would facilitate the solution of border-crossing problems in terms of transport and spatial planning. A point to keep in mind is that areas around Satolas should be reserved for the future development of the junction. Another possibility is for the state to issue a Directive Territoire d'Aménagement (DTA) to give the area around Satolas an extraordinary administrative status by which its control of the area would in principle become a responsibility of the state. There is very strong regional consensus on the necessity of administrative reorganisation.

The Most Important Themes of the Lyon Case

The Development Prospects of the Multi-modal Junction Satolas

Satolas airport seems to have excellent development prospects. A combination of positive factors puts the junction in an eminent starting position towards substantial growth and the attraction of new economic activity. To make effective capital out of the junction's potential, several necessary preconditions have to be met (see the next section). Positive factors for Satolas are the saturation of the great European airports, in particular those of Paris, the progressive liberalisation of aviation, the fact that the French government has designated Satolas as a strategic growth location (the national *schéma directeur* envisages raising the number of runways at Satolas from two to four); the availability of relatively abundant space around the junction for further growth of the airport and related activities; and the assurance of broad regional support for the further development of the junction. Growing environmental awareness and progressive congestion in European air space are likely to stimulate the substitution of HST services for air traffic. Multi-modal junctions with direct transfer opportunities between HST and aircraft are therefore considered promising projects. The airport has an advantageous geographic location: the population in the surrounding area is sparse, but important urban agglomerations such as Lyon and Geneva are within easy reach. Moreover, the economy of the Lyon urban region is prospering.

Necessary Preconditions for the Further Development of Satolas

Necessary preconditions for the prosperity of Satolas are an adequate administrative organisation structure, connection of Satolas to the regional rail network (comprising a high-grade rail connection between Satolas and Lyon), extension of the terminal capacity of the airport, and attraction of more intercontinental flights. Better coordination between the administrative policy of Lyon and Satolas is advisable in view of the progressive economic coherence between the two areas. To realise adequate mutual transport connections, adjust the spatial policies, and prevent undesirable competition between them, an administrative reorganisation is necessary. To improve the junction's internal accessibility, a rail connection between Lyon and Satolas is indispensable. It will make Part-Dieu more appealing to international business. The lack of volume of the present transport flows between the two locations should not be allowed to block that strategic investment. Expansion of the terminal and the parking capacity is needed to accommodate the growing number of passengers of the airport. That is an important precondition for attracting more intercontinental flights, a development at present held up by the airport's limited capacity. When Satolas could attract more intercontinental flights, also the attraction of more HSTs can be expected. Then, both transport modalities will play a mutual complementary role, and Satolas can develop from a multi-modal towards a real intermodal junction.

Timing and Financing of the Various Projects around Satolas

The various projects envisaged around Satolas, in particular its connection to the regional rail network and the expansion of the airport terminal, require relatively much investment. The question of priority therefore arises, but no unequivocal answer is possible since the projects are interdependent with respect to the development of the intermodal junction. The desired capacity of one element of such a junction always depends on that of the other elements. Better access by HST increases the development prospects of intercontinental flights, and a growing number of such flights makes it more attractive to have more HSTs call at the junction. An increase in the number of international transport moves (by HST or aeroplane) makes improvement of the internal accessibility (that is, connection to the regional rail transport) more urgent. And a better conventional rail connection of the junction makes the expansion of international transport moves more interesting. Both the lack of access by conventional rail services and the limited capacity of the air terminal are obstacles to the further development of the junction as a whole.

To cope with the desired growth, the relevant plans should be realised in good time. It seems to be logical that the national government, given its recognition of Satolas's strategic importance, should make a substantial contribution to the financing of the projects. The national government could also accelerate the construction of the strategically vital HST connection between Lyon and Turin. But the achievement of the necessary financing would be simplified most by a modified administrative situation allowing an integral policy for Lyon and Satolas to evolve. That modification should be given the highest priority, since hopefully it will inspire confidence among the actors involved in the effective realisation of the development prospects of Satolas.

Note

1   The text of this section is based on Van den Berg et al., 1996.

10 The HST-integration in Marseilles[1]

Introduction

HSTs do call at Marseilles, but from Valence onward they run on conventional track. By 1999, however, the line TGV-Méditerranée will be complete, linking Marseilles to Paris by new tracks. To that end, the station of Marseilles, Saint Charles, will be thoroughly renovated, and the environment of the station revitalised. A second stopping place, on a still-uncultivated plateau 20 km to the north of Marseilles, is under consideration.

Accessibility

Access to the City

At the moment, Marseilles-Saint Charles is already an HST station. It lies on the route Paris-Lyon-Rhône Valley-Côte d'Azur-Italy. The station is a head-end station. Daily, 12 HSTs leave Saint Charles for Paris, but up to Valence the HSTs travel on conventional track and cannot actually reach high speeds. The distance to Paris, by far the most important destination from Marseilles, is about 650 km. This distance can now be laid back in about four and a half hours. From 1999, with new track between Lyon and Marseilles, the travel time will be cut to three hours. The planned HST services from Marseilles to several destinations from 1999 onwards are indicated in Table 10.1.

The Commune of Marseilles looks upon the advent of the HST as a chance to give the city's economy a boost and revitalise the long-neglected centre of the city. To that end, the station is being thoroughly renovated and the capacity of the terminal considerably expanded. In addition, the overall quality of the station will be much improved (modernisation, better information, better connection to the bus station, establishment of shops in the station, better access for pedestrians, more parking spaces). The tourist potential of Marseilles

103

Table 10.1   Planned HST services from Marseilles from 1999 onwards

Destination	Daily frequency
Paris	12
Brussels	6
Dion	3
Genève	1
Montpellier	3

would benefit from a service between the HST station Saint Charles and the fast boats which sail from Marseilles to Corsica and other destinations.

Relationship with the Airport

About 25 km northwest of Marseilles lies Marignane airport. This airport dispatched 5.4 million passengers in 1996, of whom seven-tenths in national and three-tenths in international traffic. The main routes are Marseilles-Paris (2.7 million passengers) and Marseilles-Corsica (550,000 passengers). Many French and European destinations can be reached from Marignane. In addition, the airport more or less specialises in services to African destinations (Aeroport Marseille-Provence, 1997). The strategy of the airport is to become a 'hub' for Africa and Asia. This strategy is to be implemented in the coming years.

There is no rail service between Marseilles Saint-Charles and the airport. There are very frequent bus services between Saint Charles and Marignane, but most air passengers arrive at the airport by car. Basically, the expectation was that the new HST line between Paris and Marseilles could absorb a substantial portion of air travellers. Three factors play a role in the modal split between aircraft and HST in the Paris-Marseilles route:

- frequency. Marignane Airport offers a much higher frequency than the future Saint Charles. There are 44 daily flights from Marignane to Paris. The HST is expected to run at a much lower frequency: 12 times a day to Paris. From research, an HST frequency of 22 times a day is necessary to achieve a worthwhile substitution;
- tariffs. The prices of air transport have dramatically dropped in the last few years, a trend that is expected to continue with further liberalisation of air traffic in Europe. The tariffs for the HST are harder to reduce because of the tremendous investments in new infrastructure required. That, too, diminishes the substitution effect of the HST;

- travel time. The difference in travel times between HST and aircraft is an important factor in the modal split of travellers on the Paris-Marseilles stretch.

A significant missing link is a rail connection between Marseille-Saint Charles and the airport. At the moment there are no concrete plans to fill the gap. A station at the airport could much improve external access to the centre of Marseilles.

Internal Accessibility

Saint Charles station lies in the centre of the City of Marseilles. The southern part of the surrounding neighbourhood is much impoverished, and accommodates hardly any station-related economic functions.

Marseille-Saint Charles is relatively easily accessed by car. From the north, the station can be reached by the motorway. The road is sometimes congested, especially near the station. According to the plans for the new station, accessibility by car will be significantly improved by better traffic control. The principal measure in that context is the creation of a better hierarchy of the access roads to the station. In addition, the number of parking places underneath the station will be greatly extended.

The station is an important junction in the municipal public transport network, connected to the city railway, the express tramway and city buses. The number of passengers has been on the wane for years, partly owing to the establishment, in the 1970s, of large zones of economic activity on the city outskirts and in the surrounding suburbs, places hardly if at all accessible by public transport. Many working and shopping functions can thus be reached exclusively by car. The light-railway system in Marseilles performs well but the utilisation could be better; for one thing because, for safety reasons, it stops at nine o'clock in the evening. Such early closing hours inhibit the use of public transport.

Regional public transport between surrounding towns and Marseilles Saint Charles is not very developed. For example, between Marseilles and Aix, an important connection, trains run on a non-electrified single track. The frequency of the rail services is relatively low, and the travel time long in comparison to the car. Suburbs like Vitrolles and Aubagne are difficult to reach by train, particularly because trains run at low frequencies and SNCF stations are peripheral to the towns. The lack of sufficient regional public transport leads to enormous flows of car traffic between Marseilles and surrounding towns, mainly because some 50 per cent of the jobs of the Department of Bouches du Rhône are located in Marseilles.

The regional government lacks the power and resources to change the situation, and for the time being there is no other agency with the necessary means and there is no authority able to deal with the problem of coordinating the public transport policies in the area Aix/Marseille/Marignane/Vitrolles/ Aubagne. In the future some improvement may be expected once the region becomes responsible for the exploitation of regional railway lines. The only improvement in sight is the doubling of tracks on certain sections of the Marseilles-Aix line. In addition, a study on the improvement of the axes Rognac and Aubange is being undertaken, and 800 million francs is reserved for new trains.

A Second HST Stopping Place

An awkward question in Marseilles is the possible opening of a second HST station some 20 km north of Marseilles, on the plateau of Arbois. At the moment, the plateau is still a bare plain, but there are plans to create there a business park for high-grade companies, in combination with the HST station. A development pole near Arbois would enter into competition with the HST station at Marseilles, and might therefore be considered a threat. The following negative repercussions for Saint Charles can be distinguished:

- a stop at Arbois means some seven minutes extra travel time to Marseilles. In view of the critical travel time to Paris of about three hours needed to vie with the aeroplane, every minute gained counts (ITA, 1996);
- from Arbois, some HST trains could, under certain conditions, continue directly to Toulon, Nice and Italy without calling at Marseilles. The possible development of Arbois is thus a direct threat to the accessibility of Marseilles. The future construction of an HST branch towards Nice could mean a drastic reduction of the number of HSTs to Marseilles, because of the station's terminal position. HSTs might then stop only at Arbois and from there swerve to the east;
- the rise of Arbois could pose a serious threat to the economic strategy of the state and the City of Marseilles to revitalise the city's economy. The relevant plans assign to Saint Charles HST station a significant role of catalyst to attract high-quality, metropolitan service functions, from which the entire agglomeration of Marseilles could profit. A high-frequency HST service to Saint Charles is indispensable to that end, and could be put in

jeopardy by the development of Arbois;

- so far, there is no form of secondary public transport at all to the Arbois plateau. Therefore, the establishment of the Arbois HST station would either demand large investments in secondary public transport, or failing that, greatly increase car traffic in the urban area around Marseilles.

The region of Provence-Côte d'Azur supports the development of Arbois, as do the nearby towns of Aix-en-Provence and Vitrolles. Those in favour argue that Arbois is easily accessible to inhabitants north of Marseilles but also to many people from the region of Bouches-du-Rhône. The French ministry of the environment is against the development of the virgin plateau d'Arbois

Economic Potential

The economy of Marseilles has seriously declined in the past decades. The main causes are the decline of traditional industries and the loss of the colonies in North Africa, which were very important to Marseilles as southern commercial town. The loss of industrial activities has not, as in many other towns, been compensated by a reciprocal growth of tertiary activities. As a result, the city suffers from massive unemployment, made even worse by the arrival of poorly-educated immigrants. Nevertheless, the urban region of Marseilles still holds some significant trump cards. For one thing, the region boasts a strong concentration of heavy and light modern industry, particularly around Etang de Berre, west of Marseilles. The transport and logistic sector is also well represented. Marseilles is the largest port of France, strategically situated on the mouth of the Rhône. Another strong sector is the medical cluster. The companies and institutions within that cluster form together the greatest employer of Marseilles. In qualitative terms, Marseilles is moreover the leader in medical facilities in France. As a scientific centre, the area ranks third after Paris and Lyon. In terms of tourism, too, Marseilles has potential: the situation on the Mediterranean and the characteristic inner city offer chances in that respect. The image of the city is relatively bad, however, but considerable efforts are being made to change this and improvements are also being made.

The authorities have seized upon the advent of the HST to broaden and strengthen the economic basis of Marseilles. An important project in that context is Euroméditerranée. This comprehensive project initiated by the state is meant to enhance the metropolitan function of Marseilles as capital of the southern Mediterranean area. In that frame of thought, the state and the City of Marseilles are implementing a large number of coherent strategies (Etablissement Public d'Aménagement, 1996).

The popular neighbourhood near the station is being rehabilitated and better class houses are being built there. Furthermore, much is hoped from the link between the City of Marseilles and the industrial and logistic activities outside the city. The area north of the old centre is to be the site for tertiary activities related to the harbour and the industry. The activities envisaged are logistic companies, industries and port-related services such as banks, insurance companies, international trade, etc. To attract them, new modern offices will be erected. In that way efforts are being made to abolish the present strict separation between the (autonomous) port and the surrounding industrial area on the one hand and the city on the other.

An element of the strategy is to attract decision-making headquarters from Paris. The state has already promised to move decision-making government functions from Paris to Marseilles, but there is some scepticism about the actual implementation of these intentions. Furthermore, certain faculties of the University of Aix-Marseilles will be moved to this area, with a view to enlarging the knowledge basis and the vivacity of this part of the town. In addition, the centre is to be made more appealing, in the visual and tourist sense, by the creation of an opening to the Mediterranean.

There are plans to demolish certain docklands in the centre of the city as well as a viaduct parallel to the sea, and channel the local traffic through a tunnel. The state has a pioneering role in the Euroméditerranée project. For one thing, the state has committed itself to move certain headquarters to Marseilles. For another, by revitalising the area, the state creates favourable location conditions, thus reducing for private companies the risks of establishing in the area. The advent of the HST is a powerful catalyst for the project. It helps to attract certain types of high-quality tertiary activity, and in combination with Euroméditerranée adds lustre to the overall status of the city.

Quality of Life

The arrival of the HST in combination with the Euroméditerranée project is seized upon to raise the quality of the living environment around the station. To that effect, the impoverished neighbourhood is renovated. One purpose of the revitalisation policy of Marseilles is the integration of the highroads in the urban surroundings. Measures of traffic technology relieve the pressure of car traffic on the city. The plans are mostly concerned with the construction of (stretches of) roads below street level and the diminishing of congestion through better traffic control. The arrangement of green belts is another measure. The question is how far interlocal public transport will be boosted by the arrival of the HST. Considering the relatively low quality of the interlocal connections, the car will continue to play an important role. For the time being, there are no substantial concrete projects for a substantial improvement of the regional public transport.

Spatial Distribution of Activities

In recent years, there has been a major outflow of citizens and economic activities from the centre of Marseilles. The wholesale tackling of the station and the Euroméditerranée project sketched above are intended to counter that trend by enticing high-quality services and affluent citizens back to the centre of the town. Very probably these plans will lead to a strong boost to the city centre.

A very important problem in the spatial distribution of activities is the lack of a *Communauté Urbaine* to coordinate the different spatial policies. The development of different plans for the arrival of the HST is illustrative of the lack of cooperation and authority. In the City of Marseilles, the arrival of the TGV is linked to the development of the Euromediterranée project. At the same time, the department and the city of Aix are developing plans for the TGV at the Arbois-plateau. There is no coordination between these plans.

The consequences of possible stopping place at Arbois for the inner city of Marseilles will probably be limited. The project of Eurimediterrannée and the arrival of the HST are so far-reaching for the development of the inner city that the development of Arbois should not be considered as a direct threat.

Social Distribution of Effects

The construction of the new Méditerranée HST section has met with much opposition. To reduce the inconvenience, additional investments have been made. In Marseilles itself, the neighbourhood near Saint Charles will be fundamentally renovated. This neighbourhood is now for a great part inhabited by relatively poor citizens. Its rehabilitation will unavoidably be attended by rises of the rent, thus forcing certain population groups to move out. Given the vacancies in the centre of Marseilles, that need not cause undue hardship. Much money is also being sunk into the revitalisation of the direly impoverished northern quarters of Marseilles, an area plagued by unemployment and social tension, but those projects are not directly linked to the arrival of the HST.

Organising Capacity

Deficient organising capacity in the region around Marseilles is probably the cause of failure to make use of possible complementarities. A serious obstacle is the lack of coordinated planning between towns in the region around Marseilles. There is no competent agency at that level, nor have any strategic plans been drawn up for the area. As a result, the towns in the region are engaged in pointless competition for activities and people and the development of commercial, technological and tertiary centres. The greatest problem is the coordination of regional public transport. There are many organisations involved, such as the City of Marseilles, towns around Marseilles, the SNCF, the department, the region and the state, but conflicting interests and lack of leadership have so far impeded the development of adequate regional public transport. There is no effective Communauté Urbaine to bring about the mutual adjustment of transport matters and the spatial distribution of economic activities, a situation that is due mainly to the differing political colours of mayors in the urban area around Marseilles. Since 1992 there has been a Communauté de Communes Marseilles-Provence-Metropole, to which 16 towns in the urban region belong. But there is also a Communauté de Communes for Aix and Vitrolles, and a Communauté des villes for Aubagne. If more towns participated and more responsibility could be assigned to the Communauté de Communes Marseilles-Provence-Metropole, a more efficient solution of problems, in particular those related to transport, might be possible.

The state seems the obvious authority to solve coordination problems, for instance by creating a kind of town province. Moreover, such a move could effectively give substance to the position of Marseilles as metropolis of the south as desired by the state, which in the end would be for the good of the towns all over the region. A town province with generous responsibilities could give shape to an effective regional urban system, with the proper transport links and harmonised spatial planning, permitting the utilisation of complementarities on the regional level (Bonnier, 1997).

The Most Important Themes of the Marseilles Case

From 1999 onwards, Marseilles will be connected to Paris by a dedicated HST line. The advent of the HST will greatly increase the accessibility of the city. Some important themes relevant to the arrival of the HST in Marseilles will be dealt with below.

HST as a Means to Revitalise the City

In Marseilles the arrival of the HST is considered an important catalyst for the revitalisation of the city, and integral measures are being taken to put it to good use. First of all, the outdated station will be almost entirely transformed. The quality of the station will be improved and the capacity of the terminal much extended. In addition, the plans give much attention to the relationship between the station and the city. The access roads to the station will be improved, to reduce the congestion around the station. To that end, a better hierarchy of access roads to the station is aimed for.

A second concern of the revitalisation is the area around the station. The living environment of the town quarter will be improved, as well as the accessibility of the neighbouring university. And, thirdly, the advent of the HST is seized upon to revitalise the economy of the town as a whole. For that purpose some urban revitalisation projects are undertaken, aimed at attracting such promising economic sectors as port-related services and other tertiary activities. Efforts are also made to entice affluent groups of citizens back to the centre of the city, by building the more expensive types of houses and improving the living climate in the centre. The revitalisation plans are largely financed by the state.

The Role of Marseilles Saint Charles in the Context of the Region

The revitalising policies in Marseilles have a clear regional dimension. The aim of the economic strategy of the French state and the community of Marseilles is to strengthen the metropolitan functions of the city, thereby permitting the city to play a dominant role as the main French city in the southern Mediterranean area. In the context of the Euroméditerranée project, economic activities are attracted which clearly have functions that go far beyond the City of Marseilles alone, but are also supportive for cities in the southern Mediterranean area as a whole. In order to achieve this, superior connections are needed, not only with the surrounding cities in the Marseilles agglomeration but also with more remote cities, especially with Lyons and Paris. Therefore, the success of Euroméditerranée is closely related to the advent of the HST service to Marseilles-Saint Charles. This should be kept in mind with regard to the possible creation of a second HST station, some 20 km to the north of Marseilles. If the economy of Marseilles is to be successfully revitalised, the station of Saint Charles should clearly function as the main stopping HST place with a sufficient level of HST services.

A major problem is the lack of cooperation between cities in the wider Marseilles metropolitan area. Although together they constitute a potentially strong system of cities, there is no coordinating administrative body to exploit the potential benefits of a joint spatial-economic strategy. To solve that problem, a stronger regional government is required. An extension of the number of members and of the responsibilities of the existing Communauté de Communes or the creation of an effective metropolitan authority (Communauté Urbaine) as in other large cities in France (Lyons, Bordeaux, Strasbourg) might help to coordinate and harmonize the spatial-economic policies pursued in the urban area around Marseilles.

Internal Accessibility

Access to Saint Charles station from the surrounding region by secondary public transport is far from optimal. That is a cause of great concern for the functioning of Saint Charles station and the much-wanted revitalisation of the centre of Marseilles, as well as for the ambition of the Euroméditerranée project to strengthen the position of Marseilles as a metropole of the wider region. Road access to the station is not a problem yet, but in the future the worsening congestion on the road network will obstruct access to Marseilles, and moreover the growing car traffic has negative effects on the living environment, making Marseilles less attractive to citizens and business companies. In the near future, the road network in the region will become more and more saturated, and if Marseilles is to be revitalised, it must join forces with surrounding municipalities to invest in the regional public transport system. During recent years, almost no investments were made in the local public transport infrastructure. Important capacity problems are making these investments critical.

Furthermore, if the station of Marseilles Saint Charles is to be the main HST stopping place for the wider metropolitan area of Marseilles, large investments are needed in these connections in order to create a wide feeder area for the station. An improvement of the rail connections with surrounding towns like Aix and Vitrolles/Marignane especially would be most welcome, as would be an improvement of rail connections with the town of Aubagne and the creation of a direct link with the airport. Unfortunately, the cities involved and the regional government lack the financial means to realise the investment. This is another problem whose solution might be facilitated by more intra-regional cooperation in the framework of a possible Communauté Urbaine, to the benefit of the urban area around Marseilles as a whole. In addition to its present role as initiator of the revitalisation of the centre of Marseilles, the state might contribute to the improvement of inter-local transport in the region. That, too, would help the revitalisation of the Marseilles economy to the benefit of the wider region.

Note

1   Coauthor: drs W. van Winden, EURICUR.

11 The HST-integration in Nantes

Introduction

Nantes seems to have profited from joining the HST network. One zone adjoining the HST station has flourished tremendously. New activities have been drawn to the town. Much new transport infrastructure has been and is being constructed in the Nantes region. To give an example: in the last decade two tramlines have been opened and a new line is being prepared. Moreover, north of Nantes a new airport is planned. Around the HST station several infrastructural measures to improve internal accessibility are being taken.

Accessibility

External Accessibility

Since September 1989 high-speed trains have called at Nantes. The TGV-Atlantique line was completed while the wind was still fair. Further new dedicated HST infrastructure is much less easy to realise, now that the HST has no longer the highest priority with the SNCF, and the French state is carrying through an extensive retrenchment programme. Since HST lines connecting very large agglomerations such as Paris, Lyon and London are the only ones to guarantee profit, the HST investment programme has been drastically cut down.

The TGV-Atlantique has three main lines: the Aquitaine (Bordeaux, Tarbes, and the Spanish boundary at Hendaye/Irun), the Loire Valley (Nantes and La Rochelle), and the Brittany (Brest, Rennes, and Quimper) (see Strohl, 1993, p. 85). The Loire Valley boasts dedicated HST infrastructure from Paris to Le Mans. Nantes is to all intents and purposes the terminus of this branch (although a few HSTs go on to Le Croisic). Two-fifths of the HSTs on this line run to Nantes or beyond. The others finish earlier, at Le Mans or Angers.

From Nantes there are daily:

- 19 trains to Paris and back (travel time, two hours five minutes, formerly three hours by conventional train);
- three direct connections to Lille and back (travel time, three hours 45 minutes). Travel times to Brussels and London are four hours 30 minutes and six hours 30 minutes respectively;
- three 'direct' trains to and from Lyon by the Paris station Massy (travel time four hours 30 minutes;
- a direct connection with Brussels will be operational in 1997.

Section from Le Mans to Nantes

On the Le Mans-Nantes section, trains run on conventional infrastructure. The section has admittedly been improved to permit speeds up to 220 km/h. The most troublesome subsection is that from Nantes to Angers where the capacity is insufficient, because the rail infrastructure has to be shared by HSTs, freight trains (from and to the port of Nantes-St Nazaire), national and regional trains. Rail traffic from Nantes to the southeast, to Tours, also makes use of this section. The capacity shortage seriously constrains the schedule of the HST between Paris and Nantes. At the moment the HST frequency on this line cannot be increased, nor can it be regular (for instance one HST departure every full hour). Only half an hour's time can be gained by raising the Le Mans-Nantes section to full HST level. The greatest gain in time has already been achieved on the HST section from Paris to Le Mans, which has cut the duration of a train ride between Paris and Nantes from three to two hours. Indeed, the advantage of more tracks is the possibility of a flexible timetable rather than a gain of time.

At the moment, the effects of an HST line circumventing Le Mans (*contournement*) are being investigated. The time gains of such a ring line will profit both Nantes and Rennes, but is a disadvantage for Le Mans. There are already some services that pass Le Mans by, and that town fears that with the construction of the *contournement* their number will grow. As the HST network expands, there will be more and more through-trains. The SNCF has already acquired the plots of land needed for the *contournement*.

Currently, the SNCF seems to give more priority to the development of the TGV-Est than to the extension of the TGV-Atlantique. In the national master-plan of the SNCF, Le Mans-Angers and Le Mans-Rennes are mentioned as stretches to be converted into HST level sections, but not the Angers-Nantes line. Apparently, on the national level that line is not considered an important bottleneck. On the local level, on the contrary, this very section is regarded as *the* bottleneck of the rail connection between Le Mans and Nantes. A strong regional lobby to get this line included in the master-plan seems therefore indicated. Financial contributions from the local and regional authorities will also be required for its upgrading. To reduce the investment cost, from Le Mans an HST track could be constructed that in part could also be used for the connection with Rennes.

Barreau-sud

Another project of great importance to Nantes is the construction of the *barreau-sud* near Paris. That southern ring-line would permit trains to circumvent Paris to such destinations as Lille, London, Cologne and Lyon. At the moment the maximum speed there is 70 km/h. Dedicated HST infrastructure is considered of fundamental importance for the functioning of HST network and for the connection of western France with the rest of Europe. The time that can be gained here (about half an hour) favours quite a few destinations. At the moment, regions in western France are carrying on a collective lobby for the construction of the *barreau-sud*, which is opposed, however, by the *Département des Essones* that would be traversed by the new line.

The HST Station

The existing central station of Nantes serves as the stopping place for the HST. In western France there are many small and medium-sized towns: in none of them will a new HST station be built. On the south side of the Nantes station a new building has been erected to accommodate the HST trains and the extra transport flows they carry. Another motive was to enhance the station's image as an HST station. To serve the new station, certain facilities have been provided on the SNCF-grounds: a multistorey car park with 610 places, an hotel-restaurant and an office building with 2,000 square metres' floor area. Forty-five per cent of those arriving at or departing from the station use the car as secondary transport mode, 28 per cent the municipal public transport (especially the tram), nine per cent a connecting train, three per cent a taxi, and 15 per cent their own two feet (SNCF (Région de Nantes) et Villes de Nantes, 1996).

Plans have been made to reconstruct the station of Nantes. The northern station building is somewhat dated. The entrances need to be improved, several services regrouped and the information on the various transport possibilities upgraded. Besides, the traffic situation on the north side is being adjusted. The north entrance must be improved, the nuisance caused by cars reduced, and a better connection between bus and tram provided for. The south side is to become a multi-modal transfer point (*un pôle échange multimodal*). On this side there is space enough to give better car access (private cars and regional buses) by adjusting access roads and providing parking facilities. The upgrading of the station will cost about 50 million FF. The fact that Nantes will be host to some games during the football world championships in 1998 gives a strong impulse to carry out the planned improvements as soon as possible. The SNCF, the district, the region as well as the departement make financial contributions. Moreover, a *surtax local temporaire* will be imposed in the form of a temporary surcharge on the tickets to and from Nantes, to be spent on the reconstruction project. Much store is set on the upgrading of the station, because it fulfils a super-local function, serving people from all over the urban region.

The Airport

The present airport of Nantes is expected to reach its capacity of 2.5 million passengers in the year 2005. The airport fulfils an important function for western France. Since Nantes joined the HST network, the number of air passengers from and to Paris has fallen by more than 30 per cent.[1] Lately, however, there has been a slight rise in the number of air passengers to Paris. The airport is situated unfavourably in terms of nuisance to the residential areas of Nantes. For that reason and because the airport is expected to reach saturation, a new airport has been planned north of Nantes. That airport, Notre-Dames des Landes, is planned to start its operations in 2010.

Currently the train connection between Nantes and Rennes is inadequate. The train takes about two hours to span a distance of no more than 100 km. New rail infrastructure between Rennes and Nantes could also profit the new airport, because HSTs could run through the centre of Nantes on to the airport. Just to call at the airport without stopping in Nantes does not seem a real option at this moment. An HST line to the new airport will be of special interest to the people living west of Nantes, to whom it would mean a better connection with the airport. The catchment area of the airport would thus be expanded. But since the airport has no important intercontinental function, nor will have in the foreseeable future, the HST will play no significant role as a feeder line from other parts of France (east of Nantes).

Internal Accessibility

Since 1985 two tramlines have in phases been laid out in Nantes. In 1985 the first was opened, a 12.5 km long line from west to east. The second, from the centre southward over 5.2 km, became operational in 1993. Its continuation to the north (8.3 km) was opened in September 1994. Several extensions of the tramway track are planned. In 1998 works were taken in hand for a new tramline from northwest to southeast, to be completed by 2005. The HST station lies to the east of the centre, three tram stops away from the junction of the two present city lines. During peak hours the trams run at a frequency of two minutes. Since the HST connection the number of tram passengers has risen by some 30 per cent. Besides the tram network, there are in the Nantes district 50 bus lines, all coordinated with the tram network.

A few railway lines (northward from the urban area) at present serve only freight traffic. Their employability for passenger transport is being investigated. If the outcome is affirmative, municipal rail transport could be extended at relatively little cost. The SNCF regards the transport networks between the town centre and the town ring more and more as interesting sub-markets. There are not yet any concrete plans for coordinating the networks of the SNCF and SEMITAN (the regional public-transport organisation). Probably, a decision about the organisation of the combined network will be forthcoming by the end of 1997.

Economic Potential

Unemployment in Nantes is relatively high at 16.6 per cent. That is one reason why great store is set by the HST connection. The expectation is that new economic activities can be attracted by the improved accessibility. The condition is that the other location factors are adequate, otherwise business companies may precisely *because of* the better accessibility decide to settle elsewhere. In one instance an organisation indeed found the good accessibility of Nantes a reason not to establish there, namely, Arthur Andersen. According to the discussion partners, however, the positive effects of the HST integration will surpass the negative ones.

The decision to establish a congress centre in Nantes, *La Cité de Congrès*, had already been made before the HST came to Nantes. The HST did promote its development, however. Improved access made the organisation of events here more appealing. To a former industrial estate, the LU estate, some new companies have been drawn here from outside the city. The zone would probably have filled up even without the HST, but its advent has certainly stimulated the process. Several following organisations have decided to establish in Nantes, among other reasons because of its improved accessibility:

- the Waterman company (writing materials) has moved a unit with 100 job opportunities from Paris to Nantes. The following reasons can be quoted: lower location costs, lower cost of living than in Paris (hence a real rise of income), and a better quality of the living environment (see Nantes Atlantique Développement, 1996);
- Toyota decided to open an establishment at Ancenis, between Angers and Nantes. Its good accessibility, by motorway, HST and airport, has been a weighty consideration for that decision;
- in July 1997 French Mail, which is decentralising its services, will open an establishment in Nantes in the LU grounds. That will produce 500 job opportunities. The decision would probably not have been taken had there been no HST connection to Paris, since easy access is essential to a PTT establishment. Economic considerations have also played a role: settling in the Nantes region is much cheaper than in Paris.

Tourism is also stimulated by the HST connection. It enables people from Paris, for instance, to go by HST to the Côte Atlantique for the weekend. There are several lines extending to locations near the coast such as Le Croisic and La Baule.

Quality of Life

On one stretch along the TGV-Atlantique special attention has been paid to the quality of the (urban) living environment, namely, the stretch starting from Paris-Montparnasse station. That section has been constructed below ground level and is covered in part. Thus an area over the rail infrastructure could be converted into a city park with cycle tracks, foot paths and tennis courts: *la Coulée Verte du Sud Parisien* (see Tellinga and others, 1996, p. 168). The total costs involved in that environmental project were 413 million FF (see Strohl, 1993). Along the stretch of about 12 km the built-up area has been revaluated: the land and the houses along this railway stretch have gained in value.

Nantes boasts a rail tunnel under the city for the east-west connections.

As a result, the centre of Nantes suffers hardly if at all from the rail traffic. The advent of the HST was a strong impulse for the revitalisation of the quarter of Madeleine-Champ de Mars, which has heightened the city's appeal. It also stimulated the construction of the tram network and hence the use of public transport. Nevertheless, 45 per cent of visitors use the car as secondary transport mode, the station being relatively well accessible by car. To the north of the station measures will be taken to reduce the nuisance from car traffic.

Spatial Distribution of Activities

National

The HST plays a crucial role in French deconcentration. With towns in the province more easily accessible, a more balanced spatial distribution of activities can be tried for. The French rail system is of a radial structure. Almost all connections radiate from Paris to the province. The HST system, and in particular the Interconnexion, permits passengers to travel direct from one provincial place to another, without needing to go by Paris. That opens new opportunities for towns in western France to respond to economic developments east of Paris. On a lower scale there are still too few good rail connections among locations outside Paris, for instance from Nantes to Bordeaux and Lyon. Part of the section between Nantes and Lyon has not yet been electrified and cannot cope with speeds over 100 km/h.

Local

The revitalisation of the quarter of Madeleine-Champ de Mars, where many new activities have settled, has been speeded up by the HST connection. The city has substantially invested in this quarter to accommodate new activities that have in part been attracted by the HST. In the area, formerly considered peripheral, a clear revival can be observed in the real estate sector, in particular houses and offices. The town's ambition is to create a business park of national scope by enticing head offices of large companies from western France. At the moment the quarter counts 1,000 job opportunities. The ambition is to add another 1,100. Significant activities in the quarter are *la Cité de Congrès* and the CIO, the greatest regional bank.

The Malakoff quarter south of the HST station is a 'no man's land' to be developed from scratch. The condition is, however, that the area be opened up to the rest of the town and the agglomeration. Development of this area is foreseen in the longer run; 1,200 dwellings and 54,000 square metres of office accommodation may be realised there. In the area 2,000 new job opportunities could be created.

Social Distribution of Effects

Before its construction, there were protests against the TGV-Atlantique from the cities Nantes and Rennes. Protesters preferred the upgrading of the airports to the costly construction of a railroad (see Strohl, 1993, p. 86). Such protests have now died out. There have been no large-scale discussions around the HST integration, because no drastic adjustments were needed. There was no need, for instance, for a new railroad to be laid out or a new station built.

The airport is open around the clock. Flights are carried out by night as well as by day. There seem to be very few local protests against night flights. The fact that many aeroplanes have to fly over the city is one reason for the decision to build a new airport north of the town. The nuisance caused by the airport will thus be much reduced.

Organising Capacity

The SNCF and the French Ministry of Transport are the principal actors for the construction of rail infrastructure of national scope. Investment in new rail infrastructure has been drastically cut down. For new projects, a larger financial contribution than before is expected from the lower authorities, such as departments and regions. However, their influence on the national rail projects to be accomplished does not seem very great. The SNCF is in the process of a large-scale reorganisation. Regional organisations are being created, which, up to a point, can operate autonomously. That could open new opportunities for the lower authorities to join the regional SNCF-organisations in attempts to put the realisation of certain projects forward.

Different administrative levels are responsible for the several transport modes interweaving at the Nantes station:

* for the national rail services, including the HST: the French Ministry of Transport, or the SNCF;
* the *Département* for the regional trains and buses;

- the District for urban public transport.

To guarantee a good connection of the transport modes, regular coordination between the government levels is necessary. The *Département*, the *Région*, the District and the town make financial contributions to the station project.

The Most Important Themes of the Nantes Case

The HST Station, From Local to Regional Station

On the occasion of its connection to the HST, the Nantes station was expanded to accommodate the expected larger transport flows. The growing number of passengers and the changed function of the station require further extension and adjustment. In the past the station had a mainly local function, but the HST connections draw passengers from the entire agglomeration and region. That calls for urgent improvement of the regional accessibility, especially by car and collective transport. Experiences of other stations, for instance in Brussels, Lille and Nantes, show that high-grade car access is vital. Sufficient parking capacity is an important condition in that respect. Improved accessibility of the surrounding region by collective transport is another point worthy of attention. A kind of RER system, which uses partly old rail tracks for goods transport, would be an advisable proposition. For a successful transition from local to regional station, more support should also be found for complementary services such as shops, hotels and conference rooms. In Nantes, adequate space should be reserved around the HST station to accommodate such activities prompted by the HST integration.

Nantes has so far made economic profit from the HST connection, and hopes to exploit it further. A town quarter adjoining the HST station, Madeleine-Champ de Mars, has been able to attract quite a few new activities within a short period of time. A causal relation between an infrastructural connection and the region's economic development cannot in practice be absolutely deduced. According to the discussion partners however, the HST has been a distinct catalyst in the economic development of the area in question.

External Accessibility

For the Nantes region, two rail projects are of great import for the improvement of its external accessibility: expansion of the capacity on the section Angers-

Nantes, and the construction of a missing part of the *Interconnexion* near Paris, *le barreau-sud*. The Angers-Nantes stretch is used for freight transport, regular passenger trains and HSTs. Because the capacity is limited, this stretch is a troublesome bottleneck for HST services between Nantes and Paris. To expand the capacity on this stretch is therefore considered vital. The *barreau-sud*, which at present precludes speeds over 70 km/h, obstructs HST lines to the other side of Paris. In particular to strengthen the process of deconcentration now in progress, actors in western France set great store by this connection. The two projects have not yet been included (in a sufficiently concrete manner) in the national plans for construction of new rail infrastructure. The present retrenchment schemes are an obstacle to the fast construction of the sections involved. The two key questions are, therefore, how to influence the decision making in that respect, and what actors will have to finance the infrastructure. For the time being, the planned new airport of Nantes will lack the critical mass to warrant a high-grade HST connection. The situation is comparable with that of Turin. Nevertheless, for optimum international access to the region, there should be a convenient connection between the airport and the HST system. One option is a first-class regional train service. Another, perhaps preferable one, is to extend the HST services to and from the Nantes station to the new airport. This would make them more profitable, without impairing the HST services between Nantes and Paris (and beyond).

Note

1   The reduction probably cannot be entirely ascribed to the connection to the HST network. In the period concerned, the Gulf crisis caused a drop in the number of air passengers in all aviation.

12 The HST-integration in Rotterdam

Introduction

Rotterdam has been served by a high-speed train (HST) since June 1996. For the time being, the service is carried out on the existing rail track. At the beginning of the next century a new dedicated HST track will be realised, connecting Paris, Brussels, Rotterdam and Amsterdam and some other cities. That connection will substantially reduce the relative distances between those cities. The expectation is that it will generate positive spread effects for the Rotterdam region. The HST connection is considered to be an important catalyst for the broadening of the economic base of the Rotterdam region. At and around the central station, which will be the HST stopping-place, a new urban district has to be built, attracting new economic and social activities. To optimise its accessibility, *dedicated* car infrastructure between the ring road and the central station is planned.

Accessibility

External Accessibility

The present plans are to connect the Randstad by two HST lines to the ever-growing European HST network: a north-south line linking Schiphol through Rotterdam, Antwerp and Brussels to Paris and London, and an east-west line connecting Schiphol through Utrecht and Arnhem with Germany. To enhance the internal cohesion of the Randstad and to achieve a satisfactory modal split, a high-quality HST connection on the north-south line is important. For the time being, Rotterdam will be joined to a north-south HST connection only. Given its prime harbour function and the weight of its economic relations with the German hinterland, this seems to leave Rotterdam with less than advisable outside access. Presumably, the harbour city's economic potential would benefit most and specifically from an eastward high-speed connection. For Rotterdam, an eastbound connection by HST is essential for improving the location climate, given the weight of eastward economic relations.

One option would be to realise HST services via the city of Utrecht, connecting the already-planned HST services from the Amsterdam region towards Germany. An advantage of this option is the availability, in the near future, of *dedicated* HST infrastructure between Utrecht and several German cities, such as Cologne and Düsseldorf. Therefore, a relatively high commercial speed via this link could be expected. However, this connection is not a direct one for Rotterdam. A high grade rail connection to its German hinterland can be realised via shorter links. Therefore, another option would be an HST connection through Eindhoven with Cologne and other German cities. Neither option excludes the other. The latter might strengthen the already-important economic relations between Rotterdam, Eindhoven and Cologne. The cities involved should combine their efforts to convey the importance of that connection to the relevant actors. In the first instance, the potential transport demand could be fulfilled by high-grade trains on conventional infrastructure (tilting trains). As a matter of fact, there seems to be an increasing preference for the supply of high-speed rail services by new rolling stock on conventional infrastructure, mostly to save considerable cost. In France and Germany too, for example, cheap and flexible solutions are being considered to upgrade inter-regional rail services other than by constructing *dedicated* HST infrastructure. The eastward high-grade rail link could be extended to Hoek van Holland, to connect the recently-started high-speed ferry services to Harwich. Then, major network benefits of the mutual connection of high grade transport services can be expected.

For the Rotterdam region, two airports are of direct relevance: Schiphol and Rotterdam. The latter is a relatively small airport used mainly for business traffic. Once an HST train runs between Amsterdam and Rotterdam, the travel time between Rotterdam Central Station and Schiphol will be reduced from 45 to just under 20 minutes. Consequently, the accessibility of Schiphol Airport from the Rotterdam region will be excellent.

Internal Accessibility

In Rotterdam there is no discussion as to the HST stopping place: the train will halt at the present CS, the central station. There is in Rotterdam an extensive network of public transport, with CS as the hub. However, the system fails to meet such criteria as speed, frequency, punctuality, reliability and social safety. In addition, some important elements are lacking: there is, for instance, no high-grade link with the airport or with the southeastern part of the agglomeration (Ridderkerk and the Drecht cities). Various improvements are envisaged to overcome those shortcomings as much as possible. The most important are the planned integration of the local and regional rail networks of The Hague and Rotterdam (Randstad Rail), the extension of the Rotterdam city railway (metro) by three new lines (3M-project), and the upgrading of the Rotterdam tram network (TramPlus) for distances from three to seven kilometres. Free lanes, fewer stops, streamlined routing and greater frequencies are the means by which to upgrade the speed and reliability of the tram network.

Rotterdam generates and attracts much car traffic, which causes regular congestion, especially during peak hours. Thanks to, among other things, its spacious urban structure, the centre of Rotterdam can (outside peak hours) be reached quite quickly by car from the ring motorway. The planned concentration of more economic activity, houses and various services in the centre will probably intensify the car traffic. A stricter parking policy, fewer free parking places and higher parking tariffs are some of the measures being taken to guarantee and improve access by private car. To make maximum use of the development potential of Rotterdam CS, it must be readily accessible by car. The challenge is to improve the car-accessibility of the centre, without spoiling the quality of life. Therefore, selective car-accessibility has to be striven for: the centre must be accessible for those cars that 'cannot be avoided'. The criterion for avoidability has to be an economic one. An economic actor must have the possibility to enter the city centre by car, if s/he is willing to pay a relative large sum of money for this. Therefore, selective car accessibility has to be realised by using the price instrument, by raising fares for using car infrastructure and parking accommodation.

Also, dedicated car infrastructure to the central station area contributes to achieving selective car accessibility. In Rotterdam, an exit road from the ring motorway leading only to parking facilities near CS but offering no direct access to Rotterdam's internal road network is being considered. This would permit the provision of a service right in the centre of the town that normally is feasible only at the periphery. A major advantage of this solution is that no additional car traffic will be attracted to the existing internal road-network. Therefore, negative external effects of this car connection can be minimised.

An alternative would be to construct parking facilities at the rim of the city (*transferia*) and from there offer high-grade public transport to CS. However, with the latter solution, the HST would not attract additional car traffic to the centre, but on the other hand would add to the travel time. And that would spoil the travellers' perception of the HST as a high-quality transport system and make it less attractive. Stimulation of taxi transport would be yet another way to improve the town's accessibility, with the added advantage of reducing the need for parking space in the city. Free (target-group) lanes through the centre would encourage the use of taxis.

Economic Potential

The Rotterdam economy is predominantly based on the seaport and the related industry and services. However, precisely the port and industry have lost many job opportunities in the last few decades. Being only moderately differentiated, the Rotterdam economy is relatively vulnerable. Recently, the Rotterdam economy has structurally grown at a slower pace than the Netherlands as a whole. Many port-related companies have moved to the hinterland, especially to Noord-Brabant. Specialised services related to transport and distribution (logistics), the medical sector and urban tourism are considered as potential growth sectors for Rotterdam.

Because the HST provides mainly centre-to-centre connections, its socioeconomic effects will be most manifest in cities. The connection of Rotterdam to the HST system may give it an impulse towards the desired diversification of the Rotterdam economy. It would improve its international access by fast connections with Schiphol and the nearer European cities. In addition, it may be an incentive to raise the quality of the living environment and thus boost the image of Rotterdam. Some activities may be induced to establish themselves in the direct vicinity of the HST station. The zone around the HST station might well be attractive to activities that fit the concept of the '24-hour economy'. Connection to the HST system would reduce the constraint not only of distances but also of the time factor on the pursuit of economic and social activities. Thus, a lively town centre could be developed, with easy regional, national and international access and a wide and flexible supply of economic and social activities.

Quality of Life

The quality of the living environment, and more specifically its perception, is an essential factor for the successful implementation of the HST in the urban economy. The Rotterdam region lacks a positive image in terms of the living environment, mainly because of the proximity of the harbour and related industries. However, that negative image does not do justice to the real facts. Particularly in the last decade Rotterdam has pursued an energetic revitalisation policy (*New Rotterdam*), manifest in, among other things, substantial investment in the upgrading of public spaces. In addition, many houses in distressed neighbourhoods have been demolished or renovated, and quite a few houses built for the more affluent citizens. Such improvements have helped to draw citizens and companies to the centre of the town. The cultural function of the town has been strengthened as well. Joining the HST system can give a positive impulse to the upgrading of the public spaces around the station. The moment seems right, with the generation of additional transport flows in mind, to restructure the traffic infrastructure in a such way as to reduce the nuisance and guarantee access to the CS. The station is a showpiece of the city, and can therefore contribute much to its image.

To increase the standard of living and make the inner city (once more) attractive as a residential, living and working environment, much is being done to minimise the negative effects of car traffic. The goal is to reduce car traffic to the level which leaves the living climate attractive to inhabitants, visitors and workers. That principle should be kept in mind in the present reorganisation of the infrastructure in Rotterdam, and first of all with respect to *the* traffic node of the city, the central station.

Spatial Distribution of Activities

For a sustainable economic growth of the town, a balanced mix of activities (the *harmonious city*) has to be achieved. A balanced combination of activities can raise a town's accessibility and living quality. In the centre of Rotterdam, as in many other European cities, the spatial structure lacks balance. The working function is more dominant than the residential function, which results in unbalanced traffic flows and the standard of living conditions of the centre during certain periods of the day is relatively low. The present policy of reinforcing the town's residential function, for the express purpose of attracting affluent citizens, is therefore highly advisable and even essential. In addition it seems advisable – the development of certain American cities like Seattle being a fair example – to strengthen the urban tourist function. Several target groups can be aimed for, varying from the regional population (leisure shopping and visiting cinemas, theatres and sporting facilities), foreign leisure tourists (visiting the Rotterdam region: museums, the seaport, the windmills of

Kinderdijk, Dordrecht and other locations) to business tourism (exposition and convention centres). The HST station has to be considered an important junction, where the tourist elements are linked with each other. It functions as the major tourist gateway of the region, which will be strengthened by a high-grade HST connection. Therefore it is necessary to create an attractive station area (the function as the *showpiece* of the region) and adequate information facilities (here, visitors must have be able to find all the necessary information on the regional attractions and on the accessibility of these elements). The central station should play an important role in upgrading the image of Rotterdam. In this respect, passengers arriving at the central station should immediately be confronted with the visualisation of the recently-developed tourist market slogan of Rotterdam and its surroundings: Holland, rich in contrast.

Social Distribution of Effects

The creation of additional nuisance because of new traffic flows and social or economic activities should be avoided by all means. Car access, dependent on the connecting motorway infrastructure and the parking facilities, is among the most important problems. Cars should have easy access to economic and social central functions at minimum negative environmental effects. Only then can sufficient social support for plans concerning the development of the station zone be hoped for. To that end, the local population has to be involved in the making of plans and decisions. The citizens will be more inclined to accept drastic changes in the city when the communication with those involved has been satisfactory. Work for local people created by the development of the station zone may help the plans to be socially accepted. Because the extension plans of the CS are still at an early stage, no judgment can be made about the distribution of the effects among the groups of the local population involved. Attempts are being made to involve the local population as much as possible. Discussion meetings are being organised at which the locals can submit ideas for the future development of Rotterdam (New Rotterdam, Course 2005).

Organising Capacity

Many actors have a direct interest in planning and decision-making around the station zone, but so far only a small group has been effectively active. That small group includes the Municipality of Rotterdam (dS + V and the OBR) and Netherlands Railways (NS Real Estate). Together they have commissioned an investigation into the advisable development of the station zone. For a rapid development of the station, a joint vision and strategy is important. Naturally, the next step must be to carry out the plans and set the envisaged process in motion. To have an energetic and purposeful initiator and leader of the project is essential. To turn the station area into an attractive and permanent growth pole, it might be desirable to set up a specific organisation for management and exploitation. Sufficient organising capacity is a precondition for the successful implementation of the necessary measures. Other city projects in Rotterdam reflect a moderately positive picture of an energetic and decisive municipal government and regional networks.

The Most Important Themes of the Rotterdam Case

Car Accessibility

From the comparative research it can be derived that good car accessibility of the HST station is vital for optimum profit from the HST effect. The current plan of the City of Rotterdam to connect the motorway ring directly with the central station by a dedicated motorway seems to be very promising. This dedicated motorway has to connect specific parking facilities at the station area. By using an adequate price mechanism the attraction of 'unnecessary' car traffic has to be avoided. The principal criterion by which to judge the desirability of measures to enhance car access to the centre is their influence on the quality of the living environment. More and more cities are trying to make their centres relatively car-free. If the new car link could relieve other car infrastructure, then it might indeed help towards a relatively car-free centre, on condition of minimum negative environmental effects of the new connecting infrastructure. In addition, taxi transport might be stimulated by, among other things, introducing flexible systems (ticket combinations with travelling by train) and allowing more market influence. A major advantage of stimulating taxi transport is that a high grade 'individual' accessibility can be offered, without the necessity of creating spacious parking lots.

Activities at the HST Station Area

The central position, its good car accessibility and accessibility by internal public transport of the HST station generates an area with a relative large economic potential. Furthermore, the HST connection will substantially contribute to an improved image of the station area as well as the urban region. Given present market tendencies, the concept of a harmonious city is incompatible with large-scale office development around the HST station in Rotterdam, nor is such development probable. A multi-functional completion of the zone is envisaged. All urban functions – living, working, shopping and leisure activities – could be accommodated. The experience of many station development projects is that one function may become the motor of other secondary activities. The question is, then, which function could assume that role in Rotterdam. The accommodation of activities supporting a 24-hour economy is anyhow being considered. Through this, a growing need of society could be fulfilled. For the near future, in general, the most promising economic sector seem to be 'infotainment' (information, communication and entertainment). Activities in this sector might be attracted around the HST station. Furthermore, urban tourism might play an important role. This sector could generate a substantial amount of new jobs (especially for lower-educated people). This goes for leisure tourism as well as for business tourism, which are interrelated. The region of Rotterdam has some important assets which could attract tourists, such as the largest seaport of the world, the historic city of Dordrecht, the windmills of Kinderdijk, the modern architecture of Rotterdam, etc. However, accessibility and visitor-friendliness of the elements are weak. Visitors are insufficiently aware of the major attractions. The HST station can play a major role in this respect. With the HST connection, the station will be the gateway of the city for a growing number of tourists. Here, the tourist must be able to find the necessary information. Moreover, because of its showpiece function, an attractive station area has to be created. Also, an important tourist attraction that might function as an important catalyst for the urban tourism could be created at the station area.

Organisation, Development and Management of the Station Zone

To speed up the process, attempts are being made to involve as many relevant actors as possible in the station development. To protect the quality of the zone and ensure its enduring attraction to business activities, the setting-up of a specific organisation to take the responsibility for the zone's management seems to be advisable. Lessons could be learned from the experiences of Schiphol Airport. Special questions to be answered are whether the zone can be clearly delimited, whether the delimitation should be physically marked, and what kind of organisation would be wanted. At a station area, there is a mix of public and private functions. Therefore, it is desirable that public as well as private actors are represented in a separate organisation for the management and exploitation of the station area. This organisation must be sufficiently independent to operate in a decisive way.

13 The HST-integration in Strasbourg

Introduction

Strasbourg is not yet an HST stopping place. The planned line to Strasbourg, the TGV-Est Européen, is considered one of the main European HST corridors. Because of the considerable expense involved, the construction of certain parts of the HST network will probably be put off for some time, but early in the next century the TGV-Est Européen will run from Paris and Strasbourg and on to Germany, calling at Strasbourg Central Station. For a subsequent HST connection, the TGV-Rhine-Rhône, a second stopping place in Strasbourg is being considered. There are not (yet) any concrete plans for the development of new activities near the HST station.

Accessibility

External Accessibility

The TGV-Est Européen is conceived of not only as a connection between Paris and Strasbourg, but also as a future important European HST corridor. High-grade infrastructure will connect major German cities, such as Munich, Frankfurt, Mannheim and Stuttgart, with Paris and other French cities. Entirely new HST infrastructure will permit travelling from Paris to Mannheim and (by another branch) Stuttgart, in about three hours. Moreover, travel to London will be possible through the *Interconnexion* near Paris, the TGV-Nord and the Channel Tunnel. In May 1992, President Mitterrand and Chancellor Kohl met in La Rochelle, France, to sign a basic agreement on the construction of an East European HST (see Strohl, 1993, p. 205). A basic agreement expresses the intention of both governments, but does not commit them. However, France especially prefers to postpone the construction of certain financially daunting stretches. For one thing, the tunnel that needs to be cut through the Vosges will cost so much that the project, in whatever way financed, will be unprofitable for some time. The French part of the total project will cost the French about 24,000 million FF,[1] to which the regions involved and the EU will contribute.

The construction of the French part of the dedicated TGV-Est Européen line, which is to be undertaken in 1998, will probably reach to Metz/Nancy. That will reduce travel time between Paris and Strasbourg to two hours 25 minutes; a fully-renewed HST line will cut it to one hour 50 minutes. At present it takes four hours to travel by train from Paris to Strasbourg. In due course a track may be laid (*barreau-nord*) which passes Strasbourg by without stopping to permit a fast direct connection, for instance, between Paris and Stuttgart. However, this link will have a substantial negative impact on the quality of the living environment.

A second HST line that is interesting for Strasbourg is the TGV-Rhine-Rhône, planned to connect Strasbourg with Frankfurt, Cologne and Hamburg in the north and Basel, Dijon, Lyon, Turin and Barcelona in the south. This line will probably come into operation after the TGV-Est Européen. The section Strasbourg-Colmar-Basel will be upgraded to permit a speed of 220 km/h. The works are to be completed in two years' time. Another high-speed train is planned to run on the German right-hand bank of the Rhine. For the Karlsruhe-Offenburg section new dedicated HST infrastructure will be built; the track between Offenburg and Basel is being improved to accommodate higher speeds (see Strohl, 1993, p. 178). Those track improvements will also benefit travel to Switzerland by the new Gotthard rail tunnel. Two parallel HST lines (in France and in Germany) will then indeed run between Strasbourg and Basel at a distance of about 40 km from each other. For this major transport corridor (for goods and other transport) that is not considered inefficient. Indeed, generous rail capacity on this transport route is considered necessary.

The HST Stations

The TGV-Est Européen will halt at the present Strasbourg central station (CS). It seems the most logical option, for one thing because this station has the best internal accessibility by secondary public transport. The impressive station building and the large station square will be a distinct point of attraction for the town. Problems arise, however, for the TGV-Rhine-Rhône connection. To call at Strasbourg CS, high-speed trains from the south will have to double part of the section to CS, that station functioning as terminus. Three solutions have been suggested:

1   to accept the time loss of the HST. For point-to-point connections, as are most common in France, there is no problem. When Strasbourg is an intermediary stop of a through-train, a time loss (of some six minutes) has to be reckoned with. Should the transport company consider that unacceptable, the number of stops at Strasbourg may drop;

2   to create a second station to serve as an HST stop on the southern route. That would imply two HST stops at Strasbourg, since CS remains the most suitable stopping place for the TGV-Est Européen. Possible locations for a second stopping place are the present station at Kehl (on German territory), a new station to be erected between Kehl and Neudorf, or a station near the crossing of the tram line and the southern railway line (gare Neudorf). The question is, however, if Strasbourg is large enough to support two HST stations. Both locations would require investment in such necessities as terminals, sufficient parking space and adequate secondary public transport. Moreover, connection to other railway lines would be difficult to realise at the second HST station;

3   to build new rail infrastructure from CS in a northeasterly direction to connect up with the ICE section from Karlsruhe to Offenburg. That route would permit the TGV-Rhine-Rhône to stop at the CS without doubling. It is a highly expensive option and therefore realistic only in a distant perspective. Should the *barreau-nord* come about, part of it might serve this branch of the TGV-Rhine-Rhône, thus saving expenses (moreover, some other existing rail infrastructure could eventuall be reused).

Strasbourg CS consists of two separate parts: the platforms and the terminal on the one hand, and on the other the *gare bas* accommodating the maintenance, remisage (shedding) and shunting of trains. The latter services need not necessarily be established in the centre. Certain functions could be transferred to other stations, which would make room at the CS for extra platforms to accommodate HSTs, and for such complementary services as offices and shops.

The Airport

Strasbourg-Entsheim Airport lies some nine kilometres west of Strasbourg. At the moment, the airport annually dispatches two million passengers, of whom two-thirds are destined for Paris. Once the TGV-Est Européen is ready, the number of passengers for Paris is expected to drop substantially. For 2030 a total of 5.9 million passengers is foreseen, of which 35 per cent will be for Paris. With little delay, the capacity of the airport will be extended to 2.4 million passengers. The direct competitor is Basel-Mulhouse Airport, which dispatches an annual 2.1 million passengers. In the longer run the airport could suffer competition from the former military basis Söllingen. The railway station near the airport is hardly used for transport to Strasbourg centre. How far regular rail shuttle services between airport and centre would remedy that is being investigated. Another possibility to improve its attractiveness is the development of a business park near the airport. This so-called *plateforme logistique* is now under investigation. At first the creation of an HST station near the airport was considered as an option. Connecting this relatively small airport to the HST system is, however, not a very plausible option. Only if the HST line serves as a feeder to the airport does a station near it become an interesting proposition. To that end, a sufficient number of long-distance (that is, intercontinental) flights should take off from that airport.

Internal Accessibility

In 1995 a new tramway line, with modern, low-instep coaches, was opened in Strasbourg. This line connects the western district of Hautepierre with the CS and Place de l'Etoile and the southern municipality of Illkirch-Graffenstaden. Near the CS the tram enters a new tunnel to reach the tram station at a depth of 17 metres. By 2001 a second tram line is to be completed which will open up the western municipalities, the northern districts of the agglomeration and the district of Esplanade (the university). The two lines will cross in the centre near Homme de Fer, two tram stops away from the CS.

A disadvantage of the present CS is that it is not easily accessible from the western part of the agglomeration, because of the major spatial barrier formed by a motorway, fortification works and the railway yard. The tram connection has brought some relief, but access by other transport modes is still inadequate. The recently introduced park-and-ride system has been successful. Near Rotonde, west of the CS, motorists can park their vehicle for 14 FF and travel free of charge to the centre by tramway. This system has resulted in a new target group of tram passengers.

The ring motorway serves a mixture of regional, national and especially local traffic. One-tenth of traffic on the ring road is transit, nine-tenths of users are on their way to or from somewhere in the agglomeration. The ring road is regularly congested. To reduce the problems and separate the traffic modes, new ring roads (*contournements)* west of Strasbourg are planned.

Recently a multistorey car park with a capacity of 350 places was built near the CS. Its capacity could be doubled. By the time the station has to accommodate high-speed trains, car access to the CS will presumably be inadequate. Suggestions have been made for a new entrance road from the north, which should also serve to open up the western part of the agglomeration. On the north side a kind of *transferium*, a multistorey car park with supplementary services and direct access to the station could be created, bringing up the number of parking places near the CS up to over a thousand.

Economic Potential

The TGV-Est Européen and the TGV-Rhine-Rhône will enhance the international location of Strasbourg, and hopefully improve its traditionally weak relations with the German hinterland. With the ongoing European integration and the evolving European HST network in mind, Strasbourg can thus develop from a city peripheral to its homeland into an urban region central to Europe. Naturally, that opens up many new economic prospects, especially towards the adjoining German hinterland, but also towards the economically important cities which the two HST lines will bring much nearer to Strasbourg. The uncertain timing of the HST connections is one reason why Strasbourg has so far developed few concrete plans to make economic capital out of its improved accessibility. As seat of the European Parliament, Strasbourg has vital need of easy international access. It may even help the city to expand its international function.

Quality of Life

Unlike the TGV-Méditerranée, the construction of the TGV-Est Européen seems to have provoked little protest. The initial idea was to build an HST station north of Strasbourg, which could be used by France as well as Germany. That plan was abandoned, however, because it would have a negative influence on the quality of the living environment. Therefore, the construction of a *barreau-nord* will be resisted fiercely by the local population. For adequate social support for the plans, special measures may be needed to minimise nuisance from the railway. The construction of the *barreau-nord* would not be advantageous for the city of Strasbourg, because it might imply fewer stops of the HST in this city.

The spatial barrier between the western and central parts of the agglomeration formed by the railway, the fortification works and the motorway, is regarded as a major problem. A road north of the station could improve the connection between the two parts of the town. In that sense the HST integration could make a positive contribution to the quality of the urban location environment.

Spatial Distribution of Activities

Strasbourg has not yet drawn up any concrete plans to make economic capital out of the better accessibility the HST connection produces. In the centre of Strasbourg there is relatively little room for such large-scale developments as were possible at Euralille. Suggestions have been made to establish activities attracted by the HST connection in a few areas surrounding the HST station. Those suggestions have been laid down in three scenarios:

1   development of a zone north of the CS in the district of Rue des Magasins. A space of between 30,000–40,000 square metres is available here. The Rue des Magasins district is somewhat run down and needs rehabilitation;

2   creation of a business park west of the station and the ring motorway, at one tram stop's distance from CS. The question arises whether this zone, called Rotonde, which does not adjoin the HST station, holds sufficient attraction for new activities;

3   extension of the station to the west, to create space for new activities such as shops and offices. This scenario implies a complete reconstruction of the station area. Some rail activities (shedding, maintenance and shunting) will have to be moved elsewhere. This scenario envisages direct entrance from the motorway, parking facilities and a new station front on the north side. It is probably the costliest but also the most logical solution, since the spread effects will be greater as the development is nearer to the HST station. In this scenario fits a new tram stop on the level of the *gare basse*.

The above scenarios point to long-term solutions. In the short term Strasbourg has other investment priorities. The first is for new activities to settle near the Place de l'Etoile and *les fronts de Neudorf*, where there is sufficient development space. It is also easily accessible, by car as well as public transport. The tram takes passengers to the CS in about five minutes. The expectation is that 'HST-sensitive' activities too can be enticed to establish here, so that there is no immediate necessity to vacate development room right next to the CS.

Social Distribution of Effects

There will probably be no immediate drastic changes in Strasbourg as a result of the HST integration. For the longer term several scenarios have been drawn up for possible developments in the station zone. Development of the Rue des Magasins quarter to a business park (scenario 1) could, on the one hand, come into conflict with its present residential function, but might, on the other hand, enliven the city by the mixing of functions (concept of the harmonious town). Scenario 3 directly helps to open up the western part of the town, but comprises the most drastic renovation works of all three. Adequate communication with the local population about the whys and wherefores of the activities will be absolutely vital to win sufficient social support.

Organising Capacity

To realise the TGV-Est Européen, the lower government levels, in particular the regions involved, will have to make their own financial contribution. Nevertheless there is uncertainty about the point in time at which Strasbourg will be connected to the evolving European HST network. The local authorities therefore want to know how far they must anticipate the HST connection. The question is whether and when to invest in supplementary provisions needed to accommodate any new activities attracted by the HST. On the one hand a 'Satolas situation' should be avoided (premature large-scale investment to accommodate future developments), but neither should business companies be discouraged from settling in Strasbourg.

The Most Important Themes of the Strasbourg Case

New Definition of the Relevant Region

European integration and the connection to the evolving HST network are changing the relevant region of Strasbourg. Indeed, the relevant region of this town, which used to be nationally peripheral, will extend considerably. Certain parts of Germany will henceforth be added to the natural hinterland of Strasbourg. The city will also be far better connected with Paris, London, Brussels and many major German cities. Naturally, that opens new economic perspectives for the urban region. It may enhance its international function, and attract new, internationally-oriented activity.

Timing of Investment by the Public Sector

The TGV-Est Européen should be realised by 2002–04. After a lot of hesitations, the French government has in principle decided to realise it. However, the large-scale retrenchment plans of the SNCF may cause a serious delay. The elements to be completed first are the section between Paris and Metz/Nancy and the doubling of the bridge between Strasbourg and Kehl. There is some apprehension that the new section between Metz/Nancy and Strasbourg will be left out in favour of a direct extension of the line Paris-Metz/Nancy to Frankfurt. The question is whether that fear is warranted, and how Strasbourg can influence the development in its favour. Given the basic decision made by both governments and their confirmation of the importance of the Strasbourg *connection* in the European context, it is probable that there is only delay and not cancellation. Indeed, two large urban agglomerations in southern Germany, namely Stuttgart and Munich, have a great interest in a direct connection with Paris through Strasbourg (in Germany this line is called the *Magistrale für Europa*). For them and for some Austrian towns the line through Strasbourg is the obvious one. Strasbourg should, together with these towns, put pressure on the national governments involved to realise the desired TGV-Est Européen as fast as possible. A financial contribution of their own would give lower authorities an arguable claim to have some say in the spending of the money. Co-sponsorship of the TGV-Est Européen would give the Alsace region the right to set conditions for its configuration.

The uncertainty about the construction of the TGV-Est Européen is among the reasons why Strasbourg has difficulty in timing supplementary investment. On the one hand, premature investments are not advisable. On the other, potential economic effects of the HST integration must not be discouraged. The HST is for many cities an important tool to give the economy a new impulse. However, the more cities connected within a certain relevant region, the smaller the 'HST effect' will be. An HST connection will, therefore, be a necessary condition rather than a strong catalyst for economic growth. Given

Strasbourg's favourable geographic situation, however, the expectation is that the city can make economic profit from the HST connection. Therefore, timely investment in the provisions necessary to respond to that economic impulse seems vital, for one thing because it enables business companies to anticipate HST integration.

Choice of Stations

In Strasbourg, the CS is the most logical stopping place for the HST, given its situation and spread effects. For the TGV-Rhine-Rhône its situation is unfortunate, however. The possibility of a second station to cater for this HST line is being studied. The question is, however, whether Strasbourg can afford two HST stations. For one thing the investment costs would be much increased, and for another the attractiveness of the HST location would be diminished. As a matter of fact, the junction of several HST lines at one point offers synergic advantages: the available financial means can be concentrated for the supply of high-grade secondary transport from one location, and the zone immediately surrounding the station becomes more attractive as a location for business companies. In the short term, the advisable solution seems to be to have both lines stop at CS and accept the few minutes lost on the TGV-Rhine-Rhône. In the long run, infrastructural adjustment seems to be the most obvious solution to the problems.

Note

1   For comparison: the HST line between Paris and Lyon necessitated an investment of 7,850 million (in 1984 French francs).

14 The HST-integration in Turin

Introduction

In the urban region of Turin quite a few infrastructural projects which are related to the HST connection are now in progress. The economic depression in the city prompted a decisive and energetic promotion of economic revitalisation. Some important projects are the HST lines from Turin to Milan and Lyon, the planned underground main rail infrastructure (*Il Passante*), the construction of the first metropolitan railway and the idea of a ring line for freight trains. The European integration offers the urban region of Turin new economic chances, which it is trying to capitalise on by improved accessibility and an upgraded living environment.

Accessibility

HST Development in Italy

The first HST section to have been completed in Italy is that between Firenze and Rome; it permits top speeds of 250 km/h. The plans are to provide Italy with a T-shaped network of main HST infrastructure: Turin-Trieste and Milan-Naples. Extended across the border, these lines create two important international corridors: one running east-west from Lyon through Turin and Milan to Trieste, and another running north-south from Basel through the Simplon Pass and past Milan to the south of Italy. The fast development of HST sections in the east-west corridor, in particular those connecting Turin to Lyon and to Milan, respectively, is vital to Turin. An HST connection from Allessándria to Genoa would also be of great benefit to Turin, but the term of its completion is still an unknown factor. Present car users are seen as the most likely group to switch to the HST. Indeed, in Italy, the HST is expected to be a substitute for car traffic rather than for air traffic.

The HST Connection from Turin to Milan

HSTs coming from Paris are already running between Turin and Milan, for the time being on conventional track. The construction of a dedicated HST track between Turin and Milan will be taken in hand shortly and is planned to be complete by 2002. This HST section is considered essential for Turin. HSTs will cover the distance between the two towns in just 45 minutes, against one and a half to two hours at present. North of Turin, the HST will travel a little way on conventional tracks, but for the greater part new HST infrastructure will be laid out parallel to the Turin-Milan autostrada. This high-speed line is cheaper to construct than others. The new trains that will run on the new HST infrastructure can reach a top speed of 300 km/h.

The Turin-Lyon HST Connection

When the Turin-Lyon HST section will be finished is still uncertain. Completion was expected for the 2007–09 period, but may be delayed by construction problems. The line is relatively expensive (in the neighbourhood of 10,000 billion Lire) because a 52-km long tunnel has to be cut through the mountain massif. Moreover, the local population in the Susa valley is quite firmly opposed to the construction of the HST track (see the section on the social distribution of effects). The French and Italian railways have together founded a development company, Geie Alpetunnel, for the construction of the HST line between Lyon and Turin, but so far have failed to secure financial partners. The line has been estimated to yield a return of 5.5 per cent, three percentage points less than would be preferable. Therefore, ways have to be found to raise profitability.

Freight Trains

That the HST line from Turin to Lyon will be combined with a track for freight trains is a valuable argument for its construction, especially in view of the fast-growing trend in goods transport by rail, stimulated by, among other things, the transport policy pursued by Switzerland. The new track will permit goods trains to run at higher commercial speeds. The *tunnel de base*, in the new Lyon-Turin section, is especially important for goods trains, because it reduces the number of height differences to overcome. Milan is a vital junction for goods trains passing by the Gotthard and Simplon from other places in Europe. Through the Lyon-Turin link, Turin wants to improve its position in goods transport by rail, and to draw economic profit from complementary logistic services.

HST Stations

The first idea was to have the HST line circumvent the town and call at a peripheral HST station. That idea was soon abandoned as a bad solution, however, since it would only serve to generate more (avoidable) mobility. There would be much more travelling to a peripheral station than to a central station. Porta Nuova, a terminus, is at present the principal railway station of Turin. The present plan is to use it for non-through HST trains. Two other stations, Porta Susa and Porta Dora, will be moved underground. In the first instance Porta Susa, shifted somewhat, will get an important function as a stopping place for high-speed through trains. To the existing about 900 parking places another few thousand will be added. A direct, if not very fast, road will give access from the motorway. The station grounds offer room for various commercial activities, but Porta Susa lacks development space around the station. Therefore, some actors would prefer Porta Dora for the future HST station. At the Porta Dora location, there is indeed ample space for developing new economic activities (about 1,300,000 square metres). The fact that Porta Dora will not be connected to the new metropolitan railway need not be a problem as long as frequent trains on *Il Passante* can take over the function of metro. To be ready for new activity, the area around Dora, which used to house many industrial complexes, needs a costly redevelopment. North of Turin a new station, Rebaudengo, will be built to serve regional traffic. And between Lingotto and Porta Nuova and Porta Susa, a new station called Fermata Zappata will be constructed.

Metropolitan Railway

Turin is at the moment the only large town in Italy without a metropolitan railway. The population of the western part of Turin is growing very fast. In 1992 the decision was made to lay out a city railway line between east and west Turin, connecting, among other locations, Porta Nuova and Porta Susa. Turin already counts quite a few tram lines. The high-quality metropolitan railway is hoped to attract new target groups, such as present motorists. There will be transfer points (P+R) where the metro intersects with the motorway.

Airports

Two airports are relevant to Turin: Torino-Caselle and the international airport of Milan-Malpensa. Recently a new terminal was opened at Caselle airport, with a capacity of four million passengers. Most of the passengers at Turin Airport travel to Rome. Given the considerable distance between the two towns – 715 km – a substantial substitution effect from the HST seems unlikely. An HST station near Caselle has been considered. However, since Turin Airport is only a secondary airport, it lacks the critical size to warrant its combination with an HST station. It was considered adquate to connect the airport to the central HST station by a regional train. That railway section is indeed indispensable to link up the several high-grade transport modalities available satisfactorily. Near Turin Airport a railway station is being built to serve a direct train connection to Porta Dora and, via the Loopline, to the other stations in Turin. This station should be ready for use by 1998. A speedy realisation of the rail section between Susa and Dora is imperative to overcome the capacity bottleneck in the local rail infrastructure.

Economic Potential

A factor of great importance to the regional economy of Turin are Olivetti, the Fiat factories and the – partly related – metal industry. The recession in the industrial sector is one cause of Turin's present economic distress. There is much unemployment and a major part of the population is low-skilled and therefore difficult to place in new functions. For Turin, inclusion in the HST network is a valuable aid towards economic revitalisation. Important strategic elements are improvement of the external and internal accessibility, raising of the quality of the living environment, and extension of the social-economic basis.

Quality of Life

Il Passante

Turin is engaged in moving its principal rail infrastructure underground. A start had already been made prior to the decision to connect the city to the HST network. The so-called Loopline, *Il Passante*, will contribute to the reintegration of several town quarters. Quarters that have been isolated from the city centre for decades will gain attraction as a residential and business location. When the present railway track was laid, cutting through the town, there was not much objection since the far side mostly accommodated (now abandoned) factory complexes. Moving a 12 km section of the track underground is reinforcing the efforts to revitalise the centre and to renovate the abandoned factory sites. One section of the four-track Loopline, roughly that section between Porta Susa and the planned new Rebaudengo station, still awaits construction. Parallel to the railway axis, which is also called 'the spine' (*spina*), three million square metres of development space will come available. Extension of the Technical University is one project envisaged there. On top of the Loopline a *boulevard* will be laid out. When that road is opened, car traffic on several other roads will be restricted to forestall additional car traffic to the centre.

Three-quarters of the Loopline has already been constructed and the entire line should be complete in six years' time. One objective of this line is to increase the frequency of the regional trains. At present, buses are still essential in regional (suburban) traffic, but in the near future trains will take over their services. The financing of the final part of *Il Passante* is still problematic. Because the state has an interest in the completion of *Il Passante* for the realisation of the HST network, it is expected to make a major contribution to its financing. Indeed, its underground position is convenient for the state, since it implies more support from the local population for HST development, and thus a faster realisation of the HST section.

Freight Trains Led Outside the Town

Like Antwerp and other cities, Turin wants to move goods trains away from the city centre by providing a ring line. Thus rail capacity in the city will be released and the town will be spared the nuisance of more goods trains. The living environment will benefit from greater safety: dangerous substances (accounting for much of goods transport by rail) need no longer be conveyed through densely-populated areas. For the time being no financial means are available for the construction of the section, but space will anyhow be reserved for it.

Spatial Distribution of Activities

For Turin the planned new rail connection between Lyon and Turin is essential to underscore its changing geographic position within Europe. Mainly because of progressive European integration, Turin is no longer peripheral to its relevant region. The city used to hold a peripheral position in Italy. Its present more central role in the European setting opens new economic prospects, however. One of Turin's spatial-economic objectives is to strengthen the mutual relations in the *Diamant-Alpin* region, which comprises, among other places, Geneva, Turin and Lyon. The communication between those cities is geographically hampered by the mountain massif rising in their midst. The new HST line is hoped to reduce the generalised transport costs of mutual communication, and in particular, to remedy the paucity of economic relations between Lyon and Turin.

Social Distribution of Effects

The resistance of the local population is considered the greatest obstacle to the construction of the Lyon-Turin railway line. The Susa valley is already covered with various types of rail and road infrastructure, and the locals are little inclined to accept the new HST track. To enlarge the local support, research is being undertaken to find profitable aspects of the HST – profitable, that is, to the locals. Since direct benefits are hard to find, the search must be for positive external effects. One such effect could be the release of capacity on the present rail infrastructure between Turin and Lyon, which can then be used to raise the frequency of regional trains, and thus benefit the valley population. Another could be the substitution of rail traffic for part of the road freight traffic. Admittedly, the extra infrastructural capacity might attract new traffic and additional measures to avoid this may be necessary. Another suggestion is for a stopping place in the valley, which would be particularly attractive for skiers and thus benefit the local economy.

In the city of Turin, opposition to the HST connection is negligible. Because the rail tracks will be subterranean, the nuisance from trains will actually diminish. A major part of the works is already complete. Because the project will improve the residential and living climate in the city, the social support is satisfactory. The living quality will be enhanced further when goods trains are diverted to a new railway track outside the city.

Organising Capacity

A public-private partnership has been founded to build and manage the HST network: TAV SpA. TAV is a private company; two-fifths of its shares are owned by the Italian Railways (FS) and three-fifths by institutional investors. TAV has a 15-year concession for the exploitation of the HST network. A comparison with the development of Italy's motorway network is warranted. In a relatively short period of time an adequate network of motorways has been laid out in Italy, which may be due in part to the involvement of private actors. Quite possibly the Italian HST network, too, could be realised relatively fast thanks to the participation of private actors. The (re)construction of the HST stations is not included in the TAV's package of tasks. The Italian railways have delegated the development of stations to a subsidiary company: Métropolis. However, up to now no specific project has been drawn up for the development of HST stations.

For many cities, such as Liège, Cologne, Lille and Rotterdam, the HST connection is a great support to their revitalisation ambitions. Towns tend to fail to achieve those ambitions because of lack of money, but that should by no means keep them from drawing up an adequate vision and strategy. Once a city has developed a good strategy for an upward boost to the urban economy, higher authorities might be found willing to sponsor the plans. In a society where over seven-tenths of the population lives in urban surroundings, sound development of the urban economies is of national importance (see, among others, Van den Berg et al., 1996). Turin is beset by quite serious social-economic problems. The depression in the industrial sector has generated a lot of unemployment. A decisive and alert policy to attract new economic activity is therefore indispensable, and dynamic ideas for drawing new activity by improved internal and external accessibility and a pleasant living environment would seem to merit more financial support from higher authorities, such as the national government and the European Union, than received so far.

The Most Important Themes of the Turin Case

Construction of the Turin-Lyon HST Line

The HST connection with Lyon is very important for the economic development of Turin. From an urban region hitherto peripheral to its own country, Turin is moving to a more central position in the European setting. The HST line is also relevant to the growing international transportation of goods by rail. Turin can draw economic profit from that development by supplying value-adding logistic services. The time of completion is still uncertain, partly because of lack of financial resources, but mostly because the project is not wholeheartedly supported by the people in the Susa valley, who object to yet another line cutting through their territory. In this valley, compensating measures will be needed to reduce the resistance of the local population.

Subterranean Layout of the Municipal Rail Infrastructure

The city of Turin has been engaged for about a decade in constructing underground tracks for its principal rail infrastructure. The implications are, on the one hand, more rail capacity and, on the other, a positive impulse for the quality of the urban living environment. Other projects that may improve accessibility and the living environment are the construction of the metro and of a track for goods trains circumventing the urban area. The latter project is also important with a view to the (expected) increase of international goods rail traffic. Several European countries such as Switzerland, Belgium and The Netherlands are increasingly inclined to invest in dedicated infrastructure for freight trains. The projects are vital for the economic revitalisation of Turin, but the city, which is economically in distress, does not have the necessary resources. Therefore, a sizable contribution of higher (Italian and European) authorities to their financing is indicated.

Choice of the HST Stations

Turin will use centrally placed HST stations. In view of its lack of critical mass, Turin Airport will not be directly connected to the HST. Regional trains from the airport to the HST station in the centre would serve the purpose. The old central station Porta Nuova will be called at by non-through HST trains, while high-speed through trains will, for the time being, use Porta Susa. An alternative for that station would be Porta Dora, which is surrounded by much space for the development of any new economic activity drawn by the HST. Unlike Porta Susa, Porta Dora will not be connected to the planned metro, but compensation can be found in very frequent train services on *Il Passante*. Porta Dora seems to qualify as a strategic development location for the future. A good case can be made for founding a specific exploitation company for the development of the HST stations, comparable to the organisation of an airport, and separate from the exploitation of the transport services as such. In that way, HST-related economic activities can be attracted and preserved in an oriented and professional manner.

Conclusions

This research focused on the implications of connecting urban regions to the European HST network. The 14 participating cities studied, from a relatively wide perspective, the situation of their own urban region, the most important study elements being the strategic dimension of the HST integration, the station area and secondary transport, and urban planning and development. This has generated a large amount of information written down in individual monographs of the urban regions, of which the summaries are included in this book.

EURICUR has carried out analyses of the different situations in the cities involved. Additional information was obtained by visiting the 14 different cities and through discussions with key persons of these urban regions. All this information has been consolidated in the six areas of this research-deduced criteria: the impact on the external as well as internal accessibility; the economic potential; the quality of the living environment; a balanced spatial distribution of activities; a balanced social distribution of effects; and organising capacity. In this final chapter the main conclusions of this comparative research will be presented, arranged by these six criteria.

Accessibility

External Accessibility

Revival of rail transport There is a tendency to a revival in rail transport of people as well as goods. In particular, the progressive saturation of road and air transport systems, the drive for more use of relatively environment-friendly transport modes and the European integration have inspired investors to renewed interest in rail transport. Quite a lot of money is being invested in long-distance rail services among European urban areas for goods as well as passengers. For passenger transport, the focus is on high-speed connections between urban agglomerations. The rising interest in passenger and goods trains creates problems but also opens new prospects. Problems crop up at places where a limited rail capacity has to be shared by passengers and goods trains, for instance between Nantes and Angers and near Antwerp and Turin. On the other hand, the combination of the two types of transport increases the transport value and thus speeds up the realisation of new rail infrastructure, such as the Lyon-Turin section.

National authorities have a dominant influence on the realisation of HST networks. It is they who decide about, and largely fund, the construction of HST lines. Other tiers of government, such as the European government and the municipal authorities, have so far had only a marginal influence on the decisions. The dominance of the national authorities is manifest among other things in the priority given to national connections, and in the technical differences that persist between the rail networks of the European member states. To decide about and to finance internal connections is generally easier because fewer administrative actors are involved and the traffic flows mostly exceed those of international connections. Giving priority to national connections may imply that less money remains for the realisation of frontier-crossing infrastructure. Important international connections, such as the *TGV-Est Européen*, are therefore difficult to accomplish, a fact that could well delay European integration.

Realisation of HST infrastructure After a period of relatively generous investment in new rail infrastructure, a slow-down seems to have set in. Because many national governments are trying to cut down on their investment, projects are being deferred. The cuts in investment are mostly inspired by the wish to satisfy the criteria for admission to the European Monetary Union (EMU). A European paradox seems to ensue, as one facet of the European process of integration (the formation of the EMU) is preventing the progress of another (the realisation of the trans-European networks). The speedy realisation of planned HST lines is advisable, however, for one thing on account of worsening congestion on motorways and in the air. Those called upon to judge the advisability of HST investments seem over-awed by the need to sink a lot of money into new infrastructure with little delay. In the long term view, however, the investments may be soundly justified. Indeed, they are often of strategic importance for the economic development of the European cities involved as well as for European integration. Another aspect to be clear about is the time schedule of future HST lines, so that the cities to be connected can attune their policy to it. Uncertainty about the construction of HST connections is apt to make the timing of related new constructions difficult.

HST Stations

From junction to growth pole and from gare de ville to gare d'agglomération
Connection to the HST network puts stations on a higher level in the hierarchy of junctions. The connection to a high-quality transport system implies that cities must raise the quality and extend the capacity of the terminal and of the secondary transport systems. Adequate secondary transport will have to be provided not only in the surrounding city zone but in the entire region. The easy access and better image as well as the improved secondary transport system due to the HST connection may appeal to new activities. Thus, the HST station will progress from a junction of transport activities to a growth pole with a variety of activities.

Effects on the station location The 'HST effect', the change of a railway station's functions and image when connected to the HST network, can be divided into a number of partial effects:

- the accessibility effect: the connection of the HST acts like a catalyst. For optimum profit from the HST integration, access by secondary transport modes has to be enhanced. In many cities, the HST connection is therefore a powerful impulse for improvement of, among other things, the municipal and regional public-transport systems. The urban centres where most HST stations are accommodated will also profit from the easier access;
- the location effect: the station zone becomes more attractive for the establishment of various economic functions. Efforts will be made to make the most of the prospects opened up by the improved accessibility and image of the location. Measures should be taken to prevent an unbalanced urban development by exclusive investment in, for instance, offices. That would be incompatible with the drive for a harmonious development of the town centre: it may do harm to the living quality and the liveliness of the city;
- the revitalisation effect: the connection of the HST gives a powerful stimulus to the revitalisation of the zone surrounding the station and/or an entire town quarter. Efforts will be made to render the station environments, often dilapidated, more appealing to a variety of social-economic functions. Important points of attention are improvement of the living environment and balanced distribution of the social effects of the HST connection. In that line of thought, the effects of the HST connection on other parts of the urban agglomeration should also be taken into account. The location of

the HST station might, for instance, drain away economic activity from other town quarters.

The partial effects may reinforce one another, but could also cause friction. If car access to the HST station is optimised, the quality of living in the station zone may suffer and the revitalisation effect reduced.

Number of HST stations in a city To be able to equip efficiently several HST stations, a town must exceed a certain critical size and possess growth potential. To maintain several HST stations (relatively far from one another) means to equip several transport junctions. These stations cannot be efficiently connected by high grade secondary transport modes when they generate insufficient transport. Consequently, the frequency of additional transport might be too low, the destinations too few, and the rolling stock comparatively poor. Moreover, in a small city with more than one station, the HST effect will be too dispersed. Such junctions will lack appeal to new economic activity. Whether a city is large enough and has sufficient potential must be established by a multitude of criteria, such as volume of population and social-economic activities, situation with respect to other urban agglomerations, presence of supra-regional transport junctions (such as intercontinental airports), etc. From the present investigation, Amsterdam, Brussels, Lyon and Turin have emerged as cities likely to have the size and potentialities to support several (fully-fledged) HST junctions.

Connection with airports Most cities are making efforts to connect the HST system to the airport, if there is one nearby. High-speed trains and airlines can then complement each other, which will further improve the region's international accessibility. The question remains whether to create a direct HST line with the airport, or make a conventional rail link serve the demand. A decisive factor is the size of the airport. Should it fulfil a significant role in intercontinental aviation, then a direct connection between HST and airport may well be preferable, the HST becoming a vital feeder for the airport. If the airport does not attain the critical dimensions, an HST stopping place in the urban agglomeration, combined with a conventional rail link between station and airport, is usually the better choice. Two airports near the cities of our investigation have a direct HST connection, namely, Amsterdam-Schiphol Airport and Lyon-Satolas. The latter airport still accommodates too few intercontinental flights for full complementarity between the HST and the airport at this junction. A good conventional rail connection between the HST station and the airport would be advisable for, among other cities, Brno, Lille, Marseilles, Nantes and Turin.

Internal Accessibility

Collective transport systems To cope with larger transport flows and to filter down the relative high quality of the HST to the rest of the transport chain, in most of the investigated cities substantial investment in secondary transport systems is needed. Most city centres have adequate secondary public transport near an HST station. The HST tends to be a powerful catalyst for the construction of new urban public transport systems, as has happened in Rotterdam and Turin. However, (urban) areas at 5–30 kilometres from the HST station are often poorly accessible for lack of good public transport. Examples of cities whose regional public transport systems are susceptible to improvement, are Marseilles and Nantes. For cities in a frontier area, such as Liège and Lille, the adequate organisation of secondary regional transport tends to be difficult. Investment in secondary transport networks is often essential to the revitalisation of the cities, and hence of supra-regional importance. Unfortunately, the necessary financial resources are frequently lacking. Support from higher authorities is therefore necessary. To stimulate the use of public transport as a complement to the HST, combination tickets of HST and public transport would be a good incentive.

Car accessibility To stimulate the substitution of HST for car and aeroplane and to attract HST-related activity, good car access to HST stations appears indispensable, since a proportion of the potential HST travellers will use the HST only if fast and comfortable secondary transport is available. To please them, the transport characteristics of the HST (notably speed and comfort) should also be a feature of the secondary transport. Car access as excellent as that of most airports is often neither feasible nor desirable, however. Most HST stations are at the centre of urban areas, where the unlimited access of cars would spoil the living environment, the quality of which is also essential. Moreover, if public and private transport interfere with one another, the growth of urban car traffic may well put the performance of public transport at risk. That seems to be a risk in Antwerp, for one. In most cities, selective car access to the (centrally positioned) HST station seems desirable. Selective car access can be achieved by introducing or intensifying the price mechanism on access roads and/or parking facilities near the HST station. Travellers who set great store by a comfortable and fast transfer from the HST to the car will in principle be willing to pay for it, since they attribute a high value to the time factor. Another way to achieve selective car access, considered in Liège and Rotterdam, is to lay out *dedicated* access roads to so-called 'head-end car terminals'. To some cities, Antwerp and Geneva among them, the attainment of selective car access is of direct relevance. There, unlimited car access to the HST station through the present infrastructure is undesirable, producing serious threats to accessibility and living climate. Indeed, in most other towns as well, more stringent measures towards selective car access will become increasingly necessary. Promotion of taxi transport can also help to keep the HST station internally accessible. The great advantage of taxicabs is that they offer individual accessibility without the need for additional parking space.

Economic Potential

The evolving horizontal network of cities connected by the HST opens new prospects for economic development. Cities get a chance to develop certain specialities or key competencies as their relevant market regions are expanded by improved access. Especially for urban areas in border regions the developing European HST network offers new opportunities to establish economic relations with zones which have formerly been unattractive because of the relatively low quality of the mutual connections. Some cities that hope for advantage on that score are Brno, Geneva, Liège, Lille, Lyon, Strasbourg and Turin. Through the enhanced appeal of the urban junction, economic activities could be drained away from other towns not connected to the HST network, or from cities that are connected but less competitive in certain economic sectors. So even cities connected to the HST network could be confronted with draining effects; improved access may incite economic activities to move to other junctions in the network. The activities establishing in and around HST station grounds can be divided into HST-bounded, HST-using and HST-sensitive activities (see Van den Berg et al., 1996, pp. 55–65). HST-bounded are those activities that need to be established in the station grounds proper, such as a ticket office. HST-using activities are intensive users of the HST such as congress centres. HST-sensitive are extensive users of the HST who want the status of a site close to an HST station, such as business services. From the present investigation some specific activities have emerged which can be attracted to or strengthened by the HST. Under that heading come notably business services, urban tourism, and congress and fair activities. They could all be captured under the term 'infotainment', a combination of information, communication and entertainment. Some cities particularly anxious to secure business services are Amsterdam, Brussels, Lille, Nantes and Turin. Antwerp, Geneva, Lille, Lyon, Marseilles and Rotterdam are specifically interested in tempting more business and leisure tourists. Congress and fair activities are much in favour in Amsterdam, Cologne, Geneva, Liège, Lille and Turin.

Quality of Life

By replacing part of the transport modes relatively harmful to the environment, the HST helps to raise the quality of the living climate. Encouraging secondary public transport may bend the *modal split* even further towards the more environmentally-friendly modes. In some of the cities investigated, the HST connection gives a powerful impulse to the revitalisation of the station zone, for instance in Brno, Brussels, Cologne, Liège, Lille, Marseilles, Nantes, Rotterdam and Turin. That the HST connection strongly stimulates investment in the station zone, is one reason to expect the HST to reinforce the residential, working, shopping and leisure functions of the urban centres, making these centres livelier and more pleasant. Creating a high-grade living climate around the HST stations is one way to attract in particular the more affluent households to the urban centres. To enhance the living quality and avoid infrastructural barriers, the tendency is more and more to construct rail tracks and other infrastructure underground. Cities that are giving or have given much attention to that aspect are Amsterdam, Antwerp and Turin. Unbridled car traffic can frustrate attempts at creating a lively and appealing centre. Therefore, striking a good balance between adequate access and a pleasant living climate is of the essence.

Spatial Distribution of Activities

For some cities the HST connection is a powerful stimulus to develop an area in the urban region that is empty or has been vacated (for instance left by former industrial activities). Examples are the south of Amsterdam, the right bank of Cologne, Euralille, Lyon-Satolas, and Porta Dora in Turin. The assumption is then that the HST can give the areas in question a new status. Town quarters that used to be (somewhat) peripheral can now be promoted to a more central position in the spatial development and transport structure of the town. Such changes of the urban structure carry the danger, however, of other important town quarters being confined to the periphery and losing activities. In Amsterdam and Lyon that is considered a danger. Measures to prevent such unwelcome intra-urban shifts are to provide high-grade transport connections between the town quarters involved, and to guarantee the attractiveness of the threatened neighbourhoods by continued public investment.

The cities should try for a mixture of activities in and around the station grounds that makes for the balanced use (in time and in space) of the available infrastructure. If, for instance, the flows of HST travel should peak from six to eight in the morning and from seven to nine in the evening, then at other times the secondary infrastructure is available for other functions, such as shopping and leisure. Such patterns can be observed in Liège and Lille. In Cologne, the direct confrontation of work and congress functions makes it sometimes preferable to open congresses at a later, non-peak hour, to avoid serious congestion from the interference of visitors with commuter traffic.

Social Distribution of Effects

The integration of HST systems in urban regions does not in general cause great problems. In the urban area the trains often run on existing tracks, so that no drastic intervention is necessary. Logically, therefore, the HST system is most opposed in intermediate areas, where the new HST tracks tend to be laid out. The people living along the new tracks suffer the nuisance (such as transection of the landscape, horizon pollution, and excessive noise) but do not profit from the positive effects of the new transport system (such as improved access). In the face of strong resistance those responsible will try to let the protesting actors to benefit in some way or other from the HST system, or to compensate the adverse effects as much as possible by complementary measures. Between Cologne and Frankfurt, for instance, some regional stations are erected along the new HST section. Part of the HST track from Amsterdam to Rotterdam will be constructed underground to reduce negative effects on the environment. Measures are being considered to overcome resistance and increase local support in the Susa-valley for the construction of the HST line between Lyon and Turin.

In the urban areas themselves, the most noteworthy physical effects of the HST connection are the re-equipment of the station zones and the attraction of larger traffic flows. The revalidation of the station zones is mostly appreciated as positive by the local population. Quite often such an area had declined and lost much of its attractiveness during a period in which public and private investment was relatively low. Naturally, a plan to revitalise the area is then welcomed. Brno, Liège and Marseilles are cases in point. There is some anxiety that the HST integration and especially the mark-up of the area will crowd out certain activities, notably shops and low-rent housing. To achieve a balanced mix of activity, it might be advisable to keep certain existing elements in the area, and offer good alternative locations to others. By timely and adequate communication with the local population about imminent changes, the social support for the HST integration can be broadened.

Organising Capacity

Importance of Timely Response to New Prospects

The HST integration can greatly stimulate the economic revitalisation of towns. Many towns look upon it as a powerful catalyst for the reinforcement of urban functions. To make it effective, an integral strategy for the envisaged urban development which can count on the broad support among the actors involved, is imperative. For the HST connection is not, in most instances, a sufficient condition for initiating a process of urban revitalisation. A package of facilitating measures, such as the supply of accommodation for newly attracted activity, and the improvement of internal accessibility, is necessary for optimum profit from the HST connection. The timing of these measures is also important, in view of the intensifying competition among urban regions on the European level. Failure to implement a strategy in time may mean that economic activities choose another urban location. Relatively unfavourable economic conditions are often a strong incentive towards prompt and comprehensive measures in the context of the HST integration. That applies for instance to such cities as Liège, Lille and Marseilles. In their urban regions, with several economic sectors in decline, to attract new economic activity is essential. By contrast, under relatively favourable economic conditions actors may be insufficiently stimulated to respond to the opportunities opened by the HST integration. In some cities the decision-making is complicated by the fact that important junctions are outside the administrative territory of the urban region, for instance Lyon-Satolas and Brussels-Zaventem.

The Interests of Railways and Towns

There is a tendency to separate the construction and management of rail infrastructure from the exploitation of the rail networks. The construction and management of the infrastructure is increasingly becoming a purely public responsibility. It remains for the railway companies, who are cutting themselves loose from the government, to exploit the rail infrastructure. The exploitation and management of stations, on the borderline between infrastructure and exploitation, in practice are assigned to (a subsidiary company of) the railway company. The company will try to collect as much revenue as possible from the flows of travellers on the one hand, and from activities on the station grounds on the other. The station grounds are mostly owned by the railway companies. Logically, they will be inclined to develop those HST locations which promise them the most profit. That is not always the 'optimum' location from the urban point of view. The railway company's preference for *Schaerbeek-formation* near Brussels springs in part from the fact that it possesses quite a considerable amount of land there. For the urban region, a future location by the airport might be preferable, however. Cities and railway companies may also differ as to how to make the HST stations 'optimally' accessible. Good car access will be important to the railways to attract as many passengers as possible. But a city has to look out for other interests as well, for instance for a good quality of the living environment. The local authorities will therefore try to strike a balance between good (selective) car access and the quality of the urban living environment.

Management and Exploitation of HST Stations

Because the environments of HST stations, like airports, offer eminent economic opportunities, cities are interested in new organisation forms for HST stations that can adequately support those opportunities. There are, however, some complicating factors: the delimitation of the station area and the merging of public and private interests. The 'HST effect' stretches beyond the HST station. To the zone around the station a variety of HST-related activities can be attracted. Should a separate management and exploitation unit be advisable, then the 'functionally coherent station zone' will have to be determined. The delimitation will admittedly have to be somewhat arbitrary, because the station environment tends to pass gradually over into other neighbourhoods. Moreover, the station zone will be subject to continuous change. With respect to the HST station environment, public and private functions can be distinguished (see Table 15.1). These functions can be related to the partial HST effects identified above. The optimum capitalisation of the HST location effect can be considered a private function, the greatest concern being the short-term prospects of profit. Important criteria in that context are the economic potential of the urban area and the expected spatial shift of activities. To care for the revitalisation of the city is a public function, the principal concern being the long-term development of the city. Important relevant criteria are the quality of the living environment, a balanced social distribution of effects, and a balanced spatial distribution of activities. Easy access is a shared public-private concern, adequate plans needing to be developed for both the short and the long term. Important criteria in that context are the external and internal accessibility and, again, the expected spatial distribution of activities. Because public as well as private interests are involved in a HST station site, private and public parties should both be represented in a separate management and exploitation unit. For purposeful and decisive action, a degree of independence of that organisation is a must.

Table 15.1 Points of attention for management and exploitation of station environments

HST effects	Term	Function	Important criteria
Accessibility	Short term/long term	Public/private	Accessibility Spatial distribution of activities
Location	Short term	Private	Economic potential Spatial distribution of activities
Revitalisation	Long term	Public	Quality of the living environment Social distribution of effects Spatial distribution of activities

Synthesis

In many European cities efforts are being made to boost the inner cities, for instance by improving their accessibility and living climate, and by attracting new business activity. The evolving European HST network can support that kind of urban revitalisation. This comparative study has analysed the HST integration in towns by six criteria: accessibility, economic potential, quality of the living environment, balanced spatial distribution of activities, balanced distribution of the social effects, and organising capacity. Easy access needs a variety of modes, among them car, aeroplane and train. The various modes complement one another in terms of geographical reach, and offer flexibility to the traveller (free choice and no dependency on a single mode). Stimulated by European integration, the need for high-grade transport connections among the major European urban agglomerations is growing. Coinciding with the reurbanisation efforts of the major cities, the HST is eminently suitable to fill that need, since it essentially connects urban centres, and is relatively environmentally-friendly.

For the cities to make optimum capital out of their HST connection, improved access is essential. The precious time gain achieved by the HST should not be lost by failing secondary transport modes. On the other hand, better internal accessibility must not spoil the urban living environment. Many cities have therefore been inspired by the HST connection to improve their public transport in quality and quantity. To that end, investments are being made in particular in local rail networks (trams and city railways), which couple a large capacity to high quality (fast, frequent, and comfortable) and are relatively friendly to the environment. The quality of regional public transport is often the weak link in the chain. In view of the strengthened regional function of the HST station, most towns find it imperative to expand regional public transport services considerably.

Cars also contribute much to improved internal access to the HST station. The car is regarded as an essential mode of transport, a convenient complement to the speed and comfort of the HST. 'Sufficient' parking space near the HST station is therefore seen as an important precondition for the adequate performance of the junction. On the other hand, unlimited access for cars to the urban centres is incompatible with the aspirations to an appealing living environment. In other words, selective car access should be striven for, admitting 'necessary' traffic only. Suggested measures to that end are the creation of so-called head-end car terminals, dedicated highroads which from an urban ring road only offer access to parking provisions near the HST station, and the introduction or intensification of price instruments (roadpricing and parking levies). An upgraded taxicab system can also help to make the HST junction accessible. For eminent accessibility, good (public) transport connections between the HST station and the airport have to be provided as well. A direct (fully-fledged) HST stop at the airport seems necessary only when the airport accommodates sufficient intercontinental flights.

The HST contributes to the status of a city, as well as to better access, and in particular of the HST junction. A good status helps to attract new activity. A necessary condition is the presence of sufficient economic potential. Failing that, some activities may leave precisely *because* of the better accessibility, since thanks to the HST connection, establishment in a certain town becomes less of a necessity. The HST connection provides an important momentum to many towns for substantial investment in the renovation of the station environment. To enhance the living climate and the liveliness, a harmonious mix of activities is advisable in most instances. The aim should be a mixture of activities in and around the station grounds that allows a balanced use (in time and space) of the available infrastructure. One-sided development, for instance of office activities, should be avoided. Another danger to be avoided is that the development of the HST station should drain away (too many) activities from other zones of the urban region. Many cities are trying to attract more business and leisure tourists. By improving access to and raising the status of the city, the HST connection can be a significant catalyst. For decisive response to the new social-economic prospects, the creation of a separate exploitation and management unit for the station zone may be a good idea. Important points of attention in that context are the delimitation of the relevant station area, and the matching of public and private interest.

Because substantial public resources are involved, and for the sake of social support, a balanced social distribution of the benefits and costs of the integration of the HST system and the related economic and social developments should be aimed for. The HST integration should contribute to a harmonious long-term urban development, and a balance should therefore be struck, for one thing, between internal accessibility and the quality of the living environment. Different cities may adopt (widely) different approaches to optimum HST integration. Obviously, there is no such thing as a standard solution for optimum HST integration in a city. Each single city must take account of the spatial-economic structure and the criteria distinguished to find out what solution will contribute most to a balanced development of urban welfare. Moreover, to strive for the 'ideal' situation is often not realistic. Very time-consuming procedures or (too) high necessary investments may make a step-by-step, second best solution preferable. A clear vision of and a well-considered strategy for the HST integration remains essential, so as not to lose out on the profitable prospects of economic development opened to the urban region.

ANNEXES

Profile

Amsterdam has a characteristic and relatively large historic centre. In the seventeenth century, a belt of concentric canals was built around the medieval core; this structure is still largely existing. In the 1870s extensive new neighbourhoods were developed around the city centre, following the radial/concentric principle. Within a period of some 50 years, a typical turn-of-the-century area was built. There were some additions in the 1920s, but the main urban extension areas were built after 1945. New lobe-shape residential areas were developed, with substantial employment and shopping centres, separated by open green areas. In the 1970s and 1980s the emphasis in new developments was first on the wider region (new satellite towns for commuters) and later on the city again (making the city more compact). During the time when housing was increasingly dispersed, employment did not follow this trend. New employment areas were deliberately planned where accessibility by both public transport and private car was good (near railway and metro stations and also near the belt motorway).

In the next 10 years further regionalisation will be inevitable: 80 per cent of all new houses will be built outside the city. At the same time, employment growth will remain concentrated in the existing new centres, resulting in a predictable growth of regional travel. In order to get some grip on this growth, two specific development axes have been designated: a Waterfront Axis on the northern edge of the city centre, around the Central Station, and a southern Axis, from the city centre to the WTC/Amsterdam-South station.

The population size of the urban region of Amsterdam is about 722,000. The working population is about 328,600 people, of which 44,500 are jobless. 75 per cent of the labour force works in the city of Amsterdam. Amsterdam has about 330,000 working places (see Table A1.1).

The Strategic Dimension

One objective of the municipal policy is to strengthen Amsterdam's international position in spatial and economic terms. In some respects, Amsterdam already enjoys an eminent position on the international market, due, among other things to its favourable geographic situation and good connections within Europe. To keep that position, it is essential for Schiphol

Table A1.1   Jobs in the urban region of Amsterdam

Economic sector	Amount of jobs	%
Agriculture, food, textile	3,578	1.0
Publishing and printing	10,935	3.3
Industry	15,682	4.7
Construction	11,528	3.5
Commerce	57,012	17.3
Hotels/restaurants	14,896	4.5
Transport	16,492	5.0
Communication	8,815	2.7
Finance	38,243	11.6
Real estate	6,668	2.0
Commercial services	41,192	12.5
Government	25,453	7.7
Education	21,697	6.6
Health care	41,065	12.4
Culture and recreation	13,008	3.9
Other services	4,359	1.3
Other sectors	350	0.1
Total	330,964	100.0

Source: dRO, City of Amsterdam, 1997.

to develop into a 'mainport'. On the other hand, as the European network of high-speed railway lines is steadily expanding, access by train is becoming another factor of growing importance. Therefore, the connection or non-connection of Amsterdam to the HST network, and the manner of it, must be expected to become increasingly important for the city's international competitive position.

At the moment, Amsterdam holds a prominent position within Europe in both the business and the tourist market. In many respects London and Paris are far in the lead, Amsterdam vying with a lot of other cities for places in the sub-top. Most of these cities are already connected to the HST network, or are sure to be shortly. To obtain HST connections not only with Brussels and Paris, but certainly also with Germany and London, is of the essence for Amsterdam if it is to hold its own in the international competition.

Once a decision is made to realise HST connections, a marketing strategy needs to be developed which provides optimum reach to the potential sub-markets. At present, most business travellers tend to arrive by air and most tourists by car; the train only accounts for a limited portion of the tourist segment. Given the travel times by the different transport modes, the HST plays a major role in business travel to Paris, but only a minor one to London. On the other hand, the HST can offer an attractive alternative for tourists travelling to and from London. What role the HST might play for moves from and to Germany and Belgium will depend strongly on the places of origin or destination in those countries and in the Netherlands.

The most promising sub-markets for the HST are:

- business trips by air from and to France (notably Paris) and Germany (notably the Ruhr Area and Frankfurt), by Americans and Japanese among others;
- international congresses and fairs;
- short tourist trips by air from and to England, Italy and Switzerland, and by car from and to Germany and France;
- visits by Americans and Japanese tourists touring Europe.

That the HST would permit trips to Amsterdam and back in one day, with no need to stay overnight, will undoubtedly appeal to tourists and business travellers alike.

The Station Area and Secondary Transport

Most international train passengers are using public transport as a feeder mode: 55 per cent come by train and nearly 30 per cent by bus, tram or city railway. Fewer than one in 10 come to the station by car and one per cent by taxicab. The distribution diverges much from the present feeder transport of air passengers to Schiphol, where some 65 per cent arrive by car, some 30 per cent by public transport, and just over five per cent by taxicab.

At present the car has only a limited share in feeder transport to the station for international travel, it will probably become more important for HST travellers. Given the scarcity of space around the Central Station and Zuid/ WTC, to create large longtime car parks in the town near the HST stations would be inadvisable, the more so as Schiphol offers an excellent opportunity to get on the fast trains. From market research, the potential HST travellers do not insist on parking space in the town, nor are they prepared to pay much for the convenience. However, sufficient short-stay parking places near the Amsterdam HST stations will still be needed, to accommodate friends and relations accompanying passengers to and meeting them at the station.

To convey passengers from the airport or station to their destination, the car will be of less importance than in feeder transport. Most travellers will choose public transport or taxicab. Taxicabs may be prominent in taking HST passengers to destinations within the agglomeration, for instance businesspeople on one-day trips and hotel guests with a lot of luggage. As is the case with airports, the establishment of rent-a-car companies near HST stations can be a useful complement of the transport system. However, since many of the destinations of HST travellers in the city can also be reached quickly by city railway, tram or bus, chances are that public conveyances will provide a higher proportion of secondary transport from and to HST stations in Amsterdam than from and to Schiphol Airport. The central station (CS) already now constitutes a hub of public transport in all directions: nearly all parts of the agglomeration can be reached direct from that junction.

For business travellers as well as tourists, the realisation of the North-South metro-line between CS and Zuid/WTC will be of eminent importance. It will enable travellers to reach many of the major attraction points and hotels fast and comfortably, without changing, from both the central station and from Zuid/WTC station. Quite a few of the destinations relevant for international travellers are situated in the heart of the city, on the southern canal belt, or around Museum Square.

For secondary transport between the HST and areas outside the agglomeration, the train is the most important mode. Nearly all places of some importance can be reached directly by train, especially from the central station. Schiphol and Zuid/WTC are less central to the railway network; what additional requirements will develop after the introduction of the HST will have to be considered when the time comes. Some attention will also have to be paid to access from the HST stations to locations not adequate accessible by rail. Express coaches might fulfil that need.

Urban Planning and Development

No definitive decision has yet been made as to what Amsterdam stopping places will be developed into high-speed railway stations. Amsterdam CS, Schiphol and Amsterdam Zuid/WTC are being considered.

The advantage of high-speed connections over other transport modes lies in the combination of speed and proximity. The fact that centre-to-centre connections can be achieved by a fast system is to the advantage of HST in respect of air connections. By that argument, Amsterdam CS is a logical stopping place for high-speed connections from both the south and the east. The fact is that in the present situation more than half the international travellers have their origin or destination in the inner city of Amsterdam. The increasing number of workplaces on the south side of Amsterdam may cause a shift, but even then the inner city will remain the gravity centre of international transport. Moreover, the CS as a stopping place gives support to Amsterdam's efforts to develop the inner city, and in particular the southern IJ-bank as an A-location. A stop at Zuid/WTC supports the development, already set in motion, of the area into an important secondary centre. After the turn of the century, once the north-south line has been completed, the inner city will also be easily accessible from Zuid/WTC.

From experiences in France we know that in the network of high-speed lines, the combination of inner-city station, peripheral station and airport station within an agglomeration is not uncommon. Dependent on the type of connection: heart-to-heart, through, or airport-feeder, the fast trains may stop at one or more stations in the agglomeration.

The conclusion for the Amsterdam situation may be that CS as city-centre station and Schiphol as airport station are already there, and that work has been started to develop them into full-fledged HST stations. In view of the other modes of public transport, the status of the environment, and the envisaged line connection between Schiphol and the German Hinterland, Zuid/WTC can be developed into the third HST station within the Amsterdam agglomeration.

Station Environment

From the transport forecasts in the New HST Memorandum, the future HST stations in the Amsterdam region may be expected to deal with some 27,000 HST passengers a day, of whom 12,000 will be new rail travellers (generation or substitution). To that end, adjustments in quantity and quality are needed around the station.

Facilities for HST Passengers

First of all, special ticket windows will be opened for HST passengers, to which they can turn for all information and bookings. As the need evolves, facilities for carrying (lifts, conveyor belt), storage (safes, depot), and delivery of luggage will be realised. Market research indicates that safety appears to have the highest priority (half of all travellers feel unsafe at stations, against only one per cent at Schiphol). Naturally, comfortable waiting rooms are needed, with, for instance, a restaurant or buffet. Such services as shops (reading matter, delicacies, etc.), a bank (or exchange office) and a tourist office (or booking agency for hotels) will certainly fulfil a need.

Quality of the Change to Secondary Transport

There have to be short, clear walking routes from the station to the various types of secondary transport. For city and regional transport, conveniently arranged and attractive bus, coach and tram stations need to be constructed, where travellers can find out quickly and easily where and at what time the tram or bus to their destinations will depart. The route to the taxi stand is also important. For departing HST travellers, a drive-up facility for cars and cabs should be created close to a station entrance. For accompanying drivers, (paid) short-stay parking places are required. Possibly, a limited number of parking places can be made available to travellers arriving in their own cars.

Functions Around HST Stations

Within the HST station locations, efforts should be made to concentrate the functions most relevant to the HST, that is to say, whose visitors or employees will use the HST relatively most. Not only offices should come to mind, but also services. Social security and the vivacity of the station surroundings are some of the motives for recommending a blending of functions, including living and daily necessities. National and European headquarters and subsidiaries of foreign concerns are the establishments most suitable for HST locations. Among the wanted services, science, culture and sports suggest themselves. Other functions very fitting for HST stations are congress and exhibition accommodations and luxury hotels. Criteria by which to judge the suitability of functions for a location near an HST station are in particular: international orientation, number of visitors, uniqueness (a special spot calls for special functions), the relation to other functions in the area, and 24-hour availability. In the HST station locations, the most intensive use is advisable, especially directly around the station. It can be achieved by a high building intensity or double land-use (with common services for several functions).

Note

1   This chapter is based on dRO Amsterdam, 1994, *Hogesnelheidslijnen naar Amsterdam.*

Annex 2   Background Information on Antwerp[1]

Profile

Table A2.1 Population of the city and region of Antwerp

	City	District	Economic urban entity	Province	Region (Flanders)
Population (1994)	464,954	926,105	1,131,200	1,628,710	5,768,925
Average density (inhab./km^2)	4,773 (with port area: 2,282)	933.1	769.4	568	433.8
Surface area (ha)	20,373 (10,633 for port-right bank area)	100,090	147,000	286,746	1,350,964
Working population (1991)	259,708	386,045		686,914	2,290,514
Employed (1994)	235,184	346,189		548,295	1,292,527
Jobless (% of working population – Dec. 1995)		14.8		14.5	13.4
Number of businesses	14,196	24,660 (96.7% with fewer than 50 workers)		40,552	
Higher education				31,451	

Source: City of Antwerp, 1996, *Fiches de Synthèse*.

The Strategic Dimension

For a city like Antwerp, whose economic growth is dependent upon the goods transport sector, the relative priority of rail infrastructure for passenger traffic such as the HST is considered to be lower as compared to investments in freight rail. The primary objective is attempting to at least maintain the rail/ road ratio in accordance with European policy.

173

Table A2.2   Employment of salaried workers in and around Antwerp by economic sector, in % (1994)

	City	Province	Flanders	Province: % of Flemish total
Primary industry	0.07	0.6	0.7	24.0
Manufacturing sector	26.6	33.5	33.7	30.9
Construction	4.2	6.5	6.8	29.9
Petrochemical	5.7	5.4	2.8	58.0
Tertiary sector	73.3	65.9	65.6	31.3
Retail	31.3	13.3	13.1	31.8
Hotel-restaurant	14.6	2.8	3.3	26.2
Transport	15.2	9.4	7.6	38.5
Financial	6.2	3.7	2.8	41.9
Business services	10.3	8.2	7.3	34.9
Consumer services		3.1	3.1	31.6
Government		6.8	7.4	28.5
Education		9.4	10.4	28.2
Health		8.7	10.0	27.0

Source: City of Antwerp, 1996, *Fiches de Synthèse*.

HST infrastructure, primarily the north–south tunnel, could be the point of departure for a regional rail network (in keeping with the city's urban development plan). Although the SNCB is considering that possibility, current plans include rather unsatisfactory interfaces with the existing local network (in particular, plans have been made for a new station north of the city centre) and coordination with the planning of a regional network (managed at the Flemish regional level, rather than the national SNCB).

In a densely populated region it is difficult to obtain acceptance for any new infrastructure development. Indeed, it was only after a lengthy protest movement, widely supported by the concerned communities and groups, that the layout of the rail route to Amsterdam was approved by the Flemish government in June 1996.

That is why, as early as 1991, the city offered to define the parameters of the investments as part of an overall project vision which also included the infrastructure necessary for high-speed rail, freight transport and regional and urban networks. This global approach is designed to maximize efficiency, based upon the multi-modal model developed for the city by the Flemish government.

Until the present time, however, these issues have been addressed on an individual basis, which in the short term has resulted in ongoing protests and spiralling cost estimates. Currently, a study is under way for a new bypass of the city for freight traffic, without any overall study for the optimisation of the existing network following the foreseeable shift of a sizeable percentage of passenger traffic via a new underground tunnel beneath the city.

In the context of such an overall vision, several factors should be evaluated: alternatives to a costly underground tunnel (three to five billion Belgian francs depending upon the tunnel length), the efficacy of these investments in the context of a regional network and an alternative role for the central station in case of another choice of location for the HST station. At present, the city of Antwerp is restricted to maximizing the potential positive effects within the context of the single option made available by the SNCB.

The Station Area and Secondary Transport

The city is proposing a regional public transport network based upon the options outlined in its urban development plan (i.e., major east-west access) and which reinforces the role of the central station as a hub. This proposal provides for the highest possible frequency of regional links from the HST station. SNCB projections include 20 million passengers in 2010, in addition to 1.5 million international travellers. This level of traffic would be comparable to that of Brussels-Zaventem airport.

The hub is itself at the centre of a high-density economic zone of international importance. For the businesses located here, the characteristic of high urban concentration remains vital (the diamond trade in particular). The renewed urban district could also be a focal point for multipurpose amenities (recreation, zoo, convention centre facilities).

On the other hand, the central position and scale of the urban arteries calls for carefully conceived internal organisation and limited accessibility for cars. It is suggested that, in accordance with the urban development plan, this take the form of a new entrance for vehicles combined with special parking facilities for HST-users from the south (extension of the existing station).

Access for pedestrians and public transport users (bus and tram) would be from the north (pedestrian traffic from the east-west route, tram and 'pre-metro' Levels 0 and -1, with direct access to platforms).

The application of this option is presently encountering some difficulties with the SNCB, which seems to have trouble conceiving of any potential mode of access to an HST station other than the automobile. There is continued intention to locate additional parking facilities north of the station, as per current plans, in an attempt to recover part of the cost of the underground infrastructure by utilising the space above the tunnel. This despite the fact that the effects on local traffic would seriously impair local public transport access.

Urban Planning and Development

Early in 1997, a detailed plan was presented to the city featuring the following key points:

- a tunnel below the city at a depth of nearly 20 metres, passing beneath central station and rejoining the surface at a point 1.5 kilometres north (total length 3.8 kilometres), reducing travel times by seven minutes in each direction;
- conversion work on central station to double its capacity, with four platforms at underground Level -2, corresponding with the tunnel, and 10 cul-de-sac platforms spread over Level -1 (four tracks) and the current Level +1 (six tracks). The platforms would be extended to approximately 300 metres, and a new entrance would be created on the southeast side of the station. The plans also provide for the creation of two underground parking facilities, accommodating 400 cars and 500 bicycles to the north (Astridplein) and 850 cars and 400 bicycles to the south (Kievitplein). The north parking facility may hinder public transport access;
- a new station three kilometres north of central station (Groenendaallaan);
- redevelopment of public spaces in the working-class district at the point where the tunnel reaches the surface. This location is near a former railroad site slated to be abandoned in several years' time; the town has plans for the site which may potentially revitalise the surrounding districts.

Work is to begin in June 1998 and will be complete by 2005. During this period, the station will operate at 70 per cent capacity. Although Berchem station is supposed to accommodate the excess passengers during this period, project planning does not include major development work to enhance its capacity, although such plans exist. Furthermore, no satisfactory solution has yet been identified with local public transport (tram, bus) to prevent a loss of customers due to the lack of high-quality alternatives.

These plans could form the backbone of an urban development plan for the south part of the station district, a complement to that of the north section already adopted by the community council. However, in contrast to that project (district urban development plan and URBAN project), and despite the importance given to this 'strategic urban project' in the Flanders master-plan and a detailed description of the objectives to be attained, there is no commitment on the part of the Flemish government to the joint funding essential to the success of this type of quality urban planning initiative.

In addition, the concept of integrating public transport systems has not particularly taken off at the present time; coordination appears difficult, and interfaces with rapid underground tramlines ('pre-metro'), surface trams and other urban and regional transport systems are suboptimal: the Astridplein parking facility between one of the metro stations and central station, and the relatively large distance from the station to stops on major regional lines.

The plan also neglects several urban development opportunities, namely that of improved access to the zoo. The zoo would become one of the most highly visited tourist attractions if new access from the south were to be created.

However, to ensure success it will be important to maximize the efficiency of budgets allocated to this development. At present, the city is attempting to improve the plans and is counting upon the positive support of the Flemish government.

Note

1   Co-author: Mr. Frank de Bruyne, City of Antwerp.

Annex 3   Background Information on Brno[1]

Profile

Brno has almost 400,000 inhabitants; it is the second largest town in the Czech Republic. Brno is the natural centre of South Moravia. The region is the largest and most populated part of the Czech Republic, it takes up 20 per cent of the Czech Republic area and it has approximately two million inhabitants. It is one of the most productive and advanced regions in the Czech Republic. It is an important region as regards education and culture. The agglomeration forms a ring surrounding the city of Brno. The territory of the district is formed by the Czech-Moravian Highlands and Boskovice Furrow in the west and northwest, by the Drahany Highlands and Moravian Karst in the north and by the Vale of the rivers Dyje and Svratka in the east and south. The population density is 142 inhabitants per km^2.

Table A3.1   Area and population of the city and the agglomeration of Brno

	Area (km^2)	Population (to 31/12/1995)
Brno city	230	389,965
Brno agglomeration	3,153	381,000
Total	3,383	770,965

Source: City of Brno, 1996, *Fiches de synthèse*.

The Strategic Dimension

The Concept of High-speed Railway in the Czech Republic

The Czech Republic is a small state with a small number of metropolitan agglomerations. Therefore, construction of the high-speed railway solely for internal use is not economically justifiable. Nevertheless, the Czech Republic is situated in the middle of Europe and is an important for European transit. Therefore, the high-speed lines in the Czech Republic should follow the transit directions, which is important from the European point of view. The concept of the high-speed railway has its starting point in determining these European transit directions and, at the same time, the majority of the transport streams between the largest agglomerations in the Czech Republic. A study is currently under way to obtain the final specification of the future high-speed lines. Its conclusions will serve as the basis for the zoning protection of the future high-speed lines.

The principal transit directions leading through the Czech Republic are from the north to the south and southeast of Europe and from the southwest to the northeast of Europe. Therefore, high-speed lines have been proposed in these two principal directions. The lines lead through:

- (Berlin) – Dresden – Prague – Brno - Vienna;
- Nürberg – Pilsen – Prague – Brno – Ostrava – Katowice.

The lines have in common the division between Prague and Brno, the most important cities in the Czech Republic. The high-speed lines will be complemented by the main modernized railway lines. Work on this modernization has already started. To obtain recovery of the investments into the construction of the proposed high-speed lines, the daily transport streams in the individual divisions must be from 16,000 to 24,000 passengers. These requisite transport streams exceed, by several times, the values currently reached. Air transportation between large cities in the Czech Republic is practically nil and therefore we cannot count on gaining passengers taken over from air transportation. Although we expect a certain increase in the number of passengers taken over from road transportation, the requisite transport streams can be reached, above all, by gaining passengers in international transportation. Therefore, the implementation of the high-speed lines will depend upon obtaining the necessary financial means and ensuring their financial recovery.

The largest cities in the Czech Republic and their agglomerations will lie directly on the high-speed railway. They are the agglomeration of the cities of Pilsen (0.6 million inhabitants), Prague (2.2 million), Brno (0.8 million) and Ostrava (1.6 million) (see also Table A3.1). Integration of the high-speed railway into the suburban railway station is expected in these cities. The high-speed trains will slow down as they approach the suburban railway station and their stops will be in existing terminals, which have advantageous positions in the the town centres and good links to the city public transportation systems.

The Station Area and Secondary Transport

In the city of Brno the existing railway station is not convenient from a technical point of view and would require reconstruction and extension into the intensively built-up neighbouring sites, which are predominantly in private ownership. These sites in the centre of the town are unattainable from a financial and town-planning point of view. In 1994, the city of Brno decided, by approving the master-plan, that the railway station would be transferred from the historical centre by approximately 600m onto sites owned by the railway and the city that are not built-up.

The new railway station will serve all the trains, including the high-speed ones. The position of the new railway station remains in the central zone and it is accessible to the trains from the existing railway lines.

In the case of other large agglomerations situated near the high-speed lines, the construction of stops where they cross the existing lines is anticipated. Some of the high-speed trains will pass through and some will stop there. Within the framework of the agglomeration, suburban trains will be linked up with the high-speed trains which stop. At the stops necessary facilities for establishing a 'park-and-ride' system and for the integration of the municipal public transportation systems are expected to be ensured. These stops will be constructed in the agglomeration of the cities of Ústí-Teplice (0.5 million inhabitants). In the Czech Republic, we expect to build seven terminals in the high-speed railway network. Besides this, several railway connections between the high-speed railway and the other railway network will be established that will allow other important places in the Czech Republic to be served. At the same time, the high-speed railway utilization will be increased.

The high-speed railway lines are designed for a speed of 300 km/h. As regards passenger and freight trains using the high-speed railway, we expect a minimum speed of 160 km/h on parts of the lines only. The completion of the modernization of the existing lines with the aim of allowing speeds of 120–160 km/h is expected by 2007. The implementation of a high-speed railway depends on the European needs as a whole.

Motorway and Road Network in the Czech Republic

With regard to the settlement density, the Czech Republic has a very dense road network; nevertheless, the construction of a motorway network and a four-lane communication network for motor vehicles must be completed. From the structural and technical point of view, the road network condition is inconvenient and requires major reconstruction. As regards high-speed communications, the major interest is devoted to the construction of:

- D 5 – western connection with Germany (Norimberk);

- D 8 – northern connection with Germany (Dresden);
- D 47 – northern connection with Poland (Katowice and Krakow);
- D 11 – internal line leading along the Labe river, with connection to Poland (Wroclaw);
- D 3 or R 3 – southern line to Austria (Linz).

The motorway network around Brno is complete and should be complemented by high-speed communication R 43 and R 52 (under construction) in the north-south direction that would solve agglomeration links and connection to Austria (Vienna). The implementation of the motorway and road network completion to the specified extent is expected by 2007 approximately.

Railway and High-speed Railway Networks in Brno and Brno Agglomeration

In the Brno agglomeration there are seven lines, forming a star pattern with a junction in the city of Brno. They provide Brno with a connection with all the important places in the agglomeration and form a part of the national network. The lines are from:

- Brno – Havlíèkùv Brod (Germany);
- Brno – Èeská Tøebová (Germany);
- Brno – Jihlava;
- Brno – Znojmo;
- Brno – Bøeclav (Slovakia, Austria);
- Brno – Pøerov (Poland);
- Brno – Trenèianská Teplá (Slovakia).

All these lines will be preserved. The lines Brno-Èeská Tøebová and Brno-Bøeclav are currently being modernized to allow speeds of 120–160 km/h, due to the need to speed up transportation along the international European corridors Dresden-Prague-Brno-Vienna (Bratislava).

Connection of the lines in the Brno junction is made easier by the approved proposal for the construction of a new railway station, thanks to its capacity for building up an integrated transportation system, including a high-speed railway. In the Czech Republic as whole, i. e. also in the Brno agglomeration, the high-speed lines are realised as new constructions in new corridors. The principle of their connection to the suburban railway station is applied also in Brno. Due to the complexity of this connection, two variants for the city of

Brno were elaborated.

Variant I, called 'the northern' has three branches:

1 *Prague-Brno:* the line, leading along D 1 motorway, passing Brno from the west and is connected to the junction of the existing modernized line Brno-Èeská Tøebová;

2 *Ostrava-Brno*: the line, leading along the existing Brno-Pøerov line (Ostrava, Krakow), is connected to the existing railway line, after leaving the tunnel under the international airport in Brno-Tuøany. To eliminate the need for trains to reverse in this variant, it is necessary to build connecting sections for the Prague-Brno-Ostrava and Vienna-Brno-Ostrava directions in the city;

3 *Vienna-Brno:* the line, leading along the existing modernized Brno-Bøeclav line (Vienna, Bratislava) is connected, after crossing D 1 motorway, to the modernized Brno-Bøeclav line (Vienna).

Variant Ia is a subvariant of variant I that would arise were the objective of constructing the new railway station in another location and with the necessary capacity not implemented. The connection of the Prague-Brno, Vienna-Brno and Ostrava-Brno line for access to the existing railway station is identical with variant I, but there is no solution for ensuring a direct link between Vienna-Brno-Ostrava without train reversing.

Variant II, called 'the southern' has three branches:

1 *Prague-Brno*: the line, leading along D 1 motorway, remains in the motorway corridor as far as Brno and here is connected, after crossing D 1 motorway, to the existing Brno-Znojmo line and to the existing modernized Brno-Bøeclav line (Vienna);

2 *Ostrava-Brno:* the line, leading along the existing Brno-Pøerov line (Ostrava), is connected to the existing Brno-Trenèianská Teplá line (Slovakia), after passing the airport to the north;

3 *Vienna-Brno:* the line leads along the existing modernized Brno-Bøeclav line (Vienna) and is connected, after crossing the D 1 motorway, to the existing line.

There is no acceptable solution which would ensure a direct link between Prague-Brno-Vienna without train reversing.

From the point of view of landscape and environmental conservation, the 'northern' variant represents many problems along the line of the northwest bypass of the city for connecting Prague-Brno. The line following the motorway corridor is, from the point of view of environmental conservation, more advantageous. The Brno-Vienna and Brno-Ostrava lines are, as regards environmental conservation, without problems. In the 'northern' variant, the connection of the Brno-Pøerov line with the tunnel under the airport can be described as extremely problematic because it leads through a built-up area and because it is in contradiction to the city master-plan, in which this corridor is reserved for city ring road.

Public Transportation in Brno and Brno Agglomeration

The city public transportation in Brno and Brno agglomeration is solved on the basis of rail transportation. The public transportation system in the city of Brno is made up of tram, bus and trolleybus transport. The network density creates good conditions for an almost evenly-spread service in the whole built-up area in the city and supports a high percentage of utilization (80 per cent city public transportation – 20 per cent individual car transport). The tram network is double-tracked and has a total length of 74 km. The tram transportation is operated on 13 lines with a total length of approximately 260 km and with about 330 vehicles.

As supplementary elements to the city public transportation, there are bus and trolleybus services, contributing approximately 45 per cent to passenger transportation. The city public transportation development is based on the tram network stabilisation and its strengthening by the northeastern diameter of light automated metro (LAM).

The system is built-up in such a way that the city centre is accessible especially by using trams and trolleybuses, whilst circle and feeder traffic is predominantly buses. The city public transportation touches all the major stops of the regional bus transportation and reaches the railway stations and stops in the city territory. In front of the existing main railway station is the most important interchange junction in the city with trams arriving in around one minute intervals.

Eight lines out of a total of 13 reach the railway station. This interchange quality will be followed also for the railway station when it is transferred, which will be built on the north-southern diameter linking the two biggest city interchange junctions – the railway station and the regional transportation central bus station.

Currently, the central bus station has insufficient connections with the city public transportation. It is located in the position of the transferred railway station, but without completed city public transport lines (one tram line, circle bus line).

Public transportation in Brno agglomeration has, with regard to the city size and the size of the areas in the agglomeration, a strongly centripetal character. Approximately 94,000 persons commute to Brno daily. The city, with its 390,000 inhabitants, offers 243,000 jobs. The public transportation in the directions that are served by rail make full use of the railway transportation, while the directions without railway transportation are served by buses. The system is uncoordinated, the direction of the lines is often competitive, to the detriment of the railways. Transport unions and associations are only at the beginning of their formation.

From the point of view of the zoning plan and the planning of the links between individual zones, the direction is clear, i.e. the main railway transportation subsystem plus a suitable complementary and feeder bus transportation network, according to the relations in the area. In the master zoning plans there are preserved land reserves for the creation of an integrated transport system on the regional level, including central settlements.

Freight Transportation

With the transition towards privatization and a market economy, freight transportation re-orientated itself towards small-capacity vehicles, i.e. more frequent and operative deliveries. A decline in heavy industry and a reduction in the transportation of substrates contributed to the decrease in the use of railway freight transportation (a decrease to approximately 45 per cent of the 1990 value). Freight transportation in the city of Brno has favourable conditions:

- Malomìøice marshalling yard with spare capacity;
- container terminal with sufficient reserves and with space reserve for the extension of a combined transportation.

Both facilities are situated on modernized railway corridors and are accessible from high-speed lines.

Urban Planning and Development

The railway station is situated in the southern part of the city central zone, near its living historical core. The area, connecting the railway station with the historical core (so-called South Centre) is the key development area of the city central zone – the new gate to the city.

The city is supporting the development of this neighbourhood with shops, offices, services, cultural centres and housing through the development company 'Jižní centrum, a.s.' and through financing the basic technical infrastruc-ture. Private entrepreneurs will start the first commercial construction in 1997. Part of the first phase, which is being prepared, is a reconstruction of the unique industrial Vaòkovka site for business, cultural and educational purposes.

Regeneration of this area will enable the application, during the design of the new railway station, of perspective technological parameters and at the same time introduce space-demanding interchange junctions for different means of public and personal transportation in a composition of the traditional city structure. High-rise construction of the main interchange terminal hall will enable comfortable changes on to regional and local public transportation. The existing central bus station will thus be used and upgraded. These days this station serves many regional lines as well as dozens of international lines.

The location of the platforms and part of the trackage on the bridge construction enables, to a length of approximately 200 metres, direct connecting of the ground floor in the north-southern direction and extending the traditional pedestrian zone in the southern direction. This solution opens a non-barrier access into the terminal hall also for pedestrians and cars from the southern part of the town and, at the same, it enables the necessary services to be placed on the ground floor.

The proposed regeneration, with a link to Komárov city district, will form a set of functions – commercial, housing, administrative and cultural – in the area situated to the south of the new railway station, concentrating the whole of the city's facilities and services in the vicinity of the railway station (post office, etc.). Easy accessibility to the new station and the linked-up city public transportation terminal increases the commercial attractiveness of the development sites in this area.

Note

1   Co-author: Ms Marie Zezulkova, City of Brno.

Annex 4   Background Information on Brussels[1]

Profile

The Brussels capital region, along with Flanders and Walloon, is one of the three 'regions' (geographic entities) which make up federal Belgium; the region itself is composed of 19 communes (geographic entities), including the 'city of Brussels'. This division is administrative; structurally, the urban region comprises approximately 52 communes. In addition to its role as the capital of Belgium, Brussels is also the capital of 'communities' (entities of persons), including the Flemish Community (*Vlaamse Gemeenschap*), made up of the Flemish and the area's Dutch-speaking population, and the capital of the 'French Community', made up of the Walloons and Brussels' French-speaking population.

It is essential to understand that this institutional complexity, based on one hand upon the notion of land and on the other upon the notion of persons, has resulted in a great dispersion of responsibilities. These may be broken down as follows:

- the Belgian state for major public institutions such as the SNCB (railways) and the RVA (airways);
- the regions for regional development, urban planning, the environment, public works, transportation, international relations in these areas; for this reason, the airports and the major part of the ring road (known as the 'Ring'), located in the Flemish region, 'escape' the jurisdiction of the Brussels capital region;
- the communes for directives and preliminary issuing of building and environmental permits, which are then submitted to the region for approval.

For administrative purposes, the Brussels region is bilingual (French/Dutch); in actual fact, its steady internationalisation means that the use of English and other European languages continues to grow, while its eight per cent North African population has also introduced the Arabic language.

International Context: A Major Influence

As one of three European capitals, Brussels is home to the following institutions: the Commission of European Communities, the Secretariat of the Council of Ministers and the Economic and Social Committee, the

186

Committee of Regions, the European Parliament for its commissions and additional sessions.

Brussels is also a major international city and the site of: leading international organisations (NATO, WEU, BENELUX), the coordination centre of 170 multinational firms, head offices of 1,430 privately owned businesses, 67 banks, 60 foreign insurance firms, headquarters of 123 governmental organisations and 1,100 foreign non-governmental organisations, 21 international schools and approximately 1,000 conventions per year (fourth highest in the world).

Table A4.1 Some key data of the Brussels region

Population					Surface	Density
'Structural urban region': ± 1,700,000 residents					1,400 km^2	1,214 res/km^2
Region*	Belgians	Foreign EEC	Foreign N. African	Others		
950,000	665,000	129,000 **	82,000	74,000	161.4 km^2	5,888 res/km^2
100%	70%	13.5%	8.5%	8.0%		

* Administrative region of Brussels capital: average loss of 4,000 residents per year from 1980–94; recent trend towards stabilisation.

** 65% of the 20,000 who work for the EEC live within the region.

Employment
±610,000 jobs or 17% of Belgian jobs for 9.5% of the Belgian population (10,100,000)
51% of employees come from other regions (mobility problem).
Tertiary sector dominant: 7.5 million m^2 of office space or 8 m^2 per resident.

Public transport
Airport: 13.5 million passengers/year; average increase over 5 years: 7% to 8% per annum; airport capacity (currently under reconstruction): 20 million passengers per year; forecast 2007: 25 million passengers/year.
Port: (14 km of quays) connected to Antwerp and the European river network: access for ships ups to 4500 t, boats up to 9000 t, *5 million tonnes/year*; multi-modal water/rail/road 'TWR': *10 million tonnes/year*.
Railway: one of Europe's highest density networks, no cul-de-sacs, 28 stations in the urban area: see Sheet C.
Urban public transport (STIB): 430 km of network (selective service outside the region), 5,500 officials, 3 metro lines (40.5 km), 15 tram lines including 7.5 underground (premetro), 40 bus lines, 213,500,000 passengers per year (10% increase from 1985 to 95); TEC: bus lines to Wallonia. *DE LIJN*: bus lines to Flanders.

The Strategic Dimension

External Challenges

Brussels is at the centre of one of Europe's most densely populated areas, in which it is very well connected by all types of transportation infrastructure. At the European level, its geographic situation in a small, multicultural country have given Brussels its 'first among equals' status among the three European capitals which are nevertheless in continual competition.

However, being situated in a small country also creates a major disadvantage: Brussels is highly dependent upon the choices made by its larger neighbours who, in deciding to develop a particular branch of their transportation networks for example, may stimulate or reduce traffic through its territory: 'good decisions' on the part of foreign networks is therefore the first major challenge.

Today the Iberian Peninsula is developing and, most importantly, Europe is enlarging to the east with its potential growth markets. However, in terms of these new connections, Brussels remains only an alternative stop on the southern route (the lines connecting northern Germany, including Berlin, and the northern countries to western France, including Paris, and the western Iberian Peninsula, including Madrid) and on the eastern route (the lines connecting London to Central Europe via the French line through Strasbourg). Furthermore, this shift in the centre of gravity towards the east could result in a revival of the candidacy of Bonn, orphaned of its capital status, as potentially accommodating new European community institutions or the expansion, even relocation of those which do not have sufficient room for development in Brussels.

If the city hopes to maintain or further develop its function of European capital, Brussels must:

* enhance its accessibility from the south and east by the transport modes best suited to this function, that is, high-speed train and air transport. In addition to the renovation of the airport, currently under way, this would involve 'unifying' the three European capitals with a high-speed line serving Brussels-Luxembourg-(Metz) Strasbourg; however, there are currently no plans in this area and rapidly establishing a connection with Cologne, that is, the German network via construction of the HSL-East (partially under way; completion planned for 2005). This is all the more important due to the fact that this network is currently undergoing major changes, with the

DB planning to open ICE 2.2 service from Berlin and Frankfurt to Brussels following the opening of its HS-line serving Hanover-Berlin, then Cologne-Frankfurt;

- optimise the development of the European quarters in Brussels, which will necessitate the establishment of new connections between the different European quarters and with the HST and the airport, the development of new European locations and improving the image of the existing poles, particularly through the renovation of public spaces and considerable aesthetic and functional improvements to the access points (airport and train stations);
- develop cooperation strategies with five 'HST towns' in varying degrees of competition with one another: the two other European capitals, in light of their status, and also the cities of Lille, Antwerp and Liège. In light of the changes in time-space ratios which will ensure close proximity to Brussels and its European institutions, the lower land costs of these latter three cities make them potential sites for relocation.

Table A4.2   Ultimate travel times by HST for planned lines to Brussels

London-Lille	1:24	Lille-Brussels	:35	London-Brussels*	1:59		
Paris-Brussels**	1:22	Brussels-Antwerp	:29	Antwerp-Amsterdam	1:10	Brussels-Amsterdam	1:39
Paris-Brussels	1:22	Brussels-Liège	:39	Liège-Cologne	:58	Brussels-Cologne	1:38

*   Via Eurostar: current travel time: 3:15 Capacity: 40%.
** Via Thalys: current travel time: 2:03 Capacity: 70%.

The Station Area and Secondary Transport

The situation prior to the HST can be characterised as follows:

- a dense rail network crisscrossing the city (no cul-de-sac stations or lines) characterised by a centre core of four north-south lines, more or less parallel at distances 1.5 and 2.5 kilometres from each other, crossing one east-west line further north; distributing 28 stations within the metropolitan area, this network is articulated around the Nord-Midi Junction (mostly underground but nearing saturation). This is the city centre's veritable backbone, connecting the capital's three main stations: Brussels-Midi (51,000 passengers per day in 1994), Brussels-Central (59,000), Brussels-

Nord (32,000); these stations themselves enjoy close proximity to Belgium's major tertiary poles, but not to the European centres. The latter are not served by the junction but rather by the L161 Luxembourg-Brussels and the stations Schuman (8,500), Leopold Quarter (also commonly known as 'Luxembourg') (7,100) and, to a lesser extent, Delta;

- a well-developed public transport network of underground train and tram, surface tram and bus routes;
- numerous interconnections between rail and other transport networks, both through its junctions and in linear terms through shared line segments;
- close proximity to a rapidly developing airport (10 km from city centre, four km from regional limits);
- a current study under way within the context of the Regional Development Plan, to which the aspect of mobility is obviously essential.

The situation created by the HST:

- in 1995, completion of the terminal for north-south lines (Eurostar Brussels-London in service and Thalys Paris-Brussels to be fully served by HS lines in 1998) at Brussels-Midi, due to its position as the major station with the most southerly location, the best connections to public transport networks and offering the necessary land reserves. Subsequent need to expand the shuttle service (3,000 passengers per day in 1994) which previously connected Brussels-Central and Brussels-Nord to the airport, to double the frequency of service (six per hour), improve speed and comfort (thanks to improvements to lanes and equipment), especially since road access to the airport is becoming saturated;
- in 2005, traffic from PBKA trains (Paris-Brussels-Cologne-Amsterdam) from Brussels-Midi on the lines L25 (Antwerp) and 36 (Liège) via the Junction following the elimination of L28, the only alternative, for technical reasons (line allocated to goods traffic, obsolescence, greater length and degree of winding, difficult access from Brussels-Midi Terminal etc.); separation of north (Amsterdam) and east (Cologne) lines at 'Schaerbeek Formation', a vast area (350 ha) belonging to the SNCB where several functions including marshalling, siding and maintenance could be rationally regrouped, and where a multimodal rail/road/sea (port) node may be established.

However, as emphasized above:

- the Junction is already at saturation point; the addition of HST traffic therefore involves a total restructuring of the network in order to provide some relief. It also necessitates the addition of a fourth track on L36 to (Louvain and) Liège, on pain of blocking the rest of traffic (two tracks for rapid traffic, two tracks for other traffic). However, despite all of these measures and others currently being studied (Schuman Josaphat tunnel), the SNCB is forecasting the permanent saturation of the Junction, and therefore of the Brussels-Midi Terminal, by 2020; the problem of a second Terminal is thus already implicit;
- a transport plan was under development, based on the observation that access to Brussels by public transport was insufficient within a radius of ± 30 km, the source area for a majority of commuters (which explains the continuous and unmanageable increase in car traffic in the medium term). In order to bring the car/public transport ratio of 70/30 to 60/40 by 2005, the plan recommended, in addition to a dissuasive parking system coupled with public transport at access points to the city, the creation of a true RER (regional rail network). Its main stations were to be those of the Junction and whose feasibility on L36 was dependent upon the creation of a fourth track;
- the European Quarters, which are not situated upon the HST route, wish to be better connected to the airport (for example, through the construction of a Schuman/Josaphat tunnel), whose new terminal has been conceived to accommodate the HST if necessary, making the airport a potential HST stopping place, possibly even a station (although this would imply the creation of new connection loops.

The HST/RER/airport accessibility case studies are therefore closely related and the entire regional strategy in terms of mobility is now based upon parallel action on all of these fronts (along with a study of dissuasive parking measures); thus, initial construction on the RER is scheduled to go ahead within the context of work on the north and east HS lines; the junction linked to a dissuasive parking facility (Haren Station connecting L36 and L26), doubling of the single east-west service (L161 to L50 and 60 in the 'Quadrilatère') and better links between the L161 and the Nord station entrance facilities.

Urban Planning and Development

The development challenges are in relation to a twofold problem, which is itself based upon an increasing demand for land to satisfy the expansion requirements of the EEC (100,000 m^2 today, with all of the potential associated demand) along with the massive property holdings of the SNCB in Brussels (the rail company is known as Brussels' 20th community) managed by its specialized subsidiary 'Eurostation':

*   siting of a (future) second HST Terminal and its links with the airport;
*   finalization of redevelopment of the district surrounding the existing HST terminal, Brussels-Midi.

Siting of a potential second terminal is directly related to the 'permanent' saturation of the Brussels-Midi Junction and surroundings. This is forecasted to occur near 2020 due to the increase in HST traffic on one hand, and on the other, the anticipated success of the (future) RER. The SNCB considers that inland and RER traffic should stay within the Junction since it serves the three major stations which themselves provide service to Belgium's main service-sector poles.

It is not possible to physically enlarge the Junction, due to urban planning and cost considerations it will be necessary, around 2020, to redirect HST traffic passing through Brussels i.e., the PBKA (and perhaps certain trains from London with destinations to the north and east) via a reconfigured L28; however, this route necessitates a renewed emphasis on the north and east high-speed lines within the 'Quadrilatère', that is, after the Nord station, which would necessarily exclude any stop or terminal (for which there is insufficient land capacity in any event); from this point, the SNCB considers it logical to locate the second terminal upon the massive railway site known as Schaerbeek Formation, at the exact point at which the north and east branches of the high-speed lines divide. The site presents certain advantages: a location within the Brussels capital region, situation further northeast, good road access (although not by urban public transport), potential for an RER station, and the airport just four kilometres away.

The region is not yet inclined to agree with the SNCB over the Schaerbeek Formation thesis, since:

*   certain rush-hour commuter trains could free up the Junction during peak hours to facilitate regional rail links (L28, L161, L26) connecting with the

metro;

- the Schaerbeek Formation area is not considered as a potential extension for office complexes in the regional development scheme; based on the ABC policy, the region favours office development in central areas and reserves, on the contrary, peripheral locations near the canal for business expansions;
- an HST pole must be located right by a major hub for public transportation in order to promote intermodal transport and minimize the use of the car; this is not the case with Schaerbeek Formation.

On the other hand, the airport site could potentially be considered as an alternative for the second terminal, provided new 'X' connection loops ('diabolo project') are created to facilitate the stopping of HSTs. However, the terminal would then be situated outside the Brussels capital region; this location would also be considerably more complex in technical terms.

Finalization of Redevelopment of the Existing HST Terminal District

The arrival of HST at the Midi station (four Thalys tracks, two Eurostar tracks) necessitates the construction of a new terminal and the resulting 'HST effect' allows us to envisage the redevelopment of the surrounding district (Midi Quarter), at present rundown. However, this programme has fallen severely behind schedule (currently being recovered) for the following reasons:

- institutional changes: the creation of the region with its urban planning jurisdiction the same year (1989) as the conception of plans for the terminal by Eurostation; detailing by the region of a 'Regional Development Plan – RDP', a major policy statement by the new region; the unveiling in 1992 of new legislation imposing impact studies and urban planning responsibilities; overall administrative breakdown between state, SNCB and region concerning the rail company land holdings in Brussels; the fact that the terminal is located in the community whose Burgomaster is also first minister/president of the region, etc.;
- legal disputes in conjunction with the availability of land and developer financing;
- conflicts of interest between the region and developers: in order to ensure successful project integration, the region has outlined specific land-use plans and regulatory parameters for the allotment and size of developments, etc. These plans were immediately contested by various commercial

interests, including Eurostation: parking facilities (5,000 requested; 2,500 accorded), retail shops (20,000 m^2), office space (120,000 m^2) hotels (20,000 m^2), compensatory housing (10,000 m^2);

- speculative effects: the new organisation of the supply resulting from the development plans, inadequately managed at present (there is no pre-emptive right in Belgium for the control of property transactions), combined with speculation, has led to such dramatic increases in land values that even expropriation now appears difficult for public authorities;
- stagnation of real estate from 1992–94 and the lack of any dynamic buyer ready to bargain on the future and back the development of this 'difficult' area.

However, this delay carries serious consequences: the notion of a second terminal has gained momentum in the meantime, and there is an increasing risk of losing planned investments before the revitalisation of the Midi district is complete (not only to Schaerbeek Formation or the airport in connection with its HST potential, but also to sites elsewhere in the region such as Brussels-Nord, a temporary HST stopping place, or Delta). Rapid completion of the Brussels-Midi Terminal and its environment is imperative in order to ensure that the Midi district remains competitive in the medium-term in order to satisfy European needs, for example.

Note

1   Co-author: Aries Group s.c.c., Brussels.

Annex 5   Background Information on Cologne[1]

Profile

Cologne lies in the so-called 'Rhine Elbow' on the edge of one of the world's most densely populated areas, the Ruhr area with over 10 million inhabitants. The city of Cologne now counts about one million residents. In the last few years the population has shown an increase.

About three-fifths of the population of Cologne live on the left bank of the Rhine, and about two-fifths on the right bank. Administratively, the city is divided into nine districts. Unlike in many other German major towns, the central business district also has a high residential density. More than 100,000 people live there. And, also in contrast to many major towns, the inner city has an immigration surplus. The inner city (District 1) encompasses both the central railway station on the left bank and the Deutz district on the right bank with the Deutz station.

Cologne is the fourth largest town after Berlin, Munich and Hamburg, and the largest city of Northrhine-Westfalen, the most populous federal state of Germany with about 17 million residents. The urban region of Cologne has some two million residents (one million in the city of Cologne). The adjoining Cologne-related area, the surrounding *Kreise* and *kreisfrei* towns (not belonging to any *Kreis*) (Erftkreis, Rhein-Sieg-Kreis, city of Leverkusen, Oberbergischer Kreis, city of Bonn) house about one million people. The city of Cologne, as a *kreisfrei* town, comes under the government district of Cologne.

Cologne is a shopping town and the production and service location for many business companies. The central business district, the city proper, is marked most of all by its varied shopping and service function. One thousand four hundred and fifty retail businesses are accommodated there, among which 60 large-scale ones with over 1,000 m^2 of selling area. In all, 410,000 m^2 of selling area are available. To this can be added 1,350 service and 625 catering businesses. The records show a minimum of 250,000 visitors a day. There are no fewer than seven shopping arcades.

Another strong feature and point of attraction of the inner city are the many different museums (among others, the Walraff-Richarts Museum, the Ludwig Museum, the Chocolate Museum, the Anthropological Museum, and the Museum for Applied Art).

Further important institutions in the central business district are the media branch (worth mentioning is the WDR, West-German Broadcasting, with about

3,000 employees. The newly created Media Park has also found accommodation in the inner city), the Municipal Savings Bank of Cologne as one of the greatest money institutions in Germany, the Town Administration, the Rhineland Landscape Association, the German Railway Company, banks and insurance companies, and the headquarters of Kaufhof AG.

Greater Cologne and the Region

Overall, in terms of number of companies and employed, the primary sector nowadays plays no more than a subordinate part in the area. By employment figures and turnover, the steel, machine and vehicle industry is the most important in Cologne. With around 88,000 employed in the region, the industry accounts for almost 12 per cent of total regional employment. Within the region, 63 per cent of the job opportunities are concentrated in Cologne. The sector is very heterogeneous, encompassing small companies as well as world concerns, such as the Ford works.

The second-largest sector and one of the region's gravity centres is the chemical industry. Nearly one-third of those employed in this branch in the federal state of Northrhine-Westfalen have their jobs in the Cologne region, and of their number, two-thirds work in the city of Leverkusen and one-fifth in Cologne. The Bayer Company is the dominating firm.

The Strategic Dimension

In Cologne, the realisation of two important core elements of the European high-speed railway network is at hand: the international high-speed track from Paris via Brussels to Cologne/Amsterdam, and the planned new ICE track from Cologne to Rhine/Main.

Already now the central station at Cologne is the principal German railway junction coping with some 1,200 trains a day (of which about 120 IC/ICE). Its function is strengthened by the integration in the European high-speed network, which will make Cologne a main junction both in the north-south and in the east-west direction.

The Cologne-Rhine/Main track is to be completed by the year 2000; the planning procedures are in progress. Of the Paris-Brussels-Cologne/Amsterdam track, the Cologne-Düren section is to be completed, in combination with the extension of the Düren-Cologne S-railway, by 1998. The entire PBKA (Paris-Brussels-Cologne-Amsterdam) network, of which the section between Lille and Paris is already in exploitation, should be finished between 2000 and 2005. There are still some difficulties with the financing on the part of Belgium. Already in 1997 the Thalys is planned to run on that section. The travel times from Cologne to Paris will be halved to approximately three hours, those from Cologne to Frankfurt will be cut by more than half to about 55 minutes or one hour.

Special attention is due to the integration of the Cologne/Bonn Airport (Konrad-Adenauer Airport) in the ICE and the S-railway, which was demanded by the city of Cologne and has by now been accorded. It would assure as well a direct air connection between the airports of Frankfurt, Cologne/Bonn, and Dusseldorf, also to be joined to the ICE network.

Another suggestion made by the city of Cologne is to connect the Deutz station to the network configuration of the ICE in the area of Cologne, or in the Northrhine-Westfalen area, and channel certain ICE transports through that station directly into the north-south track. The Cologne area would thus boast three ICE stations: the Central Station, Deutz/Messe ICE station, and ICE airport station.

The Station Area and Secondary Transport

The channelling of certain ICE lines through Deutz Station creates an entirely right bank and thus more direct and faster north-south connection. At the same time, it provides the airports mentioned earlier with a direct and fast connection. Special airport links across the 'elbow' could be conceived of. Two-fifths of the Cologne population will in that way get opened up much better than they are now by ICE transport; a direct Messe railway station will develop. In the immediate environment of the planned Deutz/Messe IC station there are several development centres of the town, such as the Cologne Arena, the new Technical Town Hall, the development of the CFK estate and the Euroforum.

Another important aspect is the relief of the central station. A further increase in railway traffic, with five new lines running on the new section from Cologne to Rhine/Main, might easily cause an overload of the central station, in particular of the Hohenzollern bridge giving access to it. Following that train of thought, the new Deutz/Messe ICE railway station opens new options and relieves the Central Station. The Deutz site is optimally interwoven with the road network (trunk roads and federal motorways) and with the ÖPNV (S-railway and city railway). A generous parking supply is available in the neighbourhood. The costs involved in building the Deutz station and lay out the necessary railway yards are, at some 100 million DM, relatively low. Most of the present railway yards can be made to serve the new concept.

Urban Planning and Development

International Significance

With the achievement of the two ICE- connections Paris-Brussels-Cologne/ Amsterdam and Cologne-Rhine/Main, the position of Cologne in western Europe will change a great deal. The decisive factor is the ensuing reduced travel distance between the principal European metropolitan regions. Within the European high-speed network, Cologne will be linked to the European centre Brussels, to Lille, Paris, London, Amsterdam, and to the German metropolitan regions. Major business companies in the region of Cologne are very much dependent on mobility. The improved traffic constellation and the shortened travel times between the European metropolises, enhance the quality of Cologne as a business location for those very companies. Think, for instance, of the media branch, which is strongly represented in Cologne (by the broadcasting channels WDR, RTL, VOX, VIVA, among others, and by the Media Park); and of the research institutes and universities (Cologne University, Cologne Polytechnical School), the banks and insurance companies, important industrial works such as Ford Werke AG, Bayer AG, etc.

European metropolitan regions tend to penetrate into commuting distances, so that new forms of employment division and new occupational prospects can evolve. The travel times to the main metropolitan regions will be cut by about half. The Frankfurt region for instance, is only one hour's travel away, so that even occupational commuting can to some degree develop into a factor to be reckoned with.

With the incorporation of the Cologne/Bonn airport, a vital condition for the further extension of the airport will be fulfilled. Not only does it permit substituting rail transport for short-distance flights in Germany and the adjoining European areas, it also opens new opportunities for cooperation, for instance between the Cologne/Bonn and Frankfurt airports. The relevant region of the Cologne/Bonn airport will be extended. One other advantage of the airport's connection to the ICE is that it fulfils a condition for the airport's participation in freight traffic.

The Regional Context

One result of the new ICE high-speed network that favours the region is the ICE stopping place in Siegburg. Moreover, the ICE airport station will serve as a regional station. From that station, regional connections in the public transport can fan out. In the context of the high-speed network, the S-railway connections within the Cologne area will be completed or extended. In that way, the region to the west of Cologne will benefit directly from the PBKA ICE-connection through the simultaneous extension of the Cologne-Horrem-Düren S-railway. Along with the new ICE-section from Cologne to Rhine/Main, S-railway S 12 will be extended to include an S-railway connection to the Cologne/Bonn airport.

The suggestion to provide the city of Cologne with a right-bank Cologne-Deutz/Messe ICE railway station would benefit not only the city quarters on the right bank of the Rhine, but also the entire right bank region. The Deutz station provides an excellent public transport connection (S-railway, DB short-distance traffic, city railway and bus), for the city as well as the region. The region is well connected by road to the motorway network in the immediate neighbourhood of the railway station. There are parking lots available in the close vicinity of the station. The planned extension of the airport S-railway as well as the city railway will make the regional connection of the Deutz station even better. In sum, improvements may be expected in the situation of the area to the right of the Rhine, across which are spread about two-fifths of the population in the Cologne area.

Development of the Station Zone Cologne-Deutz/Messe in the Context of the ICE Station

Some important industries and public institutions are located on the right bank of the Rhine. For the city, the right bank zone is the gravity centre of development (Euroforum, Multi-Purpose Hall, Cologne Arena, the development of the CFK-estate, KHD development zones in Kalk, the new technical Town Hall in Deutz, the expansion of the Cologne Messe). Already accomplished is the re-exploitation of the KHD-tower, accommodating the Lion Company and the Meganet and Telecommunication branch.

The Messe will have direct access to its own station, connected to the ICE network. That is of particular importance since Cologne is a prominent location for major international fairs. To the visitor of the Messe who arrives by the Frankfurt, Cologne or Dusseldorf airport, the ICE network offers optimum access to the grounds of the Cologne Messe. The city's idea is to create, on the site of the old Deutz station, an entirely new station with a service and business centre. Within reach of the Messe and adjoining the station, adequate plots of land are available. The new technical town hall and the creation, already begun, of the Cologne Arena in the immediate vicinity, will find support in the ICE stopping place.

On the existent and extending city railway and bus network as well as through DB short-distance and S-railway traffic, an optimum integration with the ICE station is developing, which will also relieve the central station.

At the central station the parking accommodation is still limited. At the Deutz station, however, plenty of parking places are already available (those of the Messe included), and more are to be created in the context of the Cologne Arena and the Euroforum.

Note

1   Co-author: Mr. Lars Möller, City of Cologne.

Annex 6   Background Information on Geneva[1]

Profile

Table A6.1   Residents, working population and employment in and around Geneva, 1990–91

	Total resident population	Working resident population	Gross rate of employment, in %	Jobs (in the workplace)
I a *City of Geneva*	171,042	95,571	55.9	154,781
I b *Metropolitan Geneva*	379,190	206,919	54.6	262,715
II *Franco-Valdo-Genevan area*	633,427	337,729	53.3	337,190
Canton of Geneva	379,190	206,919	54.6	262,715
District of Nyon	50,690	27,810	54.9	19,280
Pays de Gex	50,089	26,000	51.9	11,368
Genevan Haut-Savoyard	153,458	77,000	50.2	43,827
III *Lake Geneva Region*	2,270,128	1,152,832	50.8	1,125,900
Canton of Geneva	379,190	206,919	54.6	262,715
Canton of Vaud	601,816	319,377	53.1	317,456
Canton of Valais	249,817	123,332	49.4	146,902
Ain Department	471,019	220,582	46.8	170,591
Haute-Savoie Department	568,286	282,622	49.7	228,236
IV *Region*	7,076,371	3 344,116	47.3	3,136,709
French-speaking Switzerland	1,725,670	902,331	52.3	981,846
Rhône-Alpes Region	5,350,701	2 441,785	45.6	2,154,863

Source: City of Geneva, 1996, *Fiches de Synthèse*.

The Strategic Dimension

In order to maintain its position as a 'world metropolis', Geneva must ensure it continues to benefit from exchanges with the outside world, in particular by maintaining a network of optimal air links and by developing connections to rapid rail links such as the high-speed train.

The economic future of the Geneva region will be dependent upon efforts to be undertaken to reinforce and consolidate its international position. To

Table A6.2   Transportation in the Geneva region in figures (1995 values)

Air transport:
    6,270,000 passengers/year
    108 destinations (regular lines only) (Europe 58)
    45 airlines serving Geneva

Rail transport:
    Geneva-Cornavin: 10,000,000 passengers/year (220 trains/day)
    Geneva-airport: 2,500,000 passengers/year (180 trains/day)
    HST: Paris: 5 round-trip connections/day; Montpellier 1 RT/day

Urban area transport:

length of lines:		
tramway:		12 km
trolleybus:		29 km
bus:		297 km
Number of lines:		48
Vehicle/km:		15,579,000 km/year
Passengers carried:		101,241,000/year
Personnel:		1302 employees
Budget: expenses (1994)		198,512,000 Francs
Revenues:	passenger receipts	80,100,000 Francs
	other tariff receipts	3,615,000 Francs
	funding revenues	13,078,000 Francs
	state participation	106,025,000 Francs

Source: City of Geneva, 1996, *Fiches de Synthèse*.

this end, it is necessary to preserve and improve the underlying conditions responsible for the region's appeal. The growth in the supply of supporting amenities, areas suitable for new business set-ups and living environments has been made possible by the cross-border alternative. The development of cross-border cooperation will enable the Geneva region to enhance its performance. This cooperation is founded upon the promotion and accommodation of economic activities, particularly international organisations. The Geneva region will thus be able to reinforce its strategic position at the heart of Europe and better exploit its pivotal position between Switzerland and France.

Strategic Components Impacting Different Areas

In terms of *international relations*, the position of Geneva as a city specifically oriented towards governmental and non-governmental organisations must be reinforced, while respecting decisions at the federal level as concerns the postponement of Swiss membership in Europe. These decisions represent both a handicap and proof of neutrality, which must exploited to greatest advantage.

On an economic level, neither Switzerland nor Geneva has been spared economic disruption, the financial difficulties of public authorities and the globalisation of production and trade. Within this context, choices must be oriented so as to maintain the specificity of production and exports (light goods with high added value) while encouraging innovation.

In terms of *cross-border relations*, the platform for debate instituted through the regional Franco-Genevan committee (CRFG) must be reinforced in order to obtain agreements with neighbouring departments, without overlooking higher authorities such as the Swiss Confederation and the bilateral accords which the latter is endeavouring to establish, particularly with France.

In *practical* terms, the challenge is to overcome the difficulties arising from the fact that Switzerland may be considered an island in the centre of Europe. These difficulties especially concern north-south rail traffic and the insistence on piggybacking (trucks on trains), in light of fierce competition in Brenner, on the Austrian side, along the Rhine-Rhône and routes between France and Italy (Mont Blanc and Mont Cenis). At a local level, the obstacle is evident for local and regional public transport lines that are obliged to stop at customs checkpoints.

In terms of the *environment*, federal environmental protection measures impose traffic restrictions upon the state of Geneva in the city centre. While these measures are intended to enhance the quality of life, they are sometimes perceived as a hindrance to development. However, this policy also serves to promote the use of public transport.

Finally, in terms of the *organisation of high-speed rail* transport, the present challenge is promoting the 'Lake Geneva-Mont Blanc' line (Macon-Geneva) while remaining attentive to French projects such as Lyon-Turin and connections to Geneva via the 'Alpine Furrow' (Chambéry-Geneva). It is also necessary to promote HST access via Geneva without ignoring the initiatives of other French-speaking cantons favourable to secondary urban access routes (Vallorbe, Neuchâtel).

The Station Area and Secondary Transport

At present, the station served by high-speed rail is Geneva-Cornavin. This station is situated in Geneva centre and is served by all trains originating from the rest of Switzerland; it offers an excellent interface with other transport modes. The high-speed trains also stop at Bellegarde, which is the final stop for trains serving the Vallée de l'Arve and the Chablais, along with coaches from the Pays de Gex. The separation of HST trains at Bellegarde would be welcome; however, technical constraints must be clarified, in particular, the resulting loss of time. A second HST station could be at Annemasse. Some double trains could be split in Bellegarde, with one unit going to Geneva and the other to Annemasse (Vallée de l'Arve and Chablais). A potential HST station at Geneva Airport is also being considered.

Layout of Lines

The progress of projects on the French side, along with the various outlines of connections between French-speaking Switzerland and the European high-speed train network, has enabled an HST urban access route to be 'crystallised', with connections to the CFF system either between Lathoy (SNCF line at the foot of the Salève: Bellegarde-Annemasse line) and La Praille (CFF freight line currently in cul-de-sac). This layout would enable indiscriminate connection of the Swiss network to the French TGV system, whether to the north via Macon (planned TGV line Lake Geneva-Mont Blanc) or to the south, via Chambéry-Montmélian (planned TGV line 'Alpine Furrow'). Due to the potential savings in time, the Swiss position tends to favour the 'Lake Geneva-Mont Blanc' project. Still, the bivalency of the layout of the southern urban access route La Praille-Lathoy nonetheless reinforces the value of this line.

Planned Railway Stations and Connections

We will summarise below the three most likely locations for an HST station: Geneva-Cornavin (city centre); Geneva-Airport (northeast of the city); Annemasse (southeast of the city). Alternatives not being considered by the DTPE: La Praille, Archamps and Etrembières.

* Geneva-Cornavin is the terminus for regional and rapid rail service, and a stop on the routes of intercity and certain international lines. It is also the highest-density traffic point for urban lines (bus, trams, planned light rail). This situation offers certain advantages: a high-quality distribution interface for high-speed lines. The saturation of Geneva-Cornavin is relative, and especially concerns the TGV platform. If the Geneva-Macon line is completed, the extension of certain runs to Lausanne will initially result in the saturation of the Geneva-Lausanne line. However, it should not be forgotten that the central location of Geneva-Cornavin fulfils the first HST objective.
* Geneva-Airport currently accommodates traffic from all intercity lines on the CFF network – as does Geneva-Cornavin – along with direct rail lines connecting intermediary towns to the Swiss network, such as Nyon and

Morges. The development of an HST station at the airport would enable the promotion of complementary aspects between air travel and surface routes. In particular, the 'Alpine Furrow' alternative offers more advantages in terms of improving service to the airport from secondary urban centres than disadvantages resulting from competition between HST and air transport. On the other hand, the concentration of activities around the airport site, called the 'Golden Rectangle' and including an exhibition centre, theatre, business centres and luxury hotels, would benefit from HST access in close proximity. This would also enhance the development potential of this zone on the French side.

- Annemasse represents an interesting opportunity for the Chablais Haut-Savoyard area, but whether or not it would be in the interests of Geneva itself – other than in terms of costs – is questionable, particularly given the current lack of continuous direct rail service between Annemasse and Geneva-Cornavin. No one would argue that this is the role of the planned light rail service Annemasse-Cornavin, Airport-CERN. Annemasse could therefore be considered as a terminus complementary to that of Geneva-Cornavin or Geneva Airport, not without interest for Haute Savoie traffic to Evian and the Mont-Blanc massif.

Urban Planning and Development

The expansion of Geneva-Cornavin to include a new HST station will not alter the hierarchy between stations. Indeed, the station is already the arrival point for high-speed trains. However, if the frequency of high-speed service increases dramatically (15–20 trips per day) and if this is accompanied by an increase in other traffic (intercity, international and regional trains), a degree of saturation at the station must be expected. This excess flow will necessitate a transformation of the station and, at the same time, a complete restructuring of the interface with urban transit, in the sense of a regrouping of better-located bus and tram stops. This reorganisation must be undertaken in view of reducing private car traffic in Rue de Lausanne and Place Cornavin, which could, theoretically, be used as a hub (see TPG map for Place Cornavin and surroundings).

Finally, the difference in the platform levels (+8–10 metres) as compared to Place Cornavin could determine a breakdown of interface functions on a vertical scale. Obviously, this is just a hypothesis whose feasibility has not yet been proven.

Furthermore, there is a need to transform the station (which currently constitutes a 'rupture' in the urban landscape) to create a seam between the high-profile urban facade of the city centre (between station and lake) and the city's other face, the 'Grottes' district, uptown from the station and under renovation for over 25 years. The consideration of railway factors in the urban planning process is assuming increasing importance; it is recommended by the federal office of regional planning and applied in the revised Canton-level development plan. According to this document, train stations should be viewed as high-priority development poles.

We presently consider Geneva-Cornavin station as the central station and that of Geneva Airport as peripheral, despite the fact that it is less than five kilometres away. As concerns the potential of a complementary station in Annemasse, this offers certain advantages as well as disadvantages.

The planned Annemasse CERN light-rail line in the form of heavy urban rail seems to offer sufficient structuring and federative capacity to prevent the splintering of different parties within the metropolitan area following the installation of an HST terminus on the outskirts of the city in the event that one or more stations are established in Annemasse or at the Airport.

The regional perspectives in terms of development are based on two principles:

* establishing complementarity between Geneva and secondary regional centres, both Vaudois Canton and French, by emphasising and promoting amenities and activities of all kinds;
* promoting a cross-border approach between Geneva and the French departments of Ain and Haute-Savoie.

We consider the above principles not to present a stumbling block to establishing additional HST service or decentralised secondary stations. Conversely, the rail network that structures the Geneva region and the cross-border conurbation is already being used as rabatment lines towards the HST terminus.

However, the following aspect must be closely considered. There is no unanimous agreement over these strategies as several levels are involved in the decision-making: CFF, SNCF, European Parliament, Metropolitan France, Rhône-Alpes region, the French departments, regional councils, Swiss Confederation, French- and German-speaking cantons. To this extent, it may be considered that at present, these parties are more competitive than complementary. However, a strengthening of relations between city and region may be anticipated through the set-up of additional rail services and facilities able to accommodate them.

Note

1 Co-authors: Mr Michel Jaques and Mr S. Manzoni, City of Geneva.

Annex 7   Background Information on Liège[1]

Profile

The metropolitan area of Liège has a population of 600,000. The city itself has a population of 190,000 and has set the objective of increasing that number to 200,000 residents by the year 2000. This is considered to be the strategic size for Europe's second cities. The metropolitan area of Liège and surrounding communes represents a developed continuum with one of the highest population densities in Europe: 2,740 residents per km^2.

The city of Liège has a surface area of 6,891 hectares. In comparison with its region, Liège is Wallonia's second-largest commune in terms of surface area, next to Charleroi. Liège is located at the confluence of the Meuse and the Ourthe rivers, 100 kilometres from Brussels, 30 km from Maastricht, 40 km from Aachen.

The population of Liège is characterised by a well-balanced age pyramid with a slight deficit in younger age groups. The rate of unemployment in Liège (12.7 per cent of the working population) is higher than the Belgian average (± 11 per cent). This is the result of a severe recession in the iron and steel industry (by far the predominant economic sector) throughout the period from the late 1970s to the early 1980s.

Despite the economic redeployment undertaken in the Liège area by small- and medium-size businesses operating in the metallurgy and 'high-tech' sectors, and despite the development of its tertiary sector, Liège continues to have a high rate of unemployment.

The Liège region currently comprises some 12,257 businesses, of which 90 per cent are small-to-medium-size concerns of less than 50 employees. This is an apt reflection of the trend towards new business start-ups which followed the economic recession sparked by the steelworks industry in the late 1970s. The city of Liège has more than 6,000 retail shops, 660 food-service operations and 22 hotels.

Liège has long been known as the 'Athens of the North' for its rich educational quality. Today, the higher education sector may be broken down as follows:

- university level: University of Liège and *grandes écoles* : 15,000 students;
- non-university level: 13 *grandes écoles* in Liège province, resulting from the Ministry of Education plan of grouping together these institutions in 1996.

The Strategic Dimension

Liège was able to obtain HST service following 10 years of discussions and negotiations between the European Union, federal state, local authorities and the Société Nationale de Chemins de Fer Belges (SNCB: Belgian national rail company). When it came to laying out the HST-north network (Paris-Brussels-Cologne-Amsterdam link), Liège was not part of the plans. A bypass had been skilfully outlined, with the HST passing through open country between Leuven (commune of Herentals, in Flanders) and the German border. Finally, the question of HST service via Liège was decided by the Council of Ministers.

In a country as densely populated as Belgium, where each of the three autonomous regions has its own regional development code, it did not prove easy to make room for a long HST corridor. A two-pronged principle prevailed:

- reduction of travel times between Brussels and Cologne to enable maximum use of the line, as profitability of the HST beyond Brussels towards Germany was not certain;
- maximum reuse of existing tracks, adapting them to high-speed imperatives, given the limitations of European funding for major infrastructure projects and the precarious financial situation of the SNCB.

This resulted in the following trajectory:

- Brussels to Louvain: existing track;
- Louvain to Bierset (regional airport located 10 km from Liège); dedicated track;
- Bierset to Liège: existing track;
- Liège to Vaux-sous-Chèvremont; existing track;
- Vaux-sous-Chèvremont to Soumagne and beyond to the German border: dedicated track.

In the total budget allocated to accommodating the HST in Liège, out of 6.5 billion Belgian francs, an amount of four million is dedicated to improving the railway lines from the Ans plateau to the Liège valley, including:

- improvements to the tracks on the inclined plane linking the two points, so as to enable increased speeds to 100 km/h during the approach to the HST station;

- moving the station 200 metres closer to the river;
- creation of a new station, larger and better adapted to mixed use (HST and inland traffic);
- transformation of the tracks on the edge of town, intended to accommodate HST cars;
- construction of parking facilities along the hill behind the station, directly connected by a vast concrete slab to both the station and to the motorway system.

The other 2.5 billion francs is allocated to the station structure and its architectural design.

The HST will create a 'hub' halfway between London and Berlin offering considerable relief to the saturation of Brussels (traffic, land, communications junction) and enable the creation of a corridor of small-to-medium-size businesses along a new communications axis (that is, the length of the dedicated track between Leuvain and Brussels).

The Station Area and Secondary Transport

Following an analysis by the SNCB research department, it was concluded that the present station of Guillemins should be moved 200 metres to allow it to assume the full role of an HST station. This would also enable the station to respond to technical constraints linked to the high-speed train (increased speed, extension, widening and alignment of platforms, connection of the station to the hillside parking facilities and modernisation of the station building. In order facilitate the above, it was necessary to revise the plans for the rail lines painstakingly conceived by the city's Urban Planning Department.

The moving of the station resulted in changes to the entire district:

- the shopping, hotel and restaurant functions of Guillemins Street and Square would no longer be driven by the 'locomotive' force of the station;
- the bars, lounges and cabarets of Varin Street would have to give way to accommodate the new 'Station Square';
- a new district opening out from the new station would have to be revitalised for the setting up of a new centre for shopping, business, services, housing and green spaces. At present, this environment is largely devoted to residential activities, along with nightlife (Varin Street) and storage. Traffic is poorly distributed with very little centrifugal movement. Furthermore,

in terms of the activity to be generated by the station, Varin Street is hardly the most desirable 'showcase' for Liège;

- behind the station, the 800-place hillside parking facility will be directly connected to the station by a massive floating slab and to the motorway network by an access road tangent to the tunnel connecting to motorways E25 and E40. Traffic around the station will have to be planned in order to discourage HST passengers (commuters, business people or simply occasional travellers) from using the exit hall of the station and instead take advantage of the station district. This 'cul-de-sac' effect of the new station is obviously being given a great deal of attention by planners;

- finally, the dominant ground use by buses and taxis in close proximity to the station must also be reviewed. In terms of public transport, the star-shaped network of the TEC (public transport company), already quite extensive, is unlikely to see major growth in terms of lines or traffic. Its demands on the station site should therefore not increase.

Urban Planning and Development

It would appear that all of the planning, infrastructure and technical access conditions are present in order to ensure optimal integration of the HST station into its environment. But how can it be best ensured that, with these advantages, the HST station also works to the benefit of the economy in Liège, which is today in great need? This is indeed the challenge. While the consumer base in Liège will grow with the arrival of the HST, this growth will not be sufficient to justify the wealth of precautions currently being taken by planners and project teams for the HST network and infrastructure in Liège. A policy of sustained marketing and promotion will be necessary to attract the Euregio clientele from deep within the hinterland.

To this end, the motorway link between Maastricht and Liège will be improved to offer 30-minute connections as soon as work is completed on the bypass of the E25-E40 motorways outside the city centre. Bearing in mind that it will be possible to access the new station parking facilities directly from the motorway, the new station will draw its customer base from the Euregio level. Within the context of creating a network of complementary rather than competitive cities in the same Euregional environment, the question is how to stimulate and solidify relations of support between cities rather than unfriendly, distrustful competition.

Finally, it is important that the railway companies reach an accord to improve rail connection times between the Euregion cities. For example, we know that a connection from Hasselt to Eupen (eastern Belgian cantons) takes longer than one from Liège to Maastricht. But there will be a Liège-Maastricht train with possible branch lines to the most rapid train to Brussels. We also know that the Maastricht population is demanding better connections with Luxembourg.

Other questions on a more local scale are also being raised: what importance should be given to land use as compared with the HST station function; which accompanying measures should be proposed to shopkeepers who must move away from Guillemins street to the new station commercial district, where property values will make it difficult for those seeking leases or the purchase of commercial space?

Note

1   Co-author: Mr Jean-François Sleijpen, City of Liège.

Annex 8   Background Information on Lille[1]

Profile

Table A8.1 Profile of the urban region of Lille

	Nord-Pas-de-Calais region	District of Lille
Surface area	12,430 km^2 (2.3% of national territory)	880 km^2
Population	3,965,000 (7% of French population)	1,157,113 (Lille: 172,149 or 15%)
Density (residents/ km$^{2)}$	319	1,313
Growth (82-90), (75-90)	0.1%	0.20%
Working population	1,560,000 (39.2% of total population)	489,169
Jobless rate	15%	13%
Cross-border workers	approx. 13,000	approx. 3,500 in each direction
Economic sectors		
Industry	4%	1.2%
Manufacturing	36%	29%
Tertiary	60%	69.7%

Source: INSEE census 1990, SDAU.

Table A8.2 Transport in the urban region of Lille

Urban transport 4 million daily transport moves in the district in 1988. Urban transport modal split: pedestrians 34%, public transport 8%, bicycles: 5%, cars: 52%

Air Lille-Lesquin: 800,000 passengers, 30,000 tons freight increase in total traffic since January 1996: +20%

Rail 45,000 passengers/day at Lille-Flanders (no. 1 provincial station for suburban traffic)

River 3rd largest river port in France. Total traffic: 7 million ton in 1990. Container traffic: 60,000 evp/year

Public transport 106 million passengers/year. Tramway system: 19 km, 38 stops. Metro system (V.A.L.): 28 km, 38 stations (+14 km and 20 new stations in 1999)

Source: City of Lille, 1996, *Fiches de synthèse*.

The Strategic Dimension

Approaching the turn of the century, two major infrastructure developments have had a profound impact on the north European region: the Channel Tunnel and the European high-speed rail network. They have been perceived, and have indeed become, the vehicles of a new dynamism in the Nord-Pas-de-Calais region. Back in 1986, the decision to create an HST stop in Lille was far from a reality. Competition for the rail service set the town of Amiens against the Lille metropolis. The political and economic strength of a region with a population of four million led the French government to choose a 'gravitational logic' over the 'shortest distance' argument advanced by Amiens.

This decision provided the HST with its first strategic dimension: the French concept of the high-speed train as a 'point-to-point network logic' gave way to a major regional development approach at work for a metropolis and its regional network of cities. A second strategic dimension saw the partisans of an ex nihilo localisation approach, leading to a multipolarisation of the urban environment, in competition with a development logic based upon the strengthening of existing centres. In contrast to the presupposition of the SNCF, in which the HST stop must be situated outside the dense urban environment in order to ensure optimal time and speed conditions for international connections, was a strong desire at the local level to profit from the 'HST effect' in order to reinforce the polarity of a 'fragmented' metropolitan region around its centre city, Lille.

The HST effect has also been considerably diffused by the creation of direct links to Paris from 11 towns in the region, participating in the construction of a true urban network, which is reinforced by the HST in its hierarchical organisation. However, in the Nord-Pas-de-Calais region, Lille is still the essential point of international service in a vast region incorporating a cross-border dimension (extending to Gand, possibly Antwerp), properly served by a regional communications network (rail and road).

The creation of a European high-speed rail network has thus provided an opportunity for the Nord-Pas-de-Calais region to promote its strategic position in northwestern Europe, structured around its economic and administrative centre. The increased speed offered by rail (one hour) and the frequency of HST service (17 daily round trips) between Lille and Paris have resulted in a contraction of space and time, giving birth to many aspirations, along with certain concerns, about the new relations between these two contrasting areas. The HST appeared as a powerful metropolisation factor to be exploited in order to ensure the city a place among Europe's great metropolises. The strategic dimension of the HST thus operates on several different levels and synthesises a number of voluntarist choices in terms of urban planning and development. Will the mere fact of HST service give Lille the international profile that it has lacked in the past? How can the entire region optimise the potential of this powerful vehicle for economic development? The 'development' dimension is the keystone of the HST strategy developed by local actors.

The Station Area and Secondary Transport

The advent of the HST has accentuated the saturation problems of the rail network around the Lille station. This infrastructure, which dates from the mid-nineteenth century, ends in a 'cul-de-sac', obliging the dead-ending of trains. In addition, it already handles heavy suburban traffic (as the number one provincial station in France in terms of traffic) and therefore cannot serve any new traffic created by the HST.

The decision to build a new station was therefore entirely logical. It is situated in a zone considered unsuitable for building and has been baptised 'Lille-Europe station'. The former station, located approximately 300 metres from this site, has been renamed 'Lille-Flanders station'. It continues to play an important role in handling regional traffic (RET). The decision to create this 'duality' of rail stations in Lille thus responds to the technical impossibility of accommodating international HST-service in the original station. The transfer of the total rail activity to the new Lille-Europe station has not been fully explored, nor has the potential solution of enlarging the Lille-Flanders station underground (although its saturation is already anticipated in 15 years' time). Major reorganisation work on the multi-modal junction for public transport has been completed, effectively reinforcing the role of Lille-Flanders as the network's main junction (two metro lines, tramway, bus station).

The 'juxtaposition' (300 metres or one metro station) of the two stations has generated problems in the organisation of the 'transport chain' on a regional level. The constraint in terms of HST/RET connections has undoubtedly hindered the distribution of 'high-speed' across the regional network. The large number of HSTs initiating from other regional cities (Paris destination only) must nevertheless be taken into account. This poor transport 'continuity' is further complicated in terms of cross-border connections on the HST, with Belgian travellers most often using their own vehicles along with the parking places made available in direct contact with the station. Despite the existence of the public transport junction at the level of 'Lille-Flanders', the international 'Lille-Europe' station enjoys quality service via the metro line 2 and the tramway.

The decision to stop the HST in the heart of Lille immediately ruled out the creation of any synergy with the Lille-Lesquin airport, which is now regretted. Following the conclusions of the Douffiagues report, the positioning of Lille airport in relation to Roissy (Paris-Charles de Gaulle), must be articulated with the high-speed network and based upon an optimal break of load.

The HST has thus been 'grafted' onto a well-developed metropolitan public transport network, without altering either its framework or its polarity. The project has enabled the improvement of pedestrian walkways between the centre and its near suburbs to the east (St Maurice), wiping out the break created by the ring road. On the other hand, bicycle path access to the stations has not been incorporated in the planning. The majority of changes are to the road system. Improvements in automobile traffic on the eastern ring road and the 'station site' development project necessitated the moving of this infrastructure further east. At the same time, extensive parking facilities have been built, largely exceeding the estimated needs of the stations (6,000 places at the Euralille site).

The lack of a planning tool which would enable the advent of the HST and accompanying development to be considered as part of an overall transport logic on a metropolitan scale, suggests that the accommodation of the high-speed train in Lille has served to strengthen an already well-established local road logic rather than generating a practical approach to urban transport management.

Urban Planning and Development

The HST is part of a major urban and metropolitan project designed to reinforce the polarity of its central city, Lille. As early as 1987, P. Mauroy expressed his wish 'not to stop the HST in the Pampas', as the SNCF then planned to do, promoting instead an exurbanised site 15 km south of Lille (Seclin). The intervention of the public authorities would play a determining role. A financial commitment of 800 million francs (50 per cent by the state and 50 per cent by local authorities), corresponding to the additional cost of infrastructure to accommodate the HST in the dense urban zone, convinced the SNCF of the legitimacy of urban service. However, aware that the trains could only pass through, without any local added-value, the elected representatives decided to create a substantial project: 'Euralille, a tertiary turbine' (P. Mauroy), in order to take advantage of the fallout of the high-speed train and guarantee Lille a definitive place in the 21st century.

The urban dimension of the project is therefore essential to a 'fragmented' metropolitan city. The HST offers both the opportunity to polarise an area seeking coherence and synergy, and bring back a certain dynamism to a city centre hard hit by the exurbanisation of economic activity. A site considered unsuitable for building, which housed the old Glacis of the fortifications built by Vauban, was selected to accommodate the international HST station and the new tertiary pole, a few hundred metres from the existing station and centre. The Euralille project was awarded to Dutch architect Rem Koolhaas, who was given the challenge of imagining and conceiving a 'piece of town' at an abandoned site crossed by transport infrastructure. With the total perimeter of the site covering 150 hectares, the development was designed in two phases.

The involvement of public authorities in the project has remained strong, both in terms of land management, with the creation of a ZAC (concerted development zone), and financial control, with the creation of a Société Anonyme d'Economie Mixte (semi-public company). The HST and Euralille also furnished the occasion to federate the Urban Community of Lille (86 communes, over one million inhabitants), structured around a metropolitan development project, just as the metro had been 10 years earlier. The overall project cost 5.1 billion francs, one-third of which was funded by the public sector.

Today, the majority of Phase One is operational. This includes the station itself along with the shopping centre and the 'Grand Palais' convention centre, which have rapidly found their place in local life. The project housing was quickly marketed. However, following a difficult economic period (the Gulf War, recession), there are fewer takers for office space and certain projects have yet to be completed. In particular, two small towers of the 'Station Triangle' remain to be built and the four-star hotel has yet to be realised. Currently, there is no talk of completing Phase Two of the project.

The project has nonetheless enabled Lille to be reconnected to its suburbs immediately to the east and to revitalise one of its major access points (Roubaix gateway). Links with the centre have been improved but the entire site remains fragmented in the absence of the ring road detour. This handicap should be overcome by 1998 but the 'piece of town' with its massive towers is the source of some questions and concerns. The major international groups that the 'tertiary turbine' was supposed to attract are still lacking, even though the project's notoriety (along with that of the HST and the Channel Tunnel) has elicited new interest in the city and its region.

Note

1   Co-author: Mr. Damien Caudron, City of Lille.

Annex 9 Background Information on Lyon[1]

Profile

Population (INSEE, 1990)

- City of Lyon: 415,487;
- Urban Community of Lyon: 1,134,687;
- Lyon Urban Region (RUL): 2,476,004;
- Rhône-Alpes Region: 5,350,701.

Higher Education

- 112,000 students in Lyon Urban Region (RUL) in 1994;
- 6,764 engineering students in Lyon-area schools in 1994 (Toulouse is the second city after Lyon, with 4,440 engineering students).

Table A9.1 Economic activity in and around Lyon (ASSEDIC, 1992): breakdown of private-sector employment

	Industry	Services	Retail	Building/ Public Works
RUL	35%	34%	22%	9%
Rhône-Alpes	37%	37%	17%	9%
France	32%	39%	19%	10%

Major Industrial Sectors in the RUL (ASSEDIC, 1992)

Construction, mechanics (38,552 employees); smelting, metal works (31,312); Textiles, clothing (28,477); electricity, electronics (27,911); car manufacturing and transportation equipment (20,084); parachemical, pharmaceuticals (14,296); food processing (13,055); rubber, plastics (11,401); chemicals, artificial fibres (11,110).

Total Number of Hotels in Lyon Metropolitan Area (CCIL, 1993)

** establishments:	4,520 rooms;
*** establishments:	2,930 rooms;
**** luxury:	990 rooms.

219

Air Transport: Traffic at Lyon-Satolas Airport, 1995

In 1996, traffic at Lyon-Satolas increased by 12.1 per cent compared to 1995, reaching 4,967,142 passengers. The same year, the level of 50 per cent international traffic was surpassed for the first time.

Rail Transport

Perrache: 26,500 passengers per day in 1984, 24,000 in 1992;
Part-Dieu: 27,000 passengers per day in 1984, 37,000 in 1992;
Satolas: total traffic at the airport HST station of 192,543 passengers in 1996.

Urban Transport

- surface routes: average traffic on a busy day in 1994: 498,511 trips;
- underground (four lines, 26 km): traffic on a busy day in 1994: 452,353 trips.

HST Programme

In addition to the Lyon-Paris line already in service, three new lines are provided for in the development plan: Mediterranean (to Marseille, Montpellier, Nice, Barcelona), Lyon-Turin (to Turin, Milan), Rhine-Rhône (to Strasbourg, Zurich, Frankfurt). Service on the Mediterranean line is scheduled to begin in 1999.

The Strategic Dimension

Lyon, a Growing Metropolis

The strategic dimension of the high-speed train may only be appreciated in terms of its relation to the city's overall economic profile. Lyon is second only to Paris as a major economic centre in France and it is capital of the Rhône-Alpes region, the country's second most important economic region. For the past 10 years, the city has been developing a high-level of expertise and across an increasingly large region, in the key areas of trade, logistics, management and tertiary. The results of these efforts have become apparent in recent years as the Lyon region has successfully attracted major industrial concerns (Hewlett Packard, Laffarge Coppée, etc.), marking a key change after 40 years of the postwar period.

These observations demonstrate that the Lyon and Rhône-Alpes economic base offers a strong capacity to take full advantage of the future HST service. While there is no reason to imagine that new HST lines will enable Lyon to take over the higher economic functions which are the privileged domain of Paris, the two key developments noted above are likely to grow considerably stronger.

The Strategic Dimension of the HST

On a more precise level, the strategic challenges of the high-speed train may be outlined in the following four points:

- the growth of Lyon-Satolas Airport. With the HST station operating at Satolas, the high-speed train will expand the airport's market radius and therefore contribute to the development of intercontinental flights. On this point, the challenge consists in encouraging operators (primarily the SNCF) to implement an integrated HST-air offer;
- a European star. The HST-star which is to be built in the urban area places Lyon at the centre of a transport mechanism offering access in less than three and a half hours to Europe's major metropolises. This strategic position will allow Lyon to reinforce its economic development on a European level, especially in terms of marketing and logistics;
- a strengthening of proximity. By reducing centre-to-centre travel times to less than one and a half hours between Lyon and major centres such as Marseille, Turin and Montpellier, the high-speed train will enable the Lyon metropolitan area to reinforce its influence over an area covering approximately the southeast quarter of France and a section of northern Italy. In concrete terms, the objective for Lyon is to develop tertiary, management and marketing functions across the southeast part of the country to a level competitive with those of Paris in this region;
- a multi-modal crossroads for a diversified metropolis. Lyon and Rhône-Alpes are privileged with a wide variety of economic sectors and functions. The geographic situation of Lyon on the motorway network is excellent. The construction of an HST-star and development of airport traffic are two key elements which will enable the city to operate as an area of integration for its economic sectors and functions, in a general context marked by the internationalisation of trade.

The Station Area and Secondary Transport

HST Stations Have Already been Built in Lyon

While three out of four HST lines to make up the Lyon HST-star are not yet built (Mediterranean HST is due to begin service in 1999), the metropolitan area already has three stations: Perrache (former central station), Part-Dieu (new central station, operational since 1983), Satolas (airport connection open since 1994). For Lyon, the question of accommodating the high-speed train is largely in terms of accompanying policies and operational strategies.

Determining the Role of Each Station in the Medium-to-long Term

Perrache station is losing momentum, although it continues to play an essential role for regional express trains. In light of its advantageous position on the Lyon's Presqu'île and its excellent accessibility for public transport, the station still has development potential. However, costly investments would seem necessary on the tracks which serve the station, particularly from the west.

Part-Dieu rapidly took over as Lyon's central station. Located along the major access route Paris-Lyon-Marseille, and with all the advantages of the HST dynamic combined with strong growth in employment and housing in the surrounding district, the station brings together all assets vital for development. However, this is dependent upon finding solutions to the increasing congestion of the lines which serve Part-Dieu.

Satolas station will develop along with the construction of future HST lines and growth in airport traffic. Its development will also be influenced by the completion of certain projects designed to make the station more accessible to regional express trains and improve access from Lyon city centre.

The problem of achieving growth at all three stations is therefore related to that of investment and operational considerations in connection with the HST offer. Choices must be made. These will be influenced by decisions in three areas: operational strategy of the rail junction in terms of the dual function of serving metropolitan area traffic and rail connections through the stations; the evolution of the urban public transport network; development plans for the metropolitan area.

Transport Policy

The primary problem is that of the city's two centres (Part-Dieu and Presqu'île) a poorly articulated design both in terms of rail lines and public transport. The urban accessibility of the Part-Dieu station is insufficient. Beyond service to the station itself, that of the left bank of the Rhône must be more generally evaluated. For historical reasons, the structuring network of public transportation in Lyon is articulated around Presqu'île, although the flows sent and received by the left bank are now equivalent. Table A9.2 illustrates this analysis: the number of users making connections (between metro and bus) at Part-Dieu is very low compared to that of Bellecour, Perrache or Hôtel de Ville. The city is looking at ways to correct this problem within the context of its Urban Transport Programme, currently under review.

Table A9.2 Number of users making connections on the urban public transport system in main stations of Lyon (typical weekday between 6 a.m. and 7 p.m.)

Presqu'île Stations	Connections	Left Bank Stations	Connections	Other Stations	Connections
Bellecour	39,300	Saxe-Gambetta	27,600	Bonnevay	34,100
Hôtel de Ville	25,100	Charpennes	28,500	Gorge de Loup	20,200
Perrache	21,500	Part-Dieu	7,100		
Cordeliers	12,700	Jean-Macé	18,000		

Urban Planning and Development

The Stations and their Districts

Quite classically, the Perrache and Part-Dieu stations, along with the network of tracks which serve them, create a break in the urban fabric. Since the nineteenth century, the Perrache station has prevented the southern tip of Presqu'île from developing according to an urban model corresponding with its central position in the city. In the 1960s, this rupture effect was further exaggerated with the completion of the motorway route A6–A7 which cuts across the Presqu'île parallel to the railway track, and with the construction of the Perrache trade centre. The current political direction is to develop the (highly symbolic) southern Presqu'île site. This development is in conjunction with the completion of major motorway bypasses of the city, which will enable traffic on the A6-A7 route in the city centre to be reprocessed.

The Part-Dieu district, conceived in the 1960s–70s, no longer corresponds to current urban planning criteria. Its organisation gives the automobile too great a place; it is poorly integrated into the surrounding urban fabric; and Part-Dieu station is itself insufficiently integrated within the district. Numerous urban planning operations are enabling the addressing of such defects. The changes are being made possible by virtue of the fact that the Part-Dieu district and its surrounding areas are undergoing development and increasing density at the present time.

Satolas Station and Lyon's Greater East

Satolas station, connected to the airport, is located 25 kilometres to the east of Lyon. This area is experiencing strong growth, reinforced by a high concentration of major infrastructure, particularly motorways. Further development related to the HST station and the airport in the years to come is likely to accentuate this trend.

For the urban community of Lyon, this evolution presents a twofold problem: urban sprawl and an imbalance between east and west. The question today is that of the capacity of the regional authorities to conceive and carry out a development plan for the eastern Lyon region, as the multi-modal hub of Satolas is situated outside the bounds of the urban community of Lyon, at the boundary between the Rhône and Isère departments, and in proximity to the Ain department. This institutional configuration hardly simplifies the implementation of such a development plan.

The urban community of Lyon is arguing for an expansion of its territory. This enlargement to the east would facilitate the urban planning process and shed new light upon the issues surrounding the development of the multi-modal hub at Satolas and its connection to the city centre.

Note

1   Co-author: Mr Jean-Loup Molin, Communauté Urbaine de Lyon.

Annex 10   Background Information on Marseille[1]

The Strategic Dimension

The arrival of the HST in Marseille fits perfectly into the context of the newly adopted state strategy concerning the Marseille metropolitan area and the city itself.

The greater metropolitan area of Marseille is defined by the large industrial-port and petrochemical complex of Fos to the west; Aix-en-Provence, a city with a dynamic tertiary sector and with excellent land reserves to the north; and to the east, a 'pole' of medium-size cities (Gémenos, Aubagne, La Ciotat) which has benefited from special tax exemptions as a business development zone in compensation by the state for the slump in the shipbuilding repair sector in La Ciotat.

Within this great multipolar metropolitan region, despite the demographic dominance of Marseille (53.9 per cent of the population), a classic yet undoubtedly excessive urban relaxation effect has been observed. Marseille has seen a disturbing trend towards demographic erosion and relocation of many businesses to outlying areas offering the easily developed areas which the city has been unable to provide within its own boundaries.

However, the most important factor is due to a decline in the 'metropolitan functions' of Marseille resulting from the radical transformation of its port. From its former position as a gateway to the French colonies, the port area has reoriented itself towards Fos with its petrochemical activities. The port of Marseille is today to a large extent outside the city.

Aware of this situation, and the remarkable advantages offered by Marseille, the only great French metropolis of the southern Mediterranean region, the state has entered into a 'national interest operation'. This process is designed to once again give the city a national and international role based upon its tradition as a centre of trade and international cooperation, by offering development assistance and reinforcing the tertiary sector in Marseille city centre. This is the 'Euromediterranean' project, established by a state structure (public urban development institution) of the same nature as that created to manage the *La Défense* programme in Paris.

Offering connections to the very heart of the city, the HST will also reinforce the role of Marseille in national and European communications networks and thus its position as a metropolis. It will contribute to the launching and structuring of the Euromediterranean project which encompasses the HST station and its district. It is also an opportunity to reopen the project file for a bus-lane public transport system in the Marseille urban area, which has been awaiting funding for many years.

The Station Area and Secondary Transport

The Mediterranean HST unquestionably marks a profound transformation in Marseille's transport chain.

Rail in Competition with Air

The SNCF is betting on the HST providing competition to air travel on the Paris-Marseille line, one of the country's most highly frequented and profitable air links. The high-speed train will undoubtedly provide strong competition to air service. The degree of this competition is not yet known, since the opening of the European skies to competition subsequent to the launch of the Mediterranean HST is creating a new situation whose consequences on HST/ air competition are difficult to assess.

While the airlines and Marignane Airport generally consider that the HST will likely take less market share than forecast by the SNCF, the airport has already registered a drop in national traffic (70 per cent today) and would like to increase its international connections within Europe, on one hand, and to Africa and Asia on the other (18 per cent today). Furthermore, the airport would like to offset the disadvantage of its location 25 km from Marseille by developing public transport systems, either by adding to shuttle and express bus services or, in the long term, with a bus lane transportation system which has yet to be defined.

As Regards Regional Transport

The metropolitan area suffers from a serious delay in investments in infrastructure, and rail does not play the role which it is capable of. The most typical example is that of the Aix-Marseille connection which links the department's two largest cities with a single non-electrified track. The advent of HST service seems to have reopened this file and a partnership has already formed to ensure the doubling of half of the line by 2000 as the new HST line becomes operational.

The creation of a new line penetrating the urban area parallel to the historic

Paris-Marseille line is freeing up traffic in terms of Marseille-northwest links, namely to l'Etang de Berre, a connection whose service is today poorly adapted and undersized.

The arrival of the HST has provided the occasion for a study which should lead to a reshaping of the service and redevelopment of certain local stations.

The objective of the city of Marseille is to create a dominant conception of a 'metropolitan station' in which St Charles is the nodal point of the rail network, and the arrival of HST traffic along with high-performance RTRs enabling the HST effect to be distributed throughout the urban area. All of the different public-sector actors wish to relieve surface congestion which is beginning to near saturation on major routes, in favour of rail service.

Urban Planning and Development

The advent of the HST coupled with the Euromediterranean urban development project is providing the occasion for a dynamic new urban planning policy designed to completely transform the centre of Marseille.

At present, the station district is an area which people pass through without stopping, either because they use St Charles station and the adjoining bus terminal, or access the Nord motorway system by road. This creates a large number of road trips along with a break in the urban fabric. Combined with a lack of consumer shops and services, this does not make the St Charles district a high-quality area, nor one which the people of Marseille have particularly adopted.

The Mediterranean HST is therefore an opportunity for a profound reshaping of this core district based on several basic principles:

- first of all, the station which is in many ways out of date and inconvenient for passengers is to be totally redeveloped and modernised, for a cost of approximately 230 million francs;
- to free up surface routes and facilitate access to the station, north-south traffic from the Nord motorway will be moved underground, passing beneath the station;
- a close link between the station and the adjoining university, which is to be expanded in the years to come, will be established so as to enable the student population to create its own centre of urban life. In addition to a quality pedestrian connection, a public space such as a large square is to be earmarked for this purpose between the station and the university;

- the station and its immediate vicinity are integrated into a specific urban planning project ('ZAC' concerted development zone), with overall responsibility taken by the Euromediterranean Public Institution. The area around the station will thus see a potential development of 100,000 m^2 of net surface area for office and residential space, student housing, hotels, shops and services;
- with the station currently poorly connected to the city, priority will be given to opening up the station to the Euromediterranean project and the port area, the heart of the new development project.

Note

1   Co-author: Mr Vincent Touze, City of Marseilles.

Annex 11 Background Information on Nantes[1]

Profile

Population and Employment

With 520,000 residents in 1996, the urban area of Nantes is the seventh largest metropolis in France by population size. The bipolar metropolitan area of Nantes/St Nazaire (which is called Nantes Atlantique) today numbers some 750,000 inhabitants, ranking fifth on a national basis. Nantes Atlantique has a younger population than the national average: the percentage of under 25s is equivalent to 36.5 per cent (Loire-Atlantique) compared to 34.1 per cent at a national level.

In terms of growth (1982–96) and in comparison with the top 10 French cities, Nantes takes third place with 5.7 per cent growth, after Toulouse (12.4 per cent) and Bordeaux (6.9 per cent). Generally speaking, major cities on the Atlantic coast (Rennes, Nantes Atlantique and Bordeaux) have a higher-than-average growth rate. This growth in the population is essentially created by the natural balance sheet. The migratory balance (+0.15 per cent) puts the department in a median position. In regards to this balance, incoming population flows exceed outgoing, except in the 18–30 year range. In terms of socio-professional categories, there is an equal number of incoming and outgoing movement at the managerial level.

Total employment in Loire-Atlantique is approximately 400,000 jobs, representing an average increase of 1–2 per cent per annum in recent years (1988–91), below the national average. For 1992, however, UNEDIC statistics on salaried employment show that Pays de la Loire is among the five regions least impacted by the recession, as they alone have managed to increase their number of employed persons (+0.24 per cent). With 226,000 employed, the Nantes urban area represents 56 per cent of jobs in Loire-Atlantique.

Table A11.1 Population in and around Nantes

	1986	1987	1988	1989	1990	1991	1996
Population (x 1,000)							
Nantes (urban area)	478.6	482.0	485.4	488.8	492.2	495.6	520.0
Saint-Nazaire (urban area)	130.8	131.0	131.1	131.3	131.5	131.6	132.0
Loire-Atlantique	1,023.9	1,031.0	1,038.1	1,045.3	1,052.2	1,059.5	1,100.0

Working Population

The working population residing in the urban area has grown faster than the total population +5.7 per cent between 1982 and 1990). This increase in the number of working people is dependent upon two factors: growth in the population of working-age individuals and behaviour changes related to the job market (employment among women, young people, etc.)

The former factor has had a determining effect on the city: the population of 35–45 year olds, the most active category, increased by 37 per cent from 1982 to 1990. We can observe that employment in the Nantes urban area offers increasingly greater appeal: more and more jobs are held by residents from outside areas and only 7 per cent of Nantes residents work outside the urban area. On 1 January 1994, the jobless rate for the Nantes employment area was 16.6 per cent.

Economic Sectors

There were 2,000 agriculture jobs in the Nantes district in 1990 (1.7 per cent of total employment). The number of jobs in the agricultural sector decreased dramatically between 1982 and 1990: -37 per cent. This reduction represents approximately 1,000 jobs in the district.

In the retail there were 28,500 jobs in the district in 1990 (12.7 per cent of total employment). Retail is experiencing a moderate rise in employment (1.3 per cent), which mainly concerns the supermarket food sector: +45 per cent (+1,150 jobs). A drop can be seen in convenience and speciality food stores: -28 per cent (-930 jobs).

Industry represented over 42,000 jobs in the district in 1990, (18.7 per cent of total). Industrial-sector jobs decreased by 11 per cent between 1982 and 1990. Building and public works represents 15,400 jobs (6.8 per cent of total) and remained stable up to 1990

There were 137,000 jobs in the service sector in the district in 1990 (60.9 per cent of total). Growth in this sector (+23 per cent) represents 25,300 additional jobs in the district. Major areas include general administration (public service) with 20,900 jobs, teaching (public sector) with 17,150 jobs, health (independent practitioners, clinics, hospitals) with 14,500 jobs.

The Strategic Dimension

The Nantes-Atlantique Airport

With a location in the near suburbs (seven km from the city centre) the airport enjoys excellent access via the ring road (with no traffic lights). Recently modernised, in 1995 it provided service for 1,244,360 passengers (+7.1 per cent over the previous year), 7,557 tons of freight (+2.5 per cent) and 31,697 aircraft movements (+15.1 per cent).

The autonomous Port of Nantes/Saint-Nazaire is the fourth largest port in France, it ensures 27 million tons of traffic per year. 1993 began with the bringing on line of a sand terminal and concluded with the opening of a 300,000 ton capacity fruit terminal in Montoir. The latter makes Nantes Atlantique the nation's third largest port for fruit and vegetable imports. Container traffic has increased by 300 per cent in five years. Several lines regularly serve Africa, the West Indies, South America, Spain and the Indian Ocean. The majority of traffic is of the container type.

The challenge for the Nantes/Saint-Lazaire port is reinforcing its role as the leading port on the Atlantic coast, adapting to foreseeable changes (coastal navigation and feedering) and serving businesses within its area, particularly small-and-medium size companies at the regional level, by pursuing the development of diverse containerised goods traffic.

The Atlantic HST

Operational since 1989, the Atlantic HST ensures 17 (two hour) connections with Paris per day. The new Massy station also enables direct connections from Nantes to Lyon (four and a half hours), with three round trips per day. The link with the HST North enables connections from Nantes to Lille (less than three and a half hours) (summer 1996). Regional traffic is served essentially by train.

Road Networks

A recent opening up of the road system enables rapid links with major western cities, Paris and, in the near future, Spain and the central and eastern regions. Travel time via the direct Nantes-Paris motorway link is about three and a half hours. Nantes ring road: two km longer than the Paris ring road, it enables the bypass of the urban area and links the city to the motorway network.

There are two tramway lines in the city. The first line (east/west: 12.5 km) began service in 1985. The second line (centre/south: 5.2 km) was inaugurated in 1993. Its extension (8.3 km) north to Orvault was completed in September 1994. A third line (southeast/northwest) is under construction.

The Station Area and Secondary Transport

In the twenty-first century, the growth cities will be those who manage to reconcile development demands with environmental protection. With this in mind, the district intends to ensure that all of its urban residents enjoy the services of a major modern city along with a certain quality of life. In terms of transportation, the district's 21 communes have combined their efforts to develop complementarity among transport modes (public transport, car, bicycle, pedestrian) and enable all to move about in harmony.

To control the growth which was leading to long-term air pollution problems for the city, the district with the support of its think tank, AURAN (Nantes Area Agency for Urban Studies) adopted an overall plan in 1991 to improve transport conditions by 2000. Today well under way, the ambitious plan was based upon a fundamental principle: 'creating a new balance'. This balance is that which must be achieved between cars, buses, tramways, motorcycles, bicycles and pedestrians in order to improve the transport conditions of each and make the city more pleasant for all.

Within this framework, the objectives are the following:

- promoting the use of ring road to make urban traffic safer and more fluid. An essential part of the urban infrastructure, the ring road completed in 1994 is not a motorway (90 per cent of its traffic concerns internal moves within the metropolitan area and exchanges with the exterior. Identified by gateways, it ensures links between major districts, allows the city to breathe and simplifies access to its centre;
- transforming access roads into urban boulevards. Located on the interior of the ring road, some of these routes similar to motorways are being redeveloped as urban boulevards. The city centre's second bypass ring is improving (roundabouts on the nineteenth-century boulevards). A city centre service route (*Coeur*) was set up with the objective of enabling automobile drivers arriving in town to move about intelligently alongside other transport mode users. The development of the Beaulieu interchange on the southern access route is an excellent example of this approach;

- creating new crossings on the Loire. To reinforce the urban area's various bypass alternatives and improve traffic flows, the district has built two new bridges over the Loire (Willy Brandt and Trois Continents). Other crossings are currently being studied;
- increasing use of public transport. The city's public transport system today comprises two tramway lines, and 55 bus lines and a town/airport bus link. The total offer represents 18.1 million kilometres travelled in 1995. Total traffic on the public transport system was 85 million trips in 1995. The major component of the urban area's transport program is the tramway. It is the centrepiece in promoting public transport use, a program which also involves: reinforcement and modernisation of the bus network; harmonisation of urban and inter-urban networks (TAN and ATLANTIC); use of the existing rail system in the planned creation of 'REDD', an express rail network serving the district and the department between Sucé/Erdre and Rezé-Pont-Rousseau (north-south link); and development of complementarity between private car and public transport, with the creation of commuter parking facilities close to major access stations;
- developing pedestrian and two-wheeled transport modes. Two development plans for two-wheeled and pedestrian transport created by AURAN have been adopted by the district. Jointly developed on behalf of the communes, the district is providing 75 per cent of funding for the necessary facilities.

Note

1   Co-author: Mr Jean-Paul Jacquet, City of Nantes.

Annex 12   Background Information on Rotterdam

Profile

Rotterdam is a characteristic example of a city at the 'reurbanisation' stage. After years of population losses, the records have recently once more shown a slight growth. From the end of the nineteenth century, when transport, industry and trade functions (shipbuilding, harbour works, petrochemical industry, wholesale trade, etc.) were flourishing, Rotterdam experienced a strong population growth culminating in a (record) population of 732,000 in 1965. From the 1970s onward, the rising prosperity and, in its wake, greater mobility, changing residential preferences, decreasing average dwelling occupancy and a national policy directed towards deconcentration led to a net population loss of about 160,000 inhabitants in 20 years. That very selective deconcentration ('suburbanisation') resulted, in combination with the effects of the 1973 and 1978 energy crises, in grave socioeconomic problems.

On the wave of the international economic recovery, rigorous policy changes on the national as well as the local level helped to stem the tide: by 1985 the decay of the city of Rotterdam had come to an end. At that time the city counted 571,000 inhabitants. Since then the population has grown slightly, to 599,000 in 1994. To make the Rotterdam economy less vulnerable to international and macroeconomic developments, attempts are being made to diversify the economic structure by reinforcing the specialised services related to transportation and distribution (or, to put it another way, by giving more attention to the international 'director's function' in the sector of sea and inland water transport). Since the mid-1980s, business services in particular have increased. Rotterdam has considerably improved its image as an 'office city' in relation to the pronounced Dutch office cities Amsterdam and The Hague.

The Strategic Dimension

For the purpose of constructing new infrastructure for the HST in the Netherlands, a HSL project-developing unit has been created, in which the Ministry of Traffic and Public Works and the Netherlands Railways participate. In May 1996 the government stated its preference with respect to the planned line service between Schiphol and Rotterdam. Its choice was a direct connection which was to be shorter than the present rail and road infrastructure

234

Table A12.1 Economic data of the Rotterdam region 1995

Sectors	Persons employed			Establishments		
	Amount (x 1,000)	% region Rotterdam	% The Netherlands	Amount	% Region Rotterdam	% The Netherlands
Petrochemical industry	17.9	6	4	122	<1	<1
Other industry	37.4	13	22	2,562	6	8
Construction	26.0	9	11	2,770	6	8
Wholesale trade	33.7	12	12	6,458	15	13
Retail trade	33.9	12	13	8,791	20	22
Transport	41.3	14	8	4,251	10	5
Other services	96.4	34	30	18,187	43	44
Total	287	100	100 (3,423)	43,700	100	100 (570,000)

Source: *Enquete regionale bedrijfsontwikkeling Rijnmond* 1995.

connecting the two mainports. Because the track traverses the so-called 'Green Heartland' of the Randstad, it will be led through a nine-km-long tunnel. After the completion of the new HST track, which is expected by the end of the next decade, the journey between Amsterdam and Paris will take just over three hours.

Table A12.2 Travel times by HST to Rotterdam

Rotterdam to	Schiphol	Amsterdam	Brussels	Paris	London
Present situation	0h45	1h04	1h54	5h04	8h00
Thalys (existing line)	0h43	1h00	1h38	3h46	4h39
New line	0h19	0h35	1h03	2h31	3h37

Source: Ministry of Traffic and Public Works, 1994, *New HST-note.*

The new HST-track will reduce rail travel times from Rotterdam to Brussels, Paris and London by about half (see Table A12.2), which implies a significant improvement of international accessibility. With the new HST connection, in terms of travel time Brussels will be as near to Rotterdam as Amsterdam. Table A12.3 shows the travel times to several other European cities by different transport modes, such as the HST, the car and the plane. From the table, the HST is by far the speediest mode for a trip to Brussels, while air travel is quicker to other destinations, especially those served by Rotterdam Airport. The HST seems a good alternative for transport by air over distances up to 500 km. The HST becomes more attractive as its services become more frequent. There are other elements that influence the travellers' choice of transport, such as the possibility of travelling straight to the city centres, and the chance of doing some (undisturbed) work during the journey.

As a matter of fact, the HST connection between Schiphol and Rotterdam will also reduce the travel time to cities served by Schiphol. For instance, the travel time by air to Lyon will drop from three hours 26 minutes to two hours 59 minutes, which will enhance the appeal of air travel. Moreover, with the advance of information technology, travel times by air may be expected to become shorter as some procedures (checking in, safety checks, etc.) are speeded up or left out altogether. On certain distances, the aeroplane may then win back some market share from the HST.

Estimates have been made of the expected international passenger traffic by HST from and to the Netherlands. Depending on the HST version chosen (track, stopping places and frequency), the estimates vary from 3.7 to eight million trips a year. On the Amsterdam-Rotterdam line, a maximum of 6.3 million domestic travellers are foreseen. That flow of passengers will presumably be composed of 1.6 million newly-generated passengers, 0.6 million passengers who used to travel by car, and 4.1 million who already travelled by rail (*New HSL-Note*, 1994, partial report 1).

Table A12.3 Present and future travel times from Rotterdam to different European cities via different transport modes

Rotterdam to	distance (km)	Car	Plane	Train	HST
Brussels	149	1h 41	2h 31 [1]	2h 02	1h 03
Paris	441	4h 38	2h 15 [2]	4h 56	2h 31
Lyon	858	8h 48	3h 26 [1]	7h 08	5h 42
Genève	950	9h 42	3h 16 [1]	8h 47	7h 21
Munchen	834	8h 33	3h 21 [1]		
Berlin	690	7h 12	3h 06 [1]	8h 09	
London	470 [4]	7h 14	1h 45 [3]	8h 00	3h 37
Milan	1038	11h 08	3h 36 [1]		

Sources: KLM, Atlas, NS, Ministerie van Verkeer en Waterstaat (1994).

1   Via Schiphol Airport. Calculated time for Rotterdam-Schiphol: 46 min.; calculated check-in time: 1 hour.
2   From Rotterdam Airport. Calculated check-in time: 30 min.; calculated time Paris CDG - centrum Paris: 30 min.
3   London City Airport from Rotterdam Airport. Calculated check-in time: 30 min.
4   Via Calais.

When the new HST track between Amsterdam and Rotterdam is complete, the travel time by train will be about halved (from one hour and four minutes to 35 minutes, see Table A12.2). For the domestic market such a reduction of travel time will be highly significant, for it implies a very competitive alternative to transport by car. On the HST track, extra shuttle services will be put in between the HSTs, so that every hour there will be four fast trains running between the two agglomerations.

The Randstad is a polycentric urban area, with more or less fragmented sales, labour and office markets. The HST is expected to assume a significant part of the transport between the northern and southern wings of the Randstad. A fast HST connection between the two Randstad wings can stimulate the integration of social-economic activities in such a way that the economic specialities and production environments complement and reinforce one another. However, the question which then suggests itself is in which areas in the Randstad integration is most likely to proceed? Connection to the HST network will change the pattern of relevant regions of economic activities, making them less continuous in space. Access to the areas around the HST stations will be improved, while the intervening zones will become relatively less approachable. Therefore, integration of activities due to the advent of the HST is most probable between areas within a certain radius around an HST station. The radius will depend on the quality of the secondary traffic services. The better such services are, the larger will be the zone profiting from the arrival of the HST.

The Station Area and Secondary Transport

Around the central station of Rotterdam there is a concentration of houses, services and office buildings. For some travellers the direct environment of the CS will therefore be either the point of departure or the final destination. However, they make up only a relatively small portion of the total number of passengers. The majority of travellers will need additional transport. In principle, all modes for the transportation of people by road or rail from the CS are available. Passenger cars are by far the most important transport mode. Of all moves within or from and to the region, the passenger car accounts for 58 per cent, public transport and bicycles for 17 and 25 per cent, respectively.[1]

Rail: there are 16 railway stations in the region of Rotterdam. Table A12.4 represents the passenger flows through the stations situated within the municipality of Rotterdam. The central station (CS) is by far the most important stopping place for passengers in Rotterdam. The passenger flows through CS are more than seven times those passing through Prins Alexander Station, the second in number of passengers. CS is also the principal junction for public transport in the urban region of Rotterdam. All types of public transport call at the CS. Because many new social and economic activities have settled around the Prins Alexander station in the last 10 years, the passenger flows passing through that stopping place have been tripled. Many new activities have also located around the Blaak station, which consequently has similarly drawn many more travellers than before.

Metro city railway: Rotterdam has a well-functioning system of partially underground city railways, operating at relatively high frequencies. The basic network consists of a north-south and an east-west connection. The system links the centre of Rotterdam with several suburbs, such as Zevenkamp, Ommoord, Capelle on IJssel, Spijkenisse and Hoogvliet.

Tramway: the tramway system of Rotterdam consists of 14 lines, and can be boarded at acceptable walking distances from most locations in Rotterdam. Because the tracks tend to wind and twist through the streets of Rotterdam and reserved lanes are rare, trams are not an adequate complementary means of conveyance for the HST at the moment.

Buses and coaches: from the central station of Rotterdam several bus and coach services depart to destinations outside the centre and the agglomeration. Because of relatively long travel times, these public transport services are no match for the HST. Business travellers especially do not look upon bus transport as an adequate secondary transport mode.

Table A12.4 Number of rail passengers in Rotterdam railway stations (x 1,000)

Station	1985	1993	Percentage change 1985–93
Centraal Station	7,320	13,705	87
Prins Alexander	582	1,849	218
Lombardijen	510	1,270	149
Blaak	231	839	263
Noord	170	527	210
Hofplein/Bergweg/Kleiweg	341	380	11
Zuid	91	159	75
Wilgenplas	79	120	52

Source: Centrum voor Onderzoek en Statistiek, 1995.

Urban Planning and Development

In the direct environment of the central station of Rotterdam quite a lot of new building has been going on. Especially in the last decade many modern office buildings have been erected along the Weena, buildings that reflect the image of the New Rotterdam. A new shopping arcade has also been realised here. The paving and the shop fronts of the Lijnbaan shopping promenade have been renewed, mostly in response to the realisation of the new underground shopping mall near the Beursplein (Exchange Square). The area on and around the Schouwburgplein has undergone a metamorphosis. A new theatre and a new mega-cinema have been created and the theatre square has been reorganised. Next to the Doelen concert building a congress centre and a hotel are being realised.

The square in front of the central station is thought unappealing and chaotic by most people. Several transport modes – trams, buses and taxicabs – share this public space with pedestrians and cyclists. The square is a nightmare, especially to pedestrians: there are no logical and safe walking routes between the town centre and the railway station. With its heavy crisscross traffic flows, it can hardly be called a friendly public place.

Connection to the HST system might well give a positive impulse to the improvement of the public spaces adjoining the station. In view of the additional transport flows that will be generated, the advent of the HST could be the right moment to take steps towards a safer and more comfortable integration of the traffic flows in the area. Travellers moving on foot between the station and the town centre ought to find a safe, logical and pleasant route, where the nuisance from other traffic should be reduced to a minimum. Moreover, the station square and the station building should be given the appeal and status of an HST terminal worthy of the name. The area deserves a (modern) aura on a level with the present Weena.

If the surrounding locations are to profit from the status radiating from the HST station, they must have their own positive and alluring identity, reflecting the qualities associated with an HST stopping place. Indeed, as the introduction to the city, the station can contribute much to its overall image.

Plans are now being drawn up for the development of the area around the central station. A large part of the area is the property of the national railway company NS. The municipality of Rotterdam will therefore develop plans jointly with NS for filling the area so as to respond adequately to the connection to the HST network, and make the most possible capital out of the economic potential. After intensive consultation, the municipality of Rotterdam

(Department of Urban Development and Housing) and NS have signed a covenant, the Masterplan CS 2000+, in which they agree to investigate the development prospects for the area around Rotterdam CS.

Note

1   Source: Town Planning and Housing Department, Municipality of Rotterdam.

Annex 13   Background Information on Strasbourg[1]

Profile

Table A13.1 Profile of the urban region of Strasbourg

	Alsace region	Urban community of Strasbourg
Surface area	8,280 km^2	304 km^2
	(1.5% of national territory)	(Strasbourg: 78km^2 or 25%)
Population	1,624,000	423,000
	(2.9% of French population)	(Strasbourg: 251,000 or 60%)
Density (residents/ km^2)	196	1,394
	(France: 102 hab/km^2)	(Strasbourg: 3,214)
Growth (1982–90)	+4%	+5%
Working population	749,000	198,000
Unemployment rate	7.9% (December 1994)	8.1% (December 1994)
Cross-border workers	61,500 (December 1994)	5,000 (December 1994)
Economic sectors		
Industry	2.7%	0%
Manufacturing	38.8%	27.7%
Tertiary	58.8%	73.3%

Source: INSEE census 1990.

Table A13.2 Transport in the urban region of Strasbourg

Urban transport 1.5 million daily transport moves in Strasbourg Urban Community in 1988 (33% pedestrian, 50% private car, 10% two-wheel, 7% public transport)

Air Strasbourg-Entzheim: 1.7 million passengers, 5,300 tons freight (2.1 million Bâle-Mulhouse)

Rail Passengers: 35,000 passengers/day in central station (6th largest French station, 2nd in terms of suburban traffic)

River 9.4 million tons (3rd largest Rhine port, 2nd river port in France)

Public transport (1995) 155,000 trips/day (+24% since 1994) 57,000 passengers/day on tram line A

Source: City of Strasbourg, 1996, *Fiches de synthèse*.

The Strategic Dimension

In light of the roles and functions developed by Strasbourg and the necessity of reinforcing its status, access to international high-speed networks is a vital

241

step in its internationalisation process. In a context of strong competition for the opening of these new corridors, rich in potential, it is essential that the city mobilise in order to ensure that target time frames are respected and the European dimension of projects taken into account.

Strasbourg is also participating in the promotion of a new development axis from Paris to Vienna, reinforcing solidarity between regions and beyond the interests of any particular city. The HST provides an opportunity for Strasbourg to position itself at the heart of a network of exchange, a fundamental strategic challenge. However, it is interesting to understand how this positioning and the transformation of its region can be articulated. This transformation will initially stem from an upset of scales and perimeters through the contraction of travel times. New, potentially rich relations are to be forged with the Paris area, the Greater East and Germany. Within the Alsatian region, access to high-speed rail via Strasbourg is an opportunity to redefine the nature of relations between the urban area and its hinterland.

The positioning of the city on international networks should also serve to strengthen existing development poles and the emergence of new ones in previously undeveloped sites, to be created or converted. These changes will require a new definition of the balance of the metropolitan area (creation of a network of different sites and poles.)

Finally, this access to international networks could also spark an evolution in the driving forces of regional development. This enhanced accessibility must also enable the mobilisation of outside investments to potential Strasbourg development sites. The question is then raised as to the management of such projects (will the HST bring new actors or partners?), the planning and control of development by the local authority, particularly in terms of specific timing of infrastructure projects. These new responsibilities reflect the city's new yet profound commitment in financial terms, alongside that of other Alsatian local authorities. The question is whether this partnership of circumstances can continue into the development phase.

The Station Area and Secondary Transport

In terms of access offered by different transport modes, the HST will be in keeping with a context whose principal characteristics have already anticipated its arrival. Accordingly, by revitalising the public transport offer and projecting the completion of a true tramway network by the year 2010, the Urban Transport Plan looks ahead to an environment in which the alternative to the private car has taken shape in a dense transport network across the urban landscape.

With the anticipated growth in the number of transport moves, the conditions for automobile traffic in the urban environment must be subject to the creation of bypass infrastructure. However, access to the city centre, for delivery purposes for example, will be strictly coordinated and controlled. When it finally arrives at central station, the HST will be at the centre of a regional rail 'star', facilitating connections with regional passenger services. Joining a system with a solidly founded base, the HST can only enhance this configuration and reinforce Strasbourg in its role of second-largest French station in terms of suburban traffic. At the same time, however, since the HST is at the heart of the system, it also defines a new standard of transport quality (particularly in terms of travel times). It can thus be an accelerator for profound changes impacting the transport chain.

First of all, the HST imposes a change in scale: travel previously handled by air will now be carried out by HST. At the same time, the airport will have to create HST links. This will necessitate a redistribution of roles between two poles of the urban area within the context of an expanded planning system. Similarly, the question of interconnection also implies this same expansion in terms of the cross-border urban environment, integrated as a coherent site in terms of transport organisation and spatial planning.

In addition to this change in scale there is also a potential transformation in the dynamic between transport actors. In fact, HST service implies a reinforcement of regional service. These modifications can require or indirectly lead to a total reorganisation of the local transport system, particularly in terms of service to outlying areas. These changes have an impact on three interdependent dimensions:

- service conditions (choice of equipment, rates, etc.);
- definition of strategic locations (interchange junctions, revisions in expropriation plans in case of capacity problems);
- modes of financing and partnership.

Thus the HST launches a dynamic of transformation in the transport chain, by upsetting the scale upon which we comprehend transport and creating a new approach to the question of accessibility. Insofar as they concern strategic locations on the level of an expanded urban area, these changes are directly related to the development dimension.

Urban Planning and Development

For the past six years Strasbourg has been pursuing an urban planning policy aimed at redistributing the balance of development among its districts and town centre. Within this context, the central station area plays an essential role in the relationship between the districts west of Strasbourg and its centre. Several scenarios of potential transformation may be considered: they illustrate voluntarist policies concerning different regions. They are illustrated merely as examples and are complementary in nature.

First scenario: the station district develops on its own: it ensures the necessary development in connection with the arrival of the HST. This is a continuation of changes begun in the past ten years. In this scenario, based on a framework established by the local authority, the private sector initiative provides the offer in terms of commercial space at sites which are available or require restructuring. The capacity for new construction in the district is estimated between 30,000 and 40,000 m^2. As the local authority has only a partial control of land reserves, public sector investments will primarily concern the interface between the station and its immediate surroundings, particularly in terms of a better tie-in between the glass arcade and the station concourse and improvements to the station's accessibility. This scenario presents the disadvantage of creating considerable pressure on the station district in terms of available land, generating conflicts between its traditional role as a neighbourhood accommodating low-income population groups and a new role as a business district. Furthermore, the control of the local authority is relatively limited.

Second scenario: creation of a link between the station district and the Rotonde site: pressure on the station district could be reduced by the development of the Rotonde 'out-of-town' site. This site, presently occupied by a tramway parking facility and situated one tram station away from the central station at the edge of the Cronenbourg district, would enable the construction of approximately 50,000 m^2 of space. It would involve the economic development of the district through a programme of activities, housing and amenities yet to be defined, and the articulation of the scales of the district and urban area. In addition, the development of this area could spark a larger reconstruction of the western beltway areas.

Third scenario: an expansion of the station district towards the west: this scenario involves going beyond the limits represented by the station and creating an articulation between the town centre and the western districts. It implies the reconstruction of part of the lower station and consequently, a partnership with the SNCF. The breadth and the speed of these transformations are to be defined.

This may well imply:

- creation of a new station access from the west via the bypass and additional parking facilities;
- creation of a new station facade based upon this new access and development of a service program for the least active areas of the lower station (approx. two ha enabling the construction of 50-60,000 m^2);
- creation of a new district by shifting the major part of the lower station and integrating the ramparts into Glacis Park. This district (approx. 10 ha enabling construction of 100–150,000 m^2) could be structured along a north/south boulevard, providing a link between Wodli and Koenigshoffen streets. The creation of a new underground tram station would then be conceivable; in this case, the formal link between the town centre and the districts of Cronenbourg and Koenigshoffen would be strengthened by a restructuring of Wodli and Koenigshoffen streets. This uncompromising scenario would need to be calibrated in conjunction with other metropolitan area development projects. It raises the question of the anticipated urban impact of a potential new station southeast of the centre which would be shared by the two HST lines: Rhine-Rhône and East-European.

Note

1   Co-author: Mr Jean-Yves Meunier and Mr Michel Reverdy, City of Strasbourg.

Annex 14   Background Information on Turin[1]

Profile

Table A14.1 Population in and around Turin

1994	Population	
	Residents	%
Turin	942,076	42.0
Metropolitan area	777,571	34.8
M.A.T. + Turin	1,719,647	77.0
Turin Province	2,235,707	100.0

Source: City Of Turin, *Notiziario di statistica n2*, 1995.

Table A14.2 Passengers Turin-Caselle Airport

Year	Passenger traffic Passengers	Annual Æ%
1994	1,758,936	+7.8
1995	1,836,407	+4.4
Æ% 1986–96		+ 97.6

Source: SAGAT Spa Annual Report 1994–95.

Table A14.3 Flights Turin-Caselle Airport

Scheduled flights 1994	
Domestic	11
European	23
Extra-European	4
Total	**38**

Source: SAGAT Spa Annual Report 1994–95.

Table A14.4 Train passengers via the Turin junction

Transit passengers/stations 1993	
Stations	No. passengers/year
Lingotto	391,757
Porta Nuova	3,908,622
Porta Susa	1,186,975

Source: City of Turin, *Informazioni Statistiche 1995*.

Table A14.5 Urban and suburban transport in the Turin region

Vehicle type	Network development 1994 km
Tram (ATM)	124.6
Bus (ATM)	352.4
Bus (SATTI)	1230
Train (SATTI)	70

Source: ATM and SATTI Annual Report 1994.

The Strategic Dimension

In comparison with other medium-size cities and European metropolises, Turin and its metropolitan area today play a non-negligible role. The city has 'conquered' this position in the past 20 years by expanding the historic mono-functional base represented by the automotive industry to other sectors and aspects of its socioeconomic and territorial reality. Since the early 1960s, this industrial sector alone was responsible for the national and international profile of the city. Today, the automotive industry and related businesses have been reinforced by the addition of other sectors and high-technology manufacturing (robotics, aeronautics, energy) and other activities (high-level tertiary and business services, university, research, cultural resources, sports, etc.)

This was achieved by partially overcoming the two primary aspects which have historically contributed to the marginal role of the Turin region both on the Italian and European levels: firstly, proximity to Milan, beacon of northern Italy and indeed, of the entire country, in terms of its international and European relations; and secondly, the geographical marginality of the Piedmont region in relation to the predominant north-south orientation which has characterised Italian and European development.

Turin and its region have fought against these handicaps by seeking out aspects of complementarity and diversification as compared to Milan and its zone of influence, and by taking full advantage of the new reality (especially prospects and potential) offered by east-west European relations. It has also played upon the pivotal role of the Piedmont region and especially that of the Turin area, acting as a gateway to Italy in lower-middle Europe. This involved strengthening existing elements, identifying potentialities and transforming them into tangible socioeconomic development opportunities for Turin, Piedmont and all of Italy.

However, as it evolves, the Turin region must not lose sight of the structural and economic elements which may determine a development strategy and consolidate its role. On an economic level, an underlying weakening in employment, production and revenues in general must be addressed. It is necessary to deal with the risk of a crisis in production on a large and medium scale with programs targeted at flexibility in production and especially, innovation and quality of products (given that the weakness of the lira will only allow the export sector to be used in the short term as a base for a solid production system).

In terms of territorial organisation, there is an inescapable need for programs aimed at enhancing the accessibility (air, rail, road) of the Turin pole and its connection capacity with the rest of Piedmont, Italy and other European regions. If this objective is based upon reinforcing its communications systems in order to attain a level of excellence, Turin will be poised to become a major junction within the European network.

In summary:

- in terms of international relations, the role of Turin must be strengthened to enable the city to take its place in the system of medium-sized cities and major European centres. This may be achieved by developing its qualities as a centre for productive tertiary activity, manufacturing, higher education, culture and sports. It would also be possible to base this on a national perspective of the federalist type, and on the decentralisation of the capital area for certain institutional functions; activities of national importance could be distributed in a more reticular basis across all of Italy, therefore including Turin (research, telecommunications, aerospace, etc.);
- in terms of the economic situation, neither Turin nor Piedmont have been spared the effects of the recession (which affected the majority of Italy with the exception of the northeast and part of the centre), along with difficulties in public finances, globalisation of production and trade within a framework of increased qualitative and tariff-based competition. It is necessary to maintain the productive economic base (manufacturing industry) by accentuating the added-value of products, their level of quality and innovative nature, by encouraging exports (resulting from the current underlying weakness of the domestic market) by innovating and organising and by refusing to be satisfied with the easy opportunities afforded by the present weakness of the lira;
- in terms of cross-border relations, ties must be strengthened with France and in particular with adjoining regions and departments (Rhône-Alpes,

Provence-Côte d'Azur, Savoie, Alpes Maritimes, etc.), going beyond the many 'Interreg' programmes and encouraging the development of solid relations, both in general terms and in those sectors which define the excellence of the Turin pole;

- in terms of choices, the problems and negative repercussions which may result from the specific geographic situation of Piedmont and the Turin area must be overcome: gateway and/or European bridge? Turin and the Piedmont region must not simply be a place of transit (obtaining virtually no benefit but considerable environmental impact) but rather become a crossroads for exchange, and for economic and social growth;
- in terms of the environment, it is important to conceive environmental protection and enhancement measures for Turin and its surroundings (air, ground and surface waters, green spaces, etc.), not as limits to growth but rather as ways of promoting the area's absolute quality, one of the essential conditions for the credibility of its role and position within the European urban network;
- In terms of the organisation of high-speed rail transport, it is necessary to: realise the Turin-Milan high-speed project (with ultimate connections to Trieste and Rome), beginning work by late 1996; define the complementary link to Alexandria and the Genoa-Milan crossover; and above all, complete the conceptual and economic feasibility studies in progress concerning the Lyon-Turin line (through the Susa valley), which represent the structural and strategic condition necessary for a European high-speed rail network (east-west and northwest lines); and finally, make the necessary decisions regarding the above.

The Station Area and Secondary Transport

Present Situation

The Turin and metropolitan area public transport system is characterised by a structural weakness leading to insufficient use of the rail system for regional and urban area trips. Public transport lines are served by tramway only for the urban network (with covered tracks on certain sections only) and by bus for the suburban and metropolitan area.

The road network is well developed in terms of motorways which converge upon Turin and connect the city in every direction (Fréjus-France, Aoste-Mont Blanc, Simplon-Switzerland, Milan, Genoa-Rome, Genoa-France,

Plaisance-Brescia-Venice); however, it requires some enhancement (both technically and in terms of linear development); it is rather poorly adapted in terms of national and departmental highways (primarily in its capacity to support links of the reticular type rather than just radial and polar); and it needs particular reinforcement in the north-south direction, within the urban area and the conurbation.

However, projects of strategic and structural importance are currently in advanced stages of completion. These projects revolve around the radical transformation of the regular rail system into an integrated international, national, regional and local system, based upon the completion of the Turin junction interstation urban network with quadrupling of tracks, along with the bringing on line of 'crossroads' stations, the construction of two new stations (San Paolo, Rebaudengo) and the total transformation of two others (Porta Susa and Dora).

For the Turin-Milan line continuing on to Venice, the high-speed construction work (passengers and freight) will begin in autumn-winter 1996, while the decision process and the definition of necessary projects for the strategic Lyon-Turin line (passengers and freight) through the Susa Valley is still in the planning stages, although discussions among national and local, institutional and operational decision-makers are well-advanced.

As concerns viability: plans were completed and work is to begin in autumn 1996 for the development of the new central line crossing the city from north to south and covering the interstation urban network. An integral part of the new urban development plan, this project calls for the extension of this main line towards the south; plans to complete the main north-south road along the western limits of the city, of strategic importance to the conurbation (Corso Marche), are awaiting funding.

Localisation of Plans and High-speed Lines

The planned Turin-Milan line is now definitive and calls for the operation of the interstation urban network within the city and its continuation to Milan, on a dedicated track (running almost constantly alongside the A4 motorway Turin-Milan). The source of long debate, the planned layout is that which ensures the least environmental and urban impact along with the best operational and service conditions.

The link with Lyon (which represents a strategic choice based on a general agreement negotiated in 1994 between the responsible actors) is composed of a corridor through the Susa valley and currently calls for different line layouts founded upon one constant factor: the need for a base tunnel at least 54 km long between Saint-Jean de Maurienne and Susa. In-depth conceptual and economic feasibility studies, jointly funded by Italy and France, are currently under way.

As concerns Turin and its metropolitan area, the possibility of a line layout exterior or tangential to the town for the connection of the Lyon and Milan lines was examined. With this in mind, the double hypothesis of a high-speed station located outside the city but within the western metropolitan area or northwest of Turin, near Caselle airport, was also taken into account. Neither the exterior nor tangential line layouts enjoys a high degree of consensus since, in light of the obstacles to be confronted and the problems to be resolved, their realisation would only be possible in the long term (at least 15 years); however, the exterior layout is under serious consideration thanks to its characteristics of providing functional relief through the Turin junction: freight and exchanges with the two intermodal centres in the west and north area of Turin would be handled on the exterior line, with passengers accommodated on the interstation urban network through the city.

Stations and Connections with the Transport System

Opinions converge on the necessity for two types of stations for high-speed passengers in Turin:

- the central, historical main station of Porta Nuova for the arrival and departure of trains originating from or terminating at Turin;
- the central station of Porta Susa, alongside the interstation urban network, for trains continuing beyond Turin.

The two stations offer a high degree of integration with the Turin and area public transport system both current and planned. In particular: Porta Susa would be integrated with the different functions of the interstation urban network (local, regional, national and international), with the planned metro line no. 1, currently at the financing stage, (Rivoli, Turin west, Porta Susa, Porta Nuova, Turin south, Nichelino), and with other existing Turin and area public transport lines; Porta Nuova would be served by the metro line no. 1 and by other public transport lines.

Within the context of the large urban transformation zone which will created by the development plan's central line, and in virtue of the excellent location of the Dora station in relation to Line 3 (1,300,000 m^2 of base plate pad) the hypothesis of a slight displacement of the interstation urban network station to the north is currently being evaluated.

Urban Planning and Development

The configuration of the Turin rail junction should not be subjected to major modifications with the routing of high-speed trains on the interstation urban network, currently being increased fourfold between Asti and Chivasso via Turin. The Turin interstation urban network will be mostly underground; the overall junction project calls for the total rebuilding and underground relocation of the Dora and Porta Susa stations, the profound rehabilitation of Porta Nuova, and the completion of two new stations, one at the northern outskirts of Turin (Rebaudengo) and the other in the semi west-central zone (San Paolo).

The operating plan for the rail junction outlined by FS Spa for the period from 2001 to 2020 shows compatibility between the interstation urban network and the accommodation of high-speed lines serving Lyon-Turin and Turin-Milan. The heavy load of the interstation urban network (to increase from 216 trains/day to over 280, in addition to higher number of freight trains) makes it essential to consider the hypothesis of a rail line exterior (or tangent) to the city. This is with particular reference to goods traffic and the relocation of Turin's current intermodal goods centre to the western part of the conurbation (in addition to an intermodal centre of lesser importance to be completed north of the city.)

As regards the stations:

- Porta Nuova (the historic central station) is currently the subject of a pilot study undertaken by FS Spa, as part of the main lines of a new development plan for the city which calls for: the strengthening of the commercial, reception and service functions of the current monumental building; the shifting of its rail functions to the south; the covering (with the creation of a park upon a concrete slab, also incorporating large parking areas) of the majority of tracks, in an effort to 'restitch' the station zone back into the fabric of the urban centre environment;
- the project concerning Porta Susa involves its underground integration and reinforcement of the station, within the context of work on the interstation urban network and in keeping with the structural urban project of the central line defined by the urban development plan; in this case also, the surface 'break' in the urban fabric which has divided the city

since the second half of the nineteenth century following the completion of the line to Milan will be eliminated: in fact, in connection with the tracks, the central line's new major boulevard will be developed and a public park built in place of the existing station.

Quite deservedly, the 'through' station of Porta Susa raises several concerns: indeed, it is destined to become the city's main station but precisely in connection with the section of the interstation urban network presenting the greatest number of physical and spatial limitations; the corridor of lanes presents its narrowest segment here, and the main line also presents its narrowest area at surface level (Line 2).

For these reasons, serious study is being given to the possibility of moving the high-speed station for through trains to the north, making use of the Dora station (whose current plans should be completely reviewed). This station enjoys an excellent position connecting with the area offering the best potential for transformation and construction of the central line defined by the new development plan, that is, Line 3 along the river Dora, the location of abandoned sites of the former steelworks and other industrial wasteland. The total urban land surface is over 1,300,000 sq. m, representing an area larger than *La Défense* in Paris. As concerns Line 3, the project calls for the development of a surface area of 904,400 m^2, with 253,232 m^2 allocated to residential construction (7,488 residents), 153,748 m^2 of tertiary and 497,420 m^2 (more than 50 per cent of the surface area) allocated to the creation of a technology and development pole dubbed 'EuroTorino'.

Despite these obvious advantages in comparison with Porta Susa, there are nonetheless certain limitations. These include the lack of a link between Dora Station and the planned metro line no. 1 (VAL technology), a link which on the contrary will exist with Porta Susa (situated two km from Dora station); however, this limitation is somewhat compensated for by the connection with the airport rail line at Dora station. This line has just been added to the interstation urban network at Dora, for the same reasons of physical limitations of the network section at Porta Susa, as previously emphasized.

In terms of the scenario which has been outlined up to this point and the factors which constitute it, there is general agreement and cooperation among the concerned public authorities (City of Turin, Province of Turin, Piedmont Region, state), along with FS Spa and the concessionary company TAV, even though each has its own specific visions and objectives (which do not however lead to major differences). Among the public authorities, the position of the Piedmont region is most open to alternative solutions which may enable a better distribution of territorial effects resulting from the positioning of the high-speed station for through trains; it is primarily the region which has looked into the possibility of a line outside the city of Turin and the potential location of a station in the western zone of tow or near Turin-Caselle airport; and it is also the region (and partly the province of Turin) which takes into consideration the various proceedings, concerns and disagreements among the communes of the Susa valley regarding the impact of the Lyon-Turin line which is to cross their valley.

Note

1   Co-authors: Carlo Alberto Barbieri (expert for the city of Turin), Carolina Giaimo (fellow worker), Biagio Burdizzo, Mr Allessandro Faraggiana and Mr Ilario Signoretti of the City of Turin.

Bibliography

General

Abler, D., Janelle, D., Philbrick, A. and Sommer, J. (1975), *Human Geography in a Shrinking World*, Duxbury Press, North Scituate, Mass.

Berg, L. van den (1987), *Urban Systems in a Dynamic Society*, Gower, Aldershot.

Berg, L. van den, and Klink, H.A. van (1992), 'Strategic networks as weapons in the competition among European cities and regions', *Journal of European Integration*, winter.

Berg, L. van den, Klink, H.A. van and Pol, P.M.J. (1993), *De hoge snelheidstrein vanuit regionaal-economisch perspectief: kans of bedreiging voor de regionale luchthaven*, EURICUR, Rotterdam.

Berg, L. van den, Braun, E. and Meer, J. van der (1996), *Organising Capacity of Metropolitan Cities, The cases of Antwerp, Bilbao, Bologna, Eindhoven, Lisbon, Munich, Rotterdam and Turin*, EURICUR, Rotterdam.

Brugge, R. ter and Pellenbarg, P.H. (1988), 'Een hoge snelheidstrein voor Nederland. Enkele notities over theorie, technologie, routes en effecten van het snelle spoorwegvervoer', *K.N.A.G. Geografisch Tijdschrift XXII*, Nr.1.

Hall, P. (1995), 'Towards a general urban theory' in: Brotchie, J., Batty, M., Blakely, E., Hall, P. and Newton, P. (eds), *Cities in Competition: Productive and sustainable cities for the 21st century*, Longman Australia, Melbourne.

Hall, P. (1996), *The Global City*, UNESCO, Blackwell Publishers, Oxford/Cambridge.

Janelle, D.G. (1969), 'Spatial organization: a model and concept', *Annals of the American Association of Geographers*, 59, pp. 348–64.

Klaassen, L.H. (1988), *Exercises in Spatial Thinking*, Avebury, Aldershot.

Kramer, J.H.T. (1990), *Luchthavens en hun uitstraling; een onderzoek naar de economische en ruimtelijke uitstralingseffecten van luchthavens*, Elinkwijk, Utrecht.

Lambooy, J.G. (1996), *The Urban Spatial Structure and Agglomeration Economies: Relations with real estate*, Tinbergen Instituut, TI 96–141/5.

Plassard, F. (1992), 'The relationship between regional policy and transport and communications networks', European Conference of Ministers of Transport, Round Table 93, 14 October.

Pol, P.M.J. (1996), 'The European Union and transport infrastructure policy', Proceedings 2nd TRAIL PhD Congress 1996 'Defence or attack', 28 May 1996, Feyenoord Stadium 'De Kuip', Rotterdam.

Sassen, S. (1991), *The Global City: London, New York, Tokyo*, Princeton, Princeton University Press.

Schafer, A. and Victor, D. (1997), 'The past and future of global mobility', *Scientific American*, October, pp. 36–9.

Report on Amsterdam

dRO-Ontwerpteam Amsterdam (forthcoming), *Verwacht aan de IJ-Oevers.*
dRO Amsterdam (1994), *Hogesnelheidslijnen naar Amsterdam.*
dRO Amsterdam (1996), *Ontwerp Integraal plan Zuidas; Ontwikkelingsstrategie.*
dRO Amsterdam (1996), *Ontwerp Integraal plan Zuidas; Toelichting.*
Gemeentevervoerbedrijf Amsterdam, NS Reizigers, NZH Groep and Midnet Groep (1997), *Collectief Vervoer in Knoop Zuid; Kiezen voor Kansen.*
Nederlands Economisch Instituut (NEI) (1992), *Economische Betekenis Aansluiting Noordvleugel Amsterdam op Europees Hogesnelheidsnet,* Rotterdam.
Nederlandse Spoorwegen (NS) (1996), *Sternet; Een Flonkerend Perspectief voor Stadsgewestelijke Mobiliteit in de Noordvleugel van de Randstad.*
Werkgroep HST (1996), *De Wereld van de Hogesnelheidstrein; een studie naar de ruimtelijke en economische effecten in en rond de HST knooppunten.*

Report on Antwerp

Berg, L. van den, Meer, J. van der and Pol, P.M.J. (1996), *Impact of the European Union on Metropolitan Cities, Inventories of European Policies and the experiences of the cities of Antwerp, Bilbao, Birmingham, Lisbon, Lyon and Rotterdam,* EURICUR, Rotterdam.
De Standaard (1996), 'Miljarden voor een mini-metro, De Antwerpse premetro of hoe 36 miljard onder de grond verdween', 6 April.
Groep Planning, Vennootschap van stedebouwkundigen, verkeerskundigen, architecten en ingenieurs (1996), *Verkeersleefbaarheidsplan, Urban-gebied Antwerpen, Eerste conceptnota.*
Kabinet van de schepen voor financiën, economie en toerisme (1996), 'Vragen en opmerkingen bij de eerste conceptnota "Verkeersleefbaarheidsplan, Urban-gebied Antwerpen"', 4 September.
Stad Antwerpen, Departement voor Ruimtelijke Ordening en Veiligheid (1996), *Etude comparative des gares TGV et de leurs contextes urbains,* monograph for Eurocities-TGV-research.
Vranken, J. and Abdeljelil, Y.B. (1995), *Sociale kaart van Antwerpen,* Acco, Leuven.

Report on Brno

The Brno Municipality, Chief Architect's Department (1996), *Eurocities High-speed railway, The Monograph,* August.
The Brno Municipality, Chief Architect's Department (1996), *Eurocities High-speed railway, Synthesis of the Monograph,* July.
City of Brno (1994), Master Zoning Plan.
Vitek, Ing. Jan (1997), 'Modernization and Decelopment of the Infrastructure in Czech Republic', contribution to International Symposium 20–21 January, Vienna.

Report on Brussels

Belgian Airports and Airways Agency (1994), *Brussels Airport, accessibility study, landside.*
Brussels Hoofdstedelijk Gewest (1996), *Brussels, des potentialités exceptionelles mais deux nouveaux défis: l'élargissement vers l'Est et la complexité institionelle belge.*
Brussels Hoofdstedelijk Gewest, Ontwerp voor de aanleg van zuidwijk.
Rotterdams Dagblad, HSL-station in Brussel (1997), 'Zwarte wolk boven de wijk', 12 April.

Report on Cologne

Deutsche Bahn Gruppe (1996), *Zum Thema 4/96*, Neubaustrecke Köln-Rhein/Main.
Jänsch, E. (1996), *Evolution of the ICE*, Modern Railways, August, pp. 513–5.
Möller, L., Stadt Köln (1996), *Monograph of the city of Cologne.*
Stadt Köln (1995), *Wirtschafts- und Arbeitsmarktbericht Köln 94/95.*

Report on Geneva

Comité Régional Franco-Genevoise (1995), *Les études de la plateforme concertée d'aménagement du territoire.*
Haegi, Claude (ed.) (1995), *The Europe of Regions, From French-Italian-Swiss partnership to cooperation with Eastern Europe.*
République et Canton de Genève, Département des travaux publics et de l'Energie (1996), *Monographies de Ville Genève.*
République et Canton de Genève, Département de Justice et Police et des Transports (1994), *TGV Léman Mont-Blanc*, Document de presentation.
SBB CFF FFS (1996), *Dossier extra, Réalisation et financement de l'infrastructure des transport publics*, August.
Ville Genève (1993), *Plan Directeur Communal (Genève 2001).*

Report on Liège

Berg, L. van den (1987), *Urban Systems in a Dynamic Society*, Aldershot, Gower.
Strohl, M.P. (1993), *Europe's High Speed Trains, A Study in Geo-economics*, Praeger, London.
Ville de Liège, Echevinat du Développement économique (1996), *Monography portant sur l'accueil du TGV dans l'agglomération liégoise, Etude préliminaire (Le TGV à Liège: Moteur d'un nouveau pôle de développement urbain.*

Report on Lille

l'Agence de développement et d'urbanisme de Lille Métropole (1996), *Monographie Eurocité Euralille, 1993, Brochure on development Euralille.*

l'Agence de développement et d'urbanisme de Lille Métropole (1996), *Lille après Euralille, la métropole en mutation.*

Strohl, M.P. (1993), *Europe's High Speed Trains, A Study in Geo-economics*, Praeger, London.

Report on Lyon

Berg, L. van den, Meer, J. van der and Pol, P.M.J. (1996), *Impact of the European Union on Metropolitan Cities, Inventories of European Policies and the experiences of the cities of Antwerp, Bilbao, Birmingham, Lisbon, Lyon and Rotterdam*, EURICUR, Rotterdam.

Le groupe de travail 'Satolas 2015' (1996), *Rapport de synthèse.*

Molin, J.L. (1996), *Lyon et le train à grande vitesse. Un enjeu économique majeur, des politiques d'accompagnement à préciser (monograph de Lyon).*

Report on Marseilles

Aeroport Marseille-Provence (1997), *Resultats 1996.*

Bonnier, J. (1997), *Les relations de l'aire métropolitaine Marseillaise avec les territoires voisins et plus lointains, son rayonnement.*

Bonnier, J. and Ferrier, J.P. (1993), *La Métropole Méditerranéenne de la France Européenne.*

De Courson, J, Groupe TEN Conseil (1994), *Impact TGV Marseille Saint-Charles.*

DATAR (1992), *L'Aire Métropolitaine Marseillaise: Renaissance d'une Métropole.*

Direction Départementale de l'Equipement (1995), *Aire Métropolitaine Marseillaise – Dossiers thématiques.*

Établissement Public d'Aménagement (1996), *A Marseille, Euroméditerranée, un grand projet d'aménagement et de developpement.*

Etablissement Public d'Aménagement (1996), *Concertation Euroméditerranée-ZAC St. Charles.*

ITA (1996), *Effet de differents scénarios de desserte TGV sur le trafic aérien Marseille-Paris.*

OCOTRAM (1995), *Pôle St. Charles: Plan de Déplacement-Stationnement.*

SNCF, Région Provence-Alpes-Côte d'Azur, Département des Bouches du Rhône, Euroméditerranée, Ministère de l'Equipement, Ville de Marseille (1996), *Le pôle transport Marseille Saint-Charles.*

Ville de Marseille (1995), *Accueil de la ligne nouvelle du TGV Mediterrannée à la gare St. Charles – Eléments pour un projet urbain.*

Report on Nantes

Nantes Atlantique Développement (1996), *Nantes, Etude Comparative des gares TGV et leurs contextes urbains (Monographie de Nantes)*.
Strohl, M.P., (1993), *Europe's High Speed Trains, A Study in Geo-economics*, Praeger, London.
SNCF (Région de Nantes) et Ville de Nantes (1996), *Aménagement du Site de la Gare de Nantes*.
Tellinga, J. and Mulder, A. (ed.) (1996), *l'Europe à Grande Vitesse*, NAi Uitgevers, Rotterdam.

Report on Rotterdam

Berg, L. van den and Pol, P.M.J. (1996), *TGV and Rotterdam*, monograph, Rotterdam.
Centrum voor Onderzoek en Statistiek (1995), *Statistisch Jaarboek Rotterdam en Regio 1995*, Rotterdam.
Gemeente Rotterdam, dS+V/RO-Centrum (1995), *De HST stopt op Rotterdam-CS, Stedebouwkundige studie naar de potenties van het CS-gebied in 2010*.
Ministerie van Verkeer en Waterstaat (V&W) (1994), *Nieuwe HSL-nota, deelrapporten 3, 13, 17 en 21*, The Hague.
Stadsregio Rotterdam (1995), *Regionaal Verkeers- en Vervoersplan Stadsregio Rotterdam*.

Report on Strasbourg

Service de l'Urbanisme de la Communauté Urbaine de Strasbourg et Agence de développement et d'urbanisme de l'agglomeration Strasbourgeoise (1996), *Monographie Eurocités-TGV, Le TGV à Strasbourg: enjeux et perspectives de développement*.
Service de l'Urbanisme de la Communauté Urbaine de Strasbourg et Agence de développement et d'urbanisme de l'agglomeration Strasbourgeoise, Eurocités-TGV, Données de Cadrage.
Strohl, M.P., (1993), *Europe's High Speed Trains, A Study in Geo-economics*, Praeger, London.

Report on Turin

Berg, L. van den, Meer, J. van der and Pol, P.M.J. (1996), *Impact of the European Union on Metropolitan Cities, Inventories of European Policies and the experiences of the cities of Antwerp, Bilbao, Birmingham, Lisbon, Lyon and Rotterdam*, EURICUR, Rotterdam.
City of Turin (1996), *Monograph of the City of Turin*, Turin.
Strohl, M.P., (1993), *Europe's High Speed Trains, A Study in Geo-economics*, Praeger, London.

Discussion Partners

Report on Amsterdam

Mr W. Vehmeijer, Department of Economic Affairs Amsterdam (dEZ)
Mr L.J. van Dalen, Transport Planning, Dutch Railways
Mr M. van Eijl, Chamber of Commerce of Amsterdam
Mr R.J.M. Sturm, Amsterdam Airport Schiphol
Mr H. Poelstra, Department of Spatial Planning Amsterdam (dRO)
Mr K. de Boer, Department of Spatial Planning Amsterdam (dRO)

Report on Antwerp

Mr T. van den Berghen, Districtsdirecteur District Noordoost, NMBS
Mr J. Bongaerts, Project Coördinator, Eurostation N.V.
Ms S. Ceulemans, Economie en Toerisme, Kabinet van de schepen voor financiën, economie en toerisme
Representative of the Maatschappij voor de Vernieuwing en Promotie van Antwerpen.
Ms V. De Beuckeleer, Kabinetsmedewerker ruimtelijke ordening
Mr F. Loos, De Lijn, Vlaamse Vervoermaatschappij
Mr B. van Brussel, De Lijn, Vlaamse Vervoermaatschappij
Mr Y. Vandewyer, Districtssecretaris Berchem
Mr E. Claessens, Transporteconoom, Universiteit Antwerpen UFSIA

Report on Brno

Mr J. Tréger, Head of Department of Economic Development, City of Brno
Mr P. Bajer, Chief Executive, Chamber of Commerce Brno
Mr R. Vetecník, Czech Agency for Foreign Investment, Regional Office Brno
Mr T. Placek, Director, Czech Airports Administration, Airport Brno
Mr I. Minarík, Referát Regionálního Rozvoje, Okresní Úrad Brno-Venkov
Mr V. Novácek, Head of the Department, Ministry of Transport and communications, Department of Railway Transport and Lines
Mr J. Josífek, Department of City Development, City of Brno
Ms M. Zezulkova, Department of City Development, City of Brno
Mr J. Vítek, Responsable du service de l'aménagement urbain, Direction de politique des transports et des rélations internationales, Ministère des Transports

Mr J. Benes, Service de l'aménagement urbain, Ministère des Transports

Mr P. Tikman, Directeur de la conception, Division des voies des transports, Direction générale des Chemins de fer tchèques

Mr P. Staffa, Directeur de la division de commerce et d'exploitation de Brno, Chemins de fer tchèques, s.o.

Mr Z. Macha, Directeur adjoint délégué au transport at à l'exploitation, Chemins de fer tchèques, s.o.

Mr L. Hrubes, chef de SDC (Gestion des voies des transports), Chemins de fer tchèques, s.o.

Mr J. Matus, Chef de DKV (Depôt des véhicules à rail), Chemins de fer tchèques, s.o.

Mr J. Najmon, Chef de station de chemins de fer de Brno, Chemins de fer tchèques, s.o.

Mr J. Siroký, Adjoint technique de chef de station de chemins de fer de Brno, Chemins de fer tchèques, s.o.

Report on Brussels

Mr Van Begin, Directeur-generaal Regie der Luchtwegen

Mr Clerbeau, ARIES-consultant

Mr C. van den Hove, Ministerie van het Brussels Stedelijk Gewest, Bestuur van de uitrusting en het vervoer

Mr Persoons, Directeur Eurostation (stedelijke terminals)

Mr J.P. Wouters, Directeur dienst bestuur van de uitrusting en het vervoer, Ministerie van het Brussels Stedelijk Gewest

Report on Cologne

Mr L. Möller, Director Traffic Planning and Chairman Working Groups PBKA and Köln-Rhein/Main, City of Cologne

Mr K.O. Fruhner, Alderman, Department of Economics and City Development, City of Cologne

Mr U. Vetterlein, Manager Trade, Economic Development, Planning and Transport, Chamber of Commerce of Cologne

Mr P. Gasper, Director Advertisement Department, Cologne Messe

Mr J. Bergman, Member of Direction, Cologne Messe

Report on Geneva

Mr M. Jaques, Département des Travaux publics et de l'Energie, Canton de Genève

Mr S. Manzoni, Office Fédéral des Transport, Canton de Genève

Mr Y.D. Viredaz, Head of Marketing-Communication, Geneva International Airport

Mr B. Beurret, Département des Travaux publics et de l'Energie, Division Aménagement, Canton de Genève

Mr J.P. Pilet, Swiss Federal Railways

Report on Liège

Mr J.F. Sleijpen, Développement économique, Emploi et Logement urbain, Ville de Liège
Mr J.P. Gomez, Urbaniste-Chef du Service de l'Urbanisme de la Ville de Liège
Mr G. Moreau, Echevin du Développement économique et du Commerce
Mr V. Bourlard, Administrateur-Directeur général d'Euro-Liège-TGV
Mr G. Theate, Ingénieur, Euro-Liège-TGV
Ms L. van Mechelen, Conseiller, Euro-Liège-TGV
Mr C. Dedy, Chef de Gare des Guillemins, Liège
Mr E. Artus, Adjoint au Chef de Gare des Guillemins, Liège
Mr J.L. Auguste, Direction Commerciale et Etudes, TEC, Societé de Transport en Commun,
    Liège-Verviers
Mr J. Bertrand, Directeur d'Exploitation, TEC, Societé de Transport en Commun, Liège-Verviers
Ms B. Camus, Public Relations, Liège Airport
Mr S. Moreau, Directeur Géneral, Palais des Congrès, Liège
Mr P. Bernimolin, Directeur Commercial, Palais des Congrès, Liège
Mr M. Delrez, Directeur de la Communication et des Relations, Palais des Congrès, Liège
Mr R. Comte, Président de l'Association des Commerçants de la rue des Guillemins
Mr M. Servais, Président du Comité de quartier de Bronckart
Mr R. Laruelle, Secrétaire du Comité de quartier de Bronckart
Mr P. Masson, Président du Comité de quartier Fragnée

Report on Lille

Mr J.Y. Savina, Directeur, Aéroport de Lille
Mr P. Duyck, Chargé de Mission Tertiaire, Département Etudes et Projets, Chambre de
    Commerce et d'Industrie de Lille, Roubaix and Tourcoing
Mr J.F. Stevens, Centre National de la Recherce Scientifique, Universités de Lille
Mr G. Joignaux, INRETS, Institut national de recherce sur les transports et leur securité
Mr D. Caudron, l'Agence de développement et d'urbanisme de Lille Métropole
Mr S. Coudert, Directeur d'études, l'Agence de développement et d'urbanisme de Lille
    Métropole
Mr M.J.L. Sehier, Services communautaire en Communauté Urbaine de Lille
Mr M.R. Caillau, Mairie de Lille
Mr A. Querleux, Responsable Département Marketing, Direction de Lille, SNCF
Mr J.P. Baïetto, Directeur Général, Euralille

Report on Lyon

Mr J.R. Revelin, Directeur de l'Aménagement et du Développement Commercial, Aéroport de
    Lyon-Satolas
Mr J.P. de Calbiac, SNCF

Mr G. Bolon, Directeur Général Adjoint chargé de la Voirie et des Infrastructures, Département
   du Rhône
Mr M. Rivoire, Conseil Régional
Mr J.L. Molin, Communauté Urbaine de Lyon

Report on Marseilles

Mr J. Bonnier, Prefecture de Région Provence-Alpes-Côte d'Azur, directeur d'etudes
Mr R. Croisé, Aeroport Marseille-Provence, Marketing passagers
Mr V. Marthelot, Etablissement Public d'Aménagement Euroméditerranée, chef de projet-
   St.Charles
Mr Rousseau, directeur des transports, Ville de Marseille
Mr Devouge, directeur de l'atelier d'Aménagement Urbain, Ville de Marseille
Mr Rimattei, secretaire général adjoint de la Ville de Marseille, Mr V. Touze, Chargé de Mission
   TGV, Ville de Marseille
Mr B. Wolkowitsch, Région Provence-Alpes-Côte d'Azur, chef du service transports

Report on Nantes

Mr J.P. Jacquet, Nantes Atlantique Développement
Mr A. Boeswillwald, Directeur du Développement et de l'Action Commerciale, SEMITAN
Mr Y. Guillemot, Président Général Port Autonome Nantes-St Nazaire
Mr Mareschal, Premier Adjoint au Maire, Hôtel de Ville, Nantes
Mr Matthieu, Directeur Aménagement Du Territoire, Conseil Régional
Mr Gourdy, Chef Service Infrastructures, Conseil Régional
Mr Herbreteau, Directeur Commission Tranports, District de l'Agglomeration Nantaise
Representative of the Marketing Department, SNCF
Mr Benoit, Directeur Aeroport Nantes-Atlantique
Mr Rocaboy, Directeur Aménagement du Territoire, Chambre Régionale de Commerce et
   d'Industrie
Mr Brasselet, Conseiller Général de Loire Atlantique, Président de la Commission Transport

Report on Rotterdam

Mr J. van 't Verlaat, Rotterdam City Development Corporation (OBR)
Mr T. van Ameijden, Rotterdam City Development Corporation (OBR)
Mr L. van Veen, Rotterdam City Development Corporation (OBR)
Mr J. Schrijnen, Rotterdam City Planning and Housing Department (dS+V)
Mr A.F.W.M. Zeegers, Rotterdam City Planning and Housing Department (dS+V)
Mr G. van Veggel, Rotterdam City Planning and Housing Department (dS+V)
Mr R. Volk, Rotterdam City Planning and Housing Department (dS+V)
Mr J. van Teeffelen, Rotterdam City Planning and Housing Department (dS+V)

Mr B. Postma, Rotterdam City Planning and Housing Department (dS+V)
Mr J.P.M. Dams, Rotterdam City Planning and Housing Department (dS+V)
Mr S. Buys, Ministry of Housing, Spatial Planning and Environment
Mr H.J.Th. Van Herwaarden, Real Estate Department, Dutch Railways
Mr L. van der Hoeven, Corporate Development, Dutch Railways
Mr G. Verwey, Transport Department, Province of South-Holland
Mr G. Wesselink, Transport Department, Province of South-Holland
Mr T.J.M. Spit, Faculty of Spatial Sciences, University of Utrecht
Mr L. Bertolini, Faculty of Spatial Sciences, University of Utrecht

Report on Strasbourg

Mr Meneteau, Service Transport, Communauté Urbaine de Strasbourg
Mr Barth, Région Alsace
Mr Jerome, Conseil Général
Ms Arnold, Service Affaires Economiques, Communauté Urbaine de Strasbourg
Mr Muller, Elu, Communauté Urbaine de Strasbourg
Mr Klotz, Elu, Communauté Urbaine de Strasbourg
Mr M. Reverdy, Chef du service de l'Urbanisme, Communauté Urbaine de Strasbourg
Mr J.Y. Meunier, Service Urbanisme, Communauté Urbaine de Strasbourg
Mr A. Trocme, Service des Relations internationales, Communauté Urbaine de Strasbourg

Report on Turin

Mr G. Pichetto, President Turin Chamber of Commerce Industry, Handicraft and Agriculture
Mr G. Giustetto, Member of the Board, Turin Chamber of Commerce Industry, Handicraft and
    Agriculture
Mr P. Balistreri, Responsabile Servizio Trasporti, Federazione delle Associazioni Industriali
    del Piemonte
Mr A. Manto, Direttore, Sector Transport and Planification Infrastructure, Region Piemonte
Mr A. Belloni, Responsible Marketing Strategy, TAV Treno Alta Velocità
Mr D. Melodia, Project Manager, Nodo Torino, Gruppo FS, Italferr-sis. t.a.v.
Mr E. Gorzegno, Direttore, Area Trasporto, Direzioni Regionali Piemonte E Valle d'Aosta,
    Ferrovie Dello Stato SpA
Mr A. Faraggiana, Divisione Mobilità, Città di Torino
Mr D. Masera, Transportation Department, Provincia di Torino
Mr Burdizzo, Divisione Mobilità, Città di Torino
Mr I. Signoretti, Servizio Centrale Grandi Opere, Città di Torino
Mr C.A. Barbieri, Esperto Urbanistica e Trasporti, Torino
Mr G. Ferrero, Deputy Major, Città di Torino
Mr F. Corsico, Deputy Major, Città di Torino